THE SOUND OF MEMORIES

THE SOUND OF MEMORIES

Recordings from the Oral History Centre, Singapore

Cheong Suk-Wai

NATIONAL ARCHIVES OF SINGAPORE
An institution of the National Library Board

World Scientific

Editorial:

Editor: Veronica Chee
Editor-in-Chief: Francis Dorai
Desk Editors: Triena Ong, Daniele Lee

Project Manager: Benjamin Ho

Published by:

National Archives of Singapore, an institution of the National Library Board
1 Canning Rise
Singapore 179868
email: nas@nlb.gov.sg
www.nas.gov.sg

and

World Scientific Publishing Co. Pte Ltd
5 Toh Tuck Link
Singapore 596224
USA office: 27 Warren Street, Suite 401-402, Hackensack, NJ 07601
UK office: 57 Shelton Street, Covent Garden, London WC2H 9HE

National Library Board, Singapore Cataloguing in Publication Data
Names: Cheong, Suk-Wai.
Title: The sound of memories : recordings from the Oral History Centre, Singapore / by Cheong Suk-Wai.
Description: Singapore : National Archives of Singapore : World Scientific Publishing Co. Pte. Ltd., [2019]
Identifiers: OCN 1101606520 | ISBN 978-981-12-0601-6 (paperback) | 978-981-12-0600-9 (hardcover)
978-981-120-802-7 (ebook)
Subjects: LCSH: Singapore--History--Anecdotes. | Singapore--Social conditions--History--Anecdotes.
Classification: DDC 959.57--dc23

Printed in Singapore

CONTENTS

FOREWORD

At forty, one is entitled to claim with some confidence a measure of certitude about our world and our place in it. As Confucius declared in Book II of his *Analects,* "At fifteen I wanted to learn; at thirty I had a foundation; at forty a certitude."

As the Oral History Centre (OHC) marks its 40th anniversary this year, it can claim with certainty its achievements in recording Singapore's history. The collection of over 5,000 interviews (totalling some 23,500 recorded hours), on events such as the Japanese Occupation to issues on the political development of Singapore as well as matters touching on the more ordinary rhythms and cycles of everyday life, has established the OHC's centrality in the reconstruction of Singapore's past.

This certainty of what we know and understand about our past is grounded on the foundations of what we have achieved in the preceding decades. For the OHC, this confidence at forty is grounded in its practice of oral history. It is a practice of history as an empirical study of our past, based on the systematic interviewing of witnesses to our past, which is then collated to enable a reconstruction of what actually happened, and can claim to be objective and true.

The various exhibitions that the OHC has produced over the years on the Japanese Occupation were largely based on the careful collation of oral history interviews with survivors from this period. This practice of oral history interviewing to recall truths of the past was based on the assumption that our interviewees were dispassionately and accurately recalling their memories of those three years and seven months of the Japanese Occupation – that what they were conveying to us was objective information.

But in re-listening and reflecting on these interviews today, we realise, perhaps, that our interviewees may not have been objectively recalling clearly defined memories, but rather, "stream of conscious" memories, often traumatic, in response to our interview questions. This is not a consciousness of the past that is distant and detached from the present, but an emotional and traumatic past which continues to flow into the present.

Interviewing people about our everyday social and work lives may also be less about getting our interviewees to retrieve concrete facts about how, for example, the cycles of religious festivals were celebrated in the past, but more about invoking their stream of conscious memories about how their parents celebrated these festivals as well as their own recollections of these occasions during childhood and how they are observed today.

From this perspective, oral history interviews may be less about retrieving objective and verifiable information about a distant past to reliving a historical consciousness that connects us to a present and a living past. It will involve a different mode of listening to and communicating with our interviewees, a different paradigm and practice of what oral history is perhaps about.

If we are able to rise to this challenge then we should be well prepared to move the OHC into the fourth decade of its life, and be ready to welcome the fifth.

Kwa Chong Guan
Former Director
Oral History Department, 1985–1994

While we respect and celebrate the narratives recounted by our interviewees, we recognise that all oral history accounts, by their very nature, are personal, experiential and interpretative. They are founded on the memories, perceptions and viewpoints of individuals. While all reasonable attempts have been taken to avoid inaccuracies, the excerpts of the interviews found in this book should not be understood as statements of fact endorsed by the National Archives of Singapore, an institution of the National Library Board.

CHAPTER ONE

COMMUNITIES

We are One, We are Singaporeans

The year was 1930 and Peter William Benson was beside himself with excitement. He had just scored a coup for journalism in Singapore – an interview with Sir Cecil Clementi, the new Governor of the Straits Settlements, no less.

His colleague **Khoo Teng Soon** recalled that Benson, who was Indian, "had a huge paunch, drank a lot of gin and tonic, had money problems and smoked cheap cheroots". Khoo added, however, that Benson was very good at his job as a reporter with *The Malaya Tribune* and had "great contacts" in the police force.

Khoo Teng Soon (far right, standing next to President Wee Kim Wee), better known as T.S. Khoo, at the Singapore Press Club's annual dinner and dance in 1985. Khoo was a colleague of reporter Peter William Benson at *The Malaya Tribune*.

Governor of the Straits Settlements Sir Cecil Clementi (1929–1934) was apparently disdainful of locals.

So off Benson went for the interview at Government House. Alas, he was out within seconds. "Clementi had never granted an interview to any local reporter," Khoo said. "That is, until Benson wrote to him for an interview. Clementi obviously looked at that name – Peter W. Benson – and decided that Benson must be an expat. And of course, when he got into Government House, Clementi took one look at him and ordered him out."

During his time in Singapore between 1929 and 1934, Clementi tried to stamp out the spread of anti-colonial sentiments by censoring the vernacular press. He also stopped the local Chinese community's efforts to raise funds for China in their fight against the Japanese and angered the Peranakan Chinese with his anti-Chinese education and immigration policies. After Clementi prohibited education grants for Chinese and Tamil vernacular schools, only the Malay community received free education. Khoo mused: "Those were the days when you could have these types of governors."

Such prejudice, however, went beyond racist governors of the time. **Frederick Arthur Chua**, one of Singapore's pioneering judges, recalled that when he returned to Singapore in the 1930s with a law degree from Britain's Cambridge University, he was not accepted into Singapore's circle of expatriates. Chua said: "Young people like me did not mix with the expatriates, only the older people and business people. We youngsters who just graduated, we didn't mix with the expats. We didn't socialise with them and we didn't get invited either."

Chua also recalled in the 2013 book, *Legal Tenor: Legal Voices from Singapore's Legal History 1930–1959*, that when he worked in the Straits Settlements Civil Service from 1937 till 1942 in the Municipal Building – now part of the National Gallery Singapore – he and his local colleagues had a toilet to themselves. That was because they were barred from sharing a lavatory with white folk.

Khoo remembered other forms of racial discrimination. His first job was as a ledger clerk at Cold Storage supermarket in 1938 where the Centrepoint shopping mall sits today. "Very few locals patronised it," he recalled. "Unless you were a big name, you would never have an account there because they were very, very discriminating." Luckily for the locals, shops such as Kee Mun and Koon Heng sold frozen foods to rival Cold Storage, albeit on a much smaller scale.

He added: "Nine out of 10 Cold Storage customers were expats; I knew this from going through the everyday bills in the ledger… the highest a local worker at Cold Storage could aspire to was Chief Clerk – but you still could not get a staff discount!" Despite such blatant discrimination, Khoo stuck it out as Cold Storage paid him $30 a month – big money in those days when a plate of chicken *biryani* was 25 cents. His salary, however, was nowhere near that of his expat colleagues. The average young expat earned between $200 and $250 a month then.

Khoo eventually switched to a career in journalism in August 1938 as that paid him $40 a month, with an additional monthly travel allowance of $15. His nose for news led to his promotion as the first local chief sub-editor of *The Straits Times* in 1951. By then, his expat peers were drawing between $600 and $800 a month, while he and other locals had to get by on a third of those salaries.

Joseph Anthony Desker, who worked in the Colonial Secretary's office in Singapore after World War II, recalled that in the colonial government, even locals who were graduates could not rise above the level of chief clerk. The exceptions were professionals such as doctors, or lawyers such as Chua, who became the second local-born judge of the Supreme Court of Singapore on 15 February 1957. "So," Desker added, "we knew that our career was limited. The attitude towards us was that we were to be subservient."

That all changed when Singapore attained self-government in June 1959. The new government, formed by the People's Action Party, carried out the policy of Malayanisation – the exercise of replacing expatriates with local talents in all ranks of government, especially those at senior levels. Desker found Malayanisation a sea change: "There was greater cooperation and friendliness. We knew who we were talking to. We belonged, perhaps, to the same community. We understood one another and so there was greater rapport between the junior staff and the senior officers."

There remained, however, the expectation of a certain decorum between junior and senior staff. When journalist **Tan Wee Him** first reported for work at *The Straits Times* on 1 May 1970, one of the first colleagues he met was the paper's news editor Sit Yin Fong. Tan recalled: "I went into his room and he was standing behind his desk and extending his hand. 'Sit here,' he said referring to himself by his surname. So I sat immediately in the chair in front of him – leaving a bewildered Mr Sit standing, with his hand outstretched."

The relationship between masters and their apprentices was not always straightforward. **Chua Eng Cheow**, a master potter who was an expert at firing ceramic wares in dragon kilns, recalled how master potters would guard their secrets jealously. "It was their rice bowl and if they taught their skills to others, it would threaten their livelihood. Hence, we apprentices had to depend on our imagination and secret observations instead."

Of Buffalos, Goats, Pigs and Crabs

In early Singapore, before the advent of assembly-line labour, communities were often defined by their occupations. Many Bengalis were milkmen, taking their *kerbau*, or buffalos, from door to door to provide households with the freshest milk. Tamilians tended to be goatherds who also sold their livestock's milk door to door. **Kannusamy s/o Pakirisamy**, who was born in 1914, remembered these men well. In their birth country India, some among them had been indomitable Rajput warriors (members of a high-class Hindu military caste). But by the 1930s, some businessmen in Singapore began importing Australian-bred cattle, rendering the Bengalis' business redundant. "The milkmen lost their jobs and the Bengalis among them became watchmen for bungalows and stores owned by Chinese contractors," Kannusamy recalled.

The Tamilians, he added, turned to building roads and other infrastructure. "There were eight road contractors who were very well-known in Serangoon Road," he said. "They included Muthiar Mandore, Veriah Mandore and Doraisamy Mandore." The word *mandore* is from the Portuguese *mandador*, which means "overseer" or "one who gives orders".

Sometimes, people from different communities did not address one another by their given names. **Shuki Ram Chandra née Davies** recalled how her brothers would spar with their schoolmates. "It was very common for Chinese boys to call the Indian boys *nandu*, which means 'crab' in Tamil. And the Indian boys would call the Chinese *pandi*, which is Tamil for 'pig'. There were no fights about that, nothing. But now, the moment something is a little off-colour, there's an eruption."

Newsman and ex-professional boxer **Lim Kee Chan** contrasted the behaviour of hot-headed youths these days with gangsters of yore and recalled that the gangsters, at least,

An itinerant goat milk seller in Serangoon Road seen here decanting fresh milk for customers, 1982.

abided by certain principles. "Nowadays," Lim said, "you see teenagers in a staring incident and they want to fight, kill each other. That is very sad."

"In those days," he added, "if you wanted to get a few gangsters to bash somebody up, they wouldn't do it unless you gave them a good reason. They would keep asking you, 'Why do you want to hit him?' If you didn't have a good reason, they wouldn't do it. But now, for a cup of coffee, people would hammer each other."

Mrs Chandra said remarks made by some communities about others were downright outrageous. "I have watched certain mothers telling their children in public, in their mother tongue, 'not to go there because there is that *keling kwai*'." *Keling kwai* is a derogatory Cantonese phrase referring to Indians. "Maybe some people think that Indian children might be dirty or black or whatever, so don't mix with them. But that is not good; we are one, we are Singaporeans."

However subtle racism might be these days, some feel its undercurrent. Artist **Liu Chao**, a new citizen of Singapore from Shenyang, China, said: "I have a gut feeling that even though we live in harmony, there is still some sense that we all have our own communities." Curiously, Liu added, he felt more at home with non-Chinese Singaporeans than in Chinese households. For instance, he turned down invitations to celebrate the Mooncake Festival with Chinese families "because it's a kind of a family reunion and their home is not mine". Yet he was happy to eat in the homes of his Malay friends "quite a few times".

Same but Different

Almost every city in the world has a Chinatown. **Soh Siew Cheong** grew up in Singapore's version of it and recalled how the area was carved out among the Chinese clans. In his childhood, gangsterism was rife and if, say, a Hokkien crossed into Cantonese territory, it would be at his or her peril. This was easier said than done, as one wrong turn into a street controlled by a rival gang could end in bloodshed.

Former librarian **Vilasini Perumbulavil** thought differently; she held the view that the Chinese as a whole, regardless of their clan or dialect group, had more in common than their Indian counterparts. "You have Hokkiens, Teochews, Cantonese and so on but at least you have one unifying thing, which is your script. For us, there is no unifying factor… a Punjabi and a Malayalee could be from different countries. Their customs are so different. The things that they eat are different, they look different, their colour is different. Would Tamils and Malayalees feel at home in Punjab, Sindh or Bengal? Each is completely different and they write and speak differently."

Khoo Teng Soon marvelled at how his maternal grandparents remained married for decades although neither spoke each other's language. His maternal grandfather was Chew Boon Lay, after whom Boon Lay housing estate is named. Chew spoke only Hokkien, while his wife was Peranakan and spoke only Malay. "For years," Khoo mused, "we had this curious situation where the old man could speak only Hokkien and hardly any Malay whereas my grandmother could speak only Baba Malay without being able to speak Hokkien. Despite all that, they produced 13 children." And while Chew was against gambling, he was blind and so his wife would sneak out for *chap ji kee* (Hokkien for "12 cards"), or illegal lottery sessions.

Outside the family, there were distinctive clans within the same community. In the case of Malay-Muslims, each clan was known for certain attributes, occupations and even dishes. **Haji Mohamed Sidek Bin Siraj**, a civil servant turned Haj pilgrimage officer, said that the Malays, for example, were always called on to adjudicate disputes. Such disputes might include fights between the Bugis and the Banjarese over women within the community because, as he put it, "the Banjarese brought their women along with them while the Bugis didn't." The Baweanese, he added, were often stable hands and when cars replaced horse carriages, they became chauffeurs.

The Minangkabau of Sumatra brought *nasi padang* (rice served with various side dishes) to Singapore, while those who sold *satay* or grilled skewered meat were primarily Javanese. "They were not commercial-minded and liked their businesses to stay on a small scale," he mused. And the *mee goreng* (Malay for fried noodles) so associated with the Indian Muslims today was actually introduced to Singapore by the Banjarese.

Despite these differences, Mohamed Sidek said that everyone in the Malay community were "united during *kenduris*, births, deaths, marriages, prayers and circumcision ceremonies". Beyond that, it was not uncommon to see Malays pile into bullock carts to watch *bangsawan*, or traditional Malay opera, at the Royal Theatre in North Bridge Road, for $1 to $3 per person.

Different but Same

Mohamed Sidek also recalled how the Malay community took a live-and-let-live attitude towards mainland Chinese who began settling in Kampong Glam, the seat of Malay culture in Singapore, in the 1920s. "The Chinese started moving into the Kampong Glam area from 1922 after the visit of the Prince of Wales to Singapore," he said. "Life in China was too hard so the Chinese began setting up small businesses in Kampong Glam."

The Malays, he added, were not perturbed by these newcomers because "they didn't come in hordes". He noted that the Chinese immigrants just opened sundry shops, selling provisions that *satay* sellers and other Malay stallholders needed, acquired the Malay language and could even speak Javanese.

In fact, Mohamed Sidek added, the *lingua franca* for Singapore well into the late 1960s was Malay, and both Chinese and Indian traders used Malay as the language of trade. **Dhanalakshmi Govindasamy**, daughter of the late great Singapore philanthropist P. Govindasamy Pillai, recalled her father telling her that while he couldn't speak English, whenever he came in contact with Englishmen in Singapore, he was "very good at conversing with them in Malay". And so, she added, "he was able to get a lot of help from them regarding the textile business."

In those days, a person's word was as good as a cast-iron contract, mused trader **Abdul Kader Tyebally**. "I used to accompany my father to talk to rattan factory owners. He would discuss business with them over the abacus… a matter of a few cents mattered. But very

A Javanese *satay* seller seen here with his scrumptious fare in Kampong Glam in the 1930s, when Chinese immigrants began moving into the neighbourhood.

seldom was there a black-and-white document at the end of it. Business was done mostly by word of mouth."

Rupchand Bhojwani, a former President of the Sindhi Merchants Association in Singapore, recalled how most members of his community "picked up not just Romanised Malay, but also Jawi". Sindhis, he added, were known for being hardworking and aggressive businesspeople, and came to Singapore from India at the beginning of the 20th century.

Friends in Need

Trust in the community was strongest in Singapore's villages, or *kampungs*. An epitome of the *kampung* spirit was Kampong Siglap. **Rita Fernando**, who grew up there, found "there really was no difference whether you were Malay, Chinese, Indian, Eurasian or whatever. You lived as one *kampung*." So, she added, if someone plucked 100 coconuts off their tree, every household in her *kampung* would get at least five or six fruit. It was the same with bunches of bananas. "You cut off the combs and shared those with everyone around you," she said. Children played games such as five stones and *capteh* (a game that requires keeping a feathered shuttlecock in the air for as long as possible by kicking it with the heel of the foot) together, and everyone turned up for *kenduris*, or traditional communal feasts that the Malays host for weddings and other festive occasions. Often, Mrs Fernando added, the non-Malay residents would help with preparations, or try their hand at making *ketupat*

Women in a Lim Chu Kang *kampung* cracking open coconuts in 1986, recalling Mrs Rita Fernando's happy memory of her fellow villagers sharing their coconut harvest.

(boiled rice cakes wrapped in woven coconut leaves) or *kuih lopes* (triangular glutinous rice cakes eaten with palm sugar syrup and grated coconut).

Best of all, *kampung* spirit meant you were a friend in need. Mrs Fernando said: "There was a very strong protective spirit where everyone would keep an eye open for the other person. If, say, a neighbour was at the bus stop and there were very young children there, they would walk the children home if it was getting dark. We were like one big happy family."

For veterinarian and former civil servant **Ngiam Tong Tau**, community spirit helped his family's livestock thrive. Ngiam's father died when he was three, leaving his mother to fend for five children. "We would get a tin and hang it on the gate and people would just put their food waste in the tin. We were recycling waste even then.... We would feed all that was in the tin to our chickens, ducks and pigs."

Kampung spirit often stemmed from the simple pleasure of being comfortable in the company of others. Gangster-turned-pastor **Neivelle Tan**, who grew up in Pennefather Road in eastern Singapore, recalled: "In the evenings, the ladies would come out after cooking their meals, waiting for their husbands to come back. They would sit out in the corridor, chit chat and gossip with one another.

"After dinner, in the cool of the evening, the fathers would come out and smoke their pipes and interact with neighbours. It was a good kind of community life which is not seen anymore."

Kampung spirit often stemmed from the simple pleasure of being comfortable in the company of others.

Community living did, however, have its quirks. **Lucy Chen née Lim Seok Hui**, who was from a privileged family, recalled: "We had a Sikh watchman who saw goings-on. He would tell us, 'Oh. So and so and so had helped themselves [to our things].' Some of our visitors just took whatever they wanted back to their homes. So we were able to recover some of the things they took by going to their homes and telling them the stuff was ours."

For old-money families such as hers, life was especially rarefied. Mrs Chen had a maid to herself, just like all her siblings. Her paternal grandfather Lim Nee Soon built the Garrick, Sultan and Nee Soon theatres. She said: "There were as many maids as there were children. So can you imagine if there were two tables of food, how many maids were there to serve us?" Nee Soon Estate (now known as Yishun) is named after her grandfather, while the former Chong Pang Village (now part of Yishun) is named after her father.

There was often a *kampung* spirit even when there was no *kampung* to speak of. Khoo Teng Soon recalled how his colleague Herman Rappa, a court and sports reporter for *The Straits Times*, would sit in Bidadari Cemetery at the grave of his son who had killed himself. "We would go there and force him to go home," said Khoo.

Luckily, they did not know **Awang Bin Osman**, who was warned from a young age that Bidadari Cemetery was the haunt of *pontianak*, or blood-sucking souls of women who had died in childbirth, as Malay folklore goes. "The *pontianak* had long hair and wore a

Awang Bin Osman (seated second from left), the headman of Kampong Wak Sumang, also known as Kampong Punggol, seen here at home with family members in 1985.

long dress," Awang said. "You could tell it was not human because its feet did not touch the ground." The trick to returning a *pontianak* to human form, he added, was to push a nail into the nape of its neck. Once, he said, a husband did exactly that to a *pontianak* that had been his dead wife but their young son later spotted the nail. Thinking that his mother was in pain, he pulled it out. "It changed back into a *pontianak* instantly," Awang said.

Unearthly beings aside, *kampung* spirit lived on well after bulldozers had razed villages to make way for public flats, spanking new skyscrapers and shopping malls. Childhood friends and bandmates **Jap Chong Chow Pin** and **Raymond Leong Kum Hon** were neighbours living in the old Singapore Improvement Trust flats in Tiong Bahru that the British had built in the early 20th century. Their parents paid $62 a month per household in rent, which was then big money as most of their neighbours earned a pittance. "Sometimes we didn't have money to pay electricity bills," Chong recalled. "Before we went to school, it was a must for us to have two eggs and a cup of Ovaltine or Milo – or else you went hungry."

Leong said most people they knew were "very enterprising" and thought up all sorts of ways to get by. Chong said: "We would think of some business to do, even within our homes. For example, my neighbours would rent out their *mahjong* tables to a few people at $1 per game at most. That was enough for our parents to buy food for the whole family for the day."

Leong added that in the early years after Singapore's independence in 1965, the authorities did not seem to regulate such sporadic businesses too closely. "Some people collected second-hand things, put them on the road and sold them. Others became hawkers. It was not so controlled; you could do this and that. So, somehow, you would find a way to make a living. But the important thing was that all the neighbours were very friendly with one another. Everybody seemed quite happy."

They even entrusted their house keys to one another if they went out of town. Chong recalled: "So when we came home, we'd say, 'Just go to so-and-so's house to get the keys'." Leong quipped: "There wasn't stealing because there was nothing in the house to steal as we were all quite poor." Some among them were so poor that they could not even afford the $5 monthly fee to enjoy Rediffusion (Singapore's first commercial radio station, broadcast via cable from 1949) radio programmes. Leong said the Rediffusion set came with a box into which listeners would put a few cents whenever they could to pay for the broadcast service.

Most movingly, they mused, whenever a neighbour could not pay his water or electricity bills and so could not bathe and had to light candles, everyone else would chip in, either by settling the debt or inviting the neighbour's entire household over to their homes for a bath. Chong and Leong marvelled at how helpful neighbours were despite their straitened circumstances – and especially when most of their families were large; in Chong's case, he lived with 10 family members in a three-room flat.

The Stop at Two Policy

According to the Department of Statistics, Singapore's birth rate rose from 22.1 babies per 1,000 residents to 23.1 babies per 1,000 residents between 1970 and 1972. With economic development still nascent and high unemployment rates, there was much pressure on the government to curb over-population lest there were not enough jobs to support burgeoning families.

Gynaecologist **Tow Siang Hwa**, who headed KK Hospital in the 1960s, said: "The number of babies born per family was then, on average, six to eight. The exceptional cases of 14 to 16 babies were seen in those days." Tow, who was interviewed in July 1997, added: "Today, you'd never see that."

On 20 July 1972, then Minister for Health Chua Sian Chin introduced the "Stop At Two" policy as part of the National Family Planning campaign. The policy exhorted married couples to have no more than two children. Hitting below the belt, as it were, many Singaporeans chafed at the "Stop At Two" policy. Families who had three or more children were penalised in many ways, including qualifying for less tax relief; paying more for hospital fees; having less maternity leave; and being sent to the back of the queue for Housing & Development Board flats.

Then in 1974, the Abortion Act was introduced, which made it legal for mothers-to-be to abort foetuses that they could not carry to full term for whatever reason, making abortion available to all women. That same year, complementary legislation, that is, the Voluntary Sterilisation Act, simplified the process for men seeking vasectomies. Incentives were given to those who chose sterilisation.

Due to these measures, Singapore's total fertility rate (TFR) plunged from 2.11 in 1976 to 1.82 by 1977. In fact, between 1972 and 1986, the TFR plunged from a high of 3.07 to 1.43, well below the minimum replacement rate of 2.1. The "Stop At Two" policy had proven most effective but remained controversial for many years.

Midwife-turned-nurse **Sumitera Mohd Letak** recalled having to be very tactful in communicating the policy to young married women. "We explained to them but we did not provoke them… we just told them why it should be like that."

There were, however, instances in which these married women would get "very aggressive" and yell at the nurses. She said: "And if you get it, the government will get it. I had colleagues who were really abused with words like, 'Hey, who are you to tell me that I

Possibly the first family planning poster ever produced by the Training and Health Education Board of the Ministry of Health (MOH), c. 1969. Created by Robert Tan, a former staff of MOH, the poster encouraged families to have no more than two children.

Mothers proudly showing off their babies at a baby show in 1954. Before the "Stop At Two" policy was introduced in Singapore in 1972, families had on average six to eight children, with some even having more than 10 children.

can't afford to feed my baby and all that?' So the choice of words, and the way you approach the problem, is very important."

Social worker **Nirmala Gopiendran** recalled how gingerly those in healthcare had to broach the "Stop At Two" policy with families. "A woman in her third pregnancy would be sent to social workers and these social workers had to encourage couples to stop at two, educate them on what precautions they could take – go on the pill, use an intra-uterine device or use condoms.

"We had to really work with these families," she said. "And, sometimes, it was a bit conflicting because if you were two months into your third pregnancy, we could not encourage you to go for an abortion, as it would be against your values and things like that."

The Picture that Sparked a Riot

Singapore's baby boom in the 1960s came after many fissures in society. The increasingly nationalistic fervour following the Japanese Occupation led to many social pressures mounting all at once. There was the thickening of anti-colonial sentiment, which set off the struggle for independence. There was a dearth of jobs for the Chinese-educated populace. And there was urban renewal, with *kampungs* having to make way for high-rise flats.

The worst outbreak of rioting in Singapore after World War II was on 11 December 1950. It was triggered by a custody tussle between the Muslim foster mother and the Catholic birth parents of Maria Hertogh (also known by her Malay name Nadra). The last straw for the rioters, who were mostly Muslim, was a provocative photo in *The Straits Times* that showed Nadra kneeling before the Virgin Mary in the Convent of the Good Shepherd.

Journalist Khoo Teng Soon said: "The day she was sent to the convent, ST [*The Straits Times*] sent photographers there. And this is something which I regret up till today. You know we carried a picture – it was my decision to carry that picture of her kneeling in the convent before the Virgin Mary." In his defence, Khoo said that at the time, he was "very young" – he was then 28 years old – and "did not realise that a picture like that could start a riot which resulted in the loss of a number of lives".

Maria was born in Java, Indonesia, on 24 March 1937 to Adrianus Petrus Hertogh, a Dutch army sergeant in the Royal Netherlands East Indies Army, and his Eurasian wife Adeline Hunter, who was of Scottish and Javanese extraction. The baby girl was baptised as a Catholic and took the name Maria Huberdina Bertha Hertogh. At the onset of World War II, her father was taken prisoner by the Japanese in Indonesia, leaving his wife to raise their children.

On New Year's Day in 1943, Adeline, struggling and having just delivered her sixth child, placed Maria in the care of a family friend, Che Aminah Mohammed, a well-travelled 42-year-old married woman from Kemaman, Terengganu. Maria's maternal grandmother Louise Winterberg, also known as Nor Louise, was a good friend of Che Aminah's and was present when Maria was handed over to the Malay woman.

Mobs set cars on fire downtown on 11 December 1950. They were enraged after the Supreme Court of Singapore denied Che Aminah Mohammed custody of her foster child Maria Hertogh.

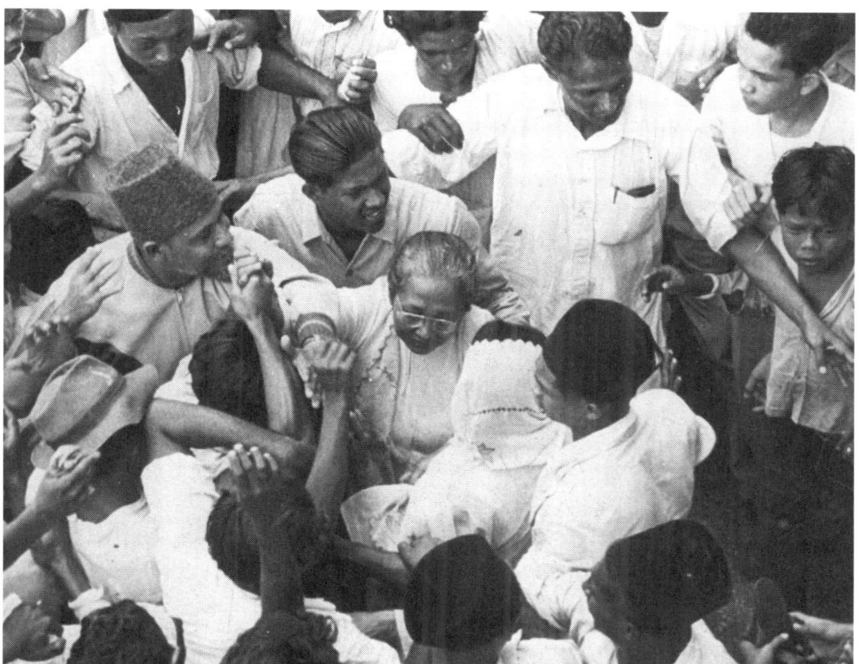

A devastated Che Aminah Mohammed seen here with her supporters right after the Supreme Court of Singapore denied her custody of Maria Hertogh on 11 December 1950.

In later years, Adeline claimed that she had only meant for her daughter to stay with Che Aminah for about five days, adding that she was on her way to take Maria home when she was detained by a Japanese sentry and sent to an internment camp.

Meanwhile, Che Aminah brought Maria up as her own, and in the Muslim way of life. It was only in September 1949 that the police and Red Cross Society tracked Maria to a *kampung* in Kemaman. Jacob Van Der Gaag, the Dutch Consul in Singapore, offered Che Aminah $500 to return Maria but she refused. His British counterpart, however, lured Che Aminah and Maria to visit Singapore. Upon their arrival, the Consul applied for custody of Maria via the court in Singapore. What ensued was a series of heart-wrenching legal twists and turns for the duo.

In April 1950, the court ordered that Maria be put in the custody of the Social Welfare Department. As Maria, who was then 13 years old, refused to leave Che Aminah's side, they were allowed to live together on York Hill. A month later, the court ruled that Maria's biological parents had custody over her, but the Chief Justice of Singapore soon reversed that decision. Che Aminah and Maria were overjoyed – but ironically, that was also when their bond began to unravel.

On 1 August 1950, Che Aminah married Maria off to trainee teacher Mansoor Adabi. He was 22 and although Maria had reached puberty, she was still only 13. The marriage outraged the girl's biological parents, who sued their daughter, her foster mother and Mansoor. At the same time, some Muslims in Singapore protested the marriage too, insisting that only girls 16 or older could marry. Maria's plight drew global attention from Egypt to Saudi Arabia to Pakistan.

Then, on 20 November 1950, Justice Brown of the Singapore High Court gave custody of Maria to the Hertoghs, reasoning that first, Maria was at an impressionable age and her views on life might change later on and, second, as her father had been interned and known nothing about his wife's arrangements with Aminah, he had not consented to Maria being fostered.

Immediately after Brown's decision, Maria and Che Aminah were sped away to a convent run by the Roman Catholic Sisters of the Good Shepherd. The nuns did not bar any reporters from entering the convent, which was how Khoo made the blunder that he would regret for the rest of his days.

That photograph of a Muslim Maria seeming to worship Mother Mary set off a torrent of threats from Muslim extremists all over the world. At one point, Karim Ghani, a Muslim leader in Singapore, said the last resort in the matter would be jihad, or holy war. Things came to such a head that the Criminal Investigation Department advised that Che Aminah and Maria move back to York Hill.

By noon on 11 December 1950, a crowd of 3,000 Muslims had gathered outside the court building, where Che Aminah's appeal against its November ruling was heard. In just five minutes, the court upheld the ruling. The brief hearing angered the crowd, who

Maria Hertogh, the girl who triggered rioting in post-World War II Singapore on 11 December 1950.

thought that the British judges were giving Muslim concerns short shrift. They began attacking Europeans and Eurasians in their path. The army had to be called in. Some later accused the Muslims within the police force of sympathising with Che Aminah, and standing by while the riots raged. By the time the riots subsided two days later, 18 people had been killed and another 173 injured, some critically so. Up to 120 vehicles and at least two buildings were damaged. The riots were subsequently known as the Maria Hertogh Riots.

Lim Kee Chan the former professional boxer was fishing on a *kelong* (an offshore fishing platform) when the riots were raging. He recalled: "I was still in school then, and fishing on a *kelong*. Suddenly, this wise guy said, 'I can smell rubber burning.' And we all said, 'Where do you see rubber burning?' Lim's friend pointed to plumes of smoke from a distance and said, 'See, see, there's a fire!' And true enough, they were burning cars." The police detained a total of 778 rioters; 100 were later convicted, and five sentenced to hang. The five, however, later had their death sentences commuted to life imprisonment.

Maria resettled in the Netherlands where, after bearing 13 children, she allegedly tried to kill her husband. She was 72 when she died of leukaemia in 2009. Che Aminah died in 1976, while Maria's first husband Mansoor died of a heart attack in 1988. He and Maria never consummated their marriage.

The Locals Grow Restive

Riots plagued the Chinese community too throughout the 1950s. These involved Chinese middle school students, who were mainly protesting against new colonial policies. One such policy was the National Service Ordinance, which was passed in December 1953. It required males in Singapore and Malaya between the ages of 18 and 20 to serve their country part-time – and to sign up by 12 May 1954 or else be fined and jailed. On 13 May 1954, representatives of the Chinese Middle School Students' Union met William Goode, the colonial Chief Secretary, at Government House. The unionists wanted to present Goode with a petition, but it all descended into chaos as they clashed with the riot police. No one died in the fracas, but 26 people were injured. More than 50 others were convicted of obstructing the police.

The Britons believed that being educated in English would open the door to better jobs. So they enhanced the benefits for English-medium schools at the expense of Chinese and other vernacular schools. The Chinese schools were starved of funding and opportunities to advance, forcing many of their students to switch to English-medium schools, in which they were most uncomfortable. At the time, many colonies in Asia and Africa were also gaining independence. The Vietnamese defeat of their French overlords in the 1954 battle of Dien Bien Phu was a significant catalyst that stoked anti-colonial sentiments further.

Such sentiments among the Chinese middle school populace set off another riot on 26 October 1956, after students in Chung Cheng High School in Tanjong Katong and Chinese High School at Dunearn Road, staged mass sit-ins, defying then Chief Minister Lim Yew Hock and the police. This time, 13 were killed in the melee, with more than 100 others injured, most badly. Teacher-turned-lawyer **Kasinather Saunthararajah**, better known as K.S. Rajah, recalled: "I lived on the third floor of a building in Tanjong Katong Road and could see the students piling up stones along the road. Their parents took food to them and the children were all sort of acting in unison."

The Chinese middle school protesters continued as rabble-rousers well into the 1960s, joining forces with the political party Barisan Sosialis that had split from the ruling People's Action Party (PAP) in 1961. **Ng Kah Ting**, who walked the ground for the PAP, recalled: "They went around tearing down posters, banners and they wrote slogans on the road, splashing paint and running down the PAP all the time." They were, he noted, "very well-organised in small teams, going around threatening people." Such violence, he added, did not seem rational.

Rajah mused: "Unfortunately, the approach of the Chinese-educated organisations was one of defiance and to turn over the apple cart. And the response of the government, of I think Lee Kuan Yew and his Cabinet, was to use the law as a weapon to harness them without at the same time appearing to be against the Chinese. So of course you had the Vandalism Act, the Trade Unions Act. The law was used to bury them in line with law and order." It was, he added, "prosecution as a means of control".

Workers, too, were growing restive. **Sin Leong**, a renowned Singaporean chef and co-creator of the Chinese New Year dish *yu sheng* (raw fish salad), recalled terrible working conditions for restaurant workers. "In those days, there was no rest, no compensation, no overtime! We even had to open our restaurants on the first and second days of Chinese New Year."

In the 1950s, he was working at the Cathay Restaurant – under the mother of Loke Wan Tho, who owned the Cathay cinema chain – and became better acquainted with his Hainanese waiters. "They were able to speak and read and knew things. So when we older workers united with them, we learnt about law and workers' rights, fixed working hours and off days. We began asking our employers for improvements to our staff benefits."

Soon, the unions stepped in to negotiate with restaurants for better working conditions. In 1949, Sin recalled, restaurant workers went on strike for two months. "The workers

Sin Leong, one among Singapore's Four Heavenly Kings of Chinese cuisine, in the kitchen of his Red Star Restaurant in Chin Swee Road, 2016. He was a witness to the 1950s riots.

squatted outside the restaurant, put up banners." But the colonial government batted away their demands, arguing that they fell under the Domestic Workers Act, which gave them fewer benefits than the Employment Act. Sensing that all was futile, Sin said, the workers ended their strike.

The drivers of the Hock Lee Bus Company did not go so quietly. On 12 May 1955, they lashed out brutally. Four were killed and 31 others injured. When **Lee Khoon Choy**, then a journalist with the *Nanyang Siang Pau* and later politician and diplomat, went down to the Hock Lee Bus Depot in Alexandra Road, he saw "thousands of students from the Chinese middle schools" plying the strikers with food and drink, and even entertaining them with songs. "About 150 strikers blocked the gates to prevent the buses from moving," he recalled. "They threw stones at the police."

The mob built to a frenzy and grabbed hold of a police officer. "They sprayed him with petrol and burned him alive," Lee said. He had witnessed that from a distance with a few other ministers and international journalists. By then, one among them, Gene Symonds, United Press manager for Southeast Asia, had broken away from Lee's group and rushed into the melee. Lee said: "Actually, we'd told him, 'Don't go near because you are European, it's too dangerous.' But he said, 'Never mind. I want to have a scoop.' The mob beat Symonds to death. Two other Chinese men, a special constable and a volunteer, also met a similar fate."

Lee thought Singapore's then Chief Minister David Saul Marshall had been "a little too soft". Marshall ordered the police not to fire on the strikers and, as a result, the cops

Police are seen here putting up barricades against protestors during the Hock Lee bus riots of 1955. Journalist Lee Khoon Choy witnessed the protest's violent climax at Alexandra Road.

appeared lax to the rioters. The way Lee saw it, Marshall was caught between a rock and a hard place: "He wanted the students' support and so was not firm enough in administering law and order."

More riots were to break out in the 1960s. Lim Kee Chan was almost caught in the riots of 21 July 1964, which was the birthday of the Prophet Muhammad. "I was at Gay World, where the Indoor Stadium is today. I went there in the afternoon for a meeting to revive the Singapore Boxing Board of Control, which prevented promoters from cheating the public.

"I parked my car at the Gay World carpark. As I was early and hungry, I had *mee* [noodles] at a stall there. Just as I was finishing the *mee*, I saw two people running along the main road… I saw people bashing stalls. I saw a lot of things. I saw some Chinese fellows running towards me and yelling, '*kiu meng, kiu meng*' (Cantonese for 'save my life, save my life'). What could I do? I couldn't do anything. I asked them to run into the carpark. I don't know what happened after that. Wah, it was terrible." Meanwhile, his wife had taken her mother and their daughter out. Lim waited with bated breath till they reached home much later, unscathed.

Lawyer **Syed Esa Almenoar** was among the Muslims marching peacefully in the procession downtown towards Geylang Serai to commemorate the Prophet Muhammad's birthday in the afternoon of 21 July 1964. Syed Esa, whose law firm partner Ahmad Ibrahim became Singapore's first local Attorney-General, recalled that Singapore's first president Yusof Ishak was in the crowd that day too. The Muslim celebrants had first congregated on the site where the Esplanade sits today. Syed Esa was among the speakers addressing the crowd that fateful afternoon. "So then we had our flag-off. We marched down all the way, past Beach Road and into Bras Basah Road," he recalled. "We went round to Victoria Street and Arab Street and nothing happened except a fight near the gasworks. I was leading the United Malays National Organisation (UMNO) party in the parade and I ordered my men not to interfere with the fight, but to march on."

They marched on to Kallang with the PAP contingent. By then, he said, the fight which had broken out between "several Malays and several Chinese" at the junction of Victoria and Lavender streets, fuelled a full-blown riot. People were being "hammered", he said, while he continued leading his UMNO contingent up to Lorong 12 Geylang, where they took shelter. There, he got a call from Malaysia's then Deputy Prime Minister Tun Abdul Razak, who was in charge of the defence forces. "He told me to go with the police immediately to see that there would be no massacre." Another UMNO strongman, Syed Jaafar Albar, then instructed him to "go to all the mosques and see that nothing happens between the Malays and the Chinese".

So Syed Esa, accompanied by three policemen in five patrol cars, went to all the mosques on the island to calm everyone down. "According to the car metre, I travelled 105 miles that day. I stopped at every mosque to see that nothing happened and I took two to three Chinese people home in the police car." Their peacekeeping mission stretched till 2 am. "We were so hungry and had no cigarettes to smoke. So we went to my house and had coffee and a carton of cigarettes there. All the police canteens were closed that night." At the end of it all, the death toll was 36, with 556 injured.

Shortly after the fracas, the government set up a Commission of Inquiry headed by lawyer Arumugam Ponnu Rajah, better known as A.P. Rajah. Syed Esa was among those called on to testify at the inquiry but that never came to pass. "Singapore separated from Malaysia and the commission died a natural death," he said.

If he could have testified and had been asked what he thought had triggered the riots, his view would have been as follows: "I think at that time, the urban renewal scheme had started... And the Malays knew that sooner or later Geylang

Supreme Court judge A.P. Rajah seen here at the opening of Legal Year 1987, headed the Commission of Inquiry (COI) into the 1964 riots. The COI, however, never took place because Singapore and Malaysia separated subsequently.

Serai or Serangoon Road or wherever it may be, one by one, their houses would go. And of course, as the English would say, those were their castles and they didn't want those disturbed. And so they went all out about it."

With that in mind and what he called "the religious vim" during that fateful Prophet Muhammad procession, everything, as he put it, went "puuup! Just like wildfire, nothing could stop it". Syed Esa noted, however, that the fight that started it all had happened in a quiet spot, near the Kallang gasworks. Otherwise, the violence could have been far worse. In a symbolic move to guard against internecine violence in future, the government later designated 21 July as Racial Harmony Day.

In 1964, Lim Kee Chan the boxer-turned-newsman and his family lived in Joo Chiat Place – right opposite a Malay *kampung* – but never came to any harm before, during or after the riots. "During the riots, we had no problem; we still came out and talked to each other," he said. "There was no fighting at all. It was only the bad guys, the gangsters, who started the riots."

Sin Leong also bore no ill-will towards those who were not Chinese. But after 1964, not all in his community shared his sentiments. Among Sin's helpers was one Ahmad, who kept an eye on Sin's family like they were his own. One day in the 1960s, Sin was teaching an open-air cooking class at Kallang. As the crowd around him swelled, he put his eldest daughter Hui Zhu, then a toddler, atop a table so she would not be lost among the audience.

Yet the girl was soon nowhere to be seen. "Ahmad was a clever fellow. He went straight to the police post. Hui Zhu was there and recognised him right away. But when Ahmad tried to claim her, the police didn't believe him because he was Malay and the girl was Chinese." They insisted on accompanying Ahmad back to where Sin was. "It was really troublesome," Sin huffed.

Khoo Teng Soon recalled: "At one time, the mere mention of Prime Minister Lee Kuan Yew's name or a picture of him in ST would rouse the anger of some of the extremists, who thought that we were trying to play it up."

Relations between the Malays and other races were so strained that the police took no chances, as teacher and writer **Chan Kwee Sung** learnt to his disappointment. "Immediately after the 1964 riots, I went to the police station on behalf of a Chinese martial arts association to apply for a permit to hold a lion dance in public. The officer in command at the Central Police Station flatly refused it, giving the reason that… the situation was still abnormal… Normally, the licence would have been granted with no questions asked."

Five years later, across the border in Kuala Lumpur, riots broke out in Petaling Street in the evening of 13 May 1969. Khoo was working at *The Straits Times* office there, in Jalan Riong. He recalled a colleague named Sandy recruiting rioters to print the next day's edition of the newspaper. "Sandy got the entire mob into the office and said he would pay them $50 a night to produce the paper. So the mob took their parangs home, came back and went to work, producing the ST."

The violence in Kuala Lumpur spread to Singapore. Between 31 May and 6 June 1969, a spate of racial riots left four dead, 80 injured. In Kuala Lumpur and Petaling Jaya, the official toll was 196 killed and 350 injured, with Malaysia declaring a state of emergency that was lifted only in 1971. In Singapore, ties between the communities frayed, but the police and Internal Security Department officers fanned out islandwide to contain the inciting of communal violence, and peace was soon restored.

Don't Just Whizz by in Patrol Cars

In 1983, Commissioner of Police **Goh Yong Hong** introduced Neighbourhood Police Posts. He recalled the rationale for it: "Before that, we depended a lot on patrol cars; hardly did we ever go into the public housing estates. We also patrolled the streets... All we did was whizz along in a car and so we didn't know the people and the people didn't know us."

Goh, in fact, overhauled the way the police force operated. "We revamped the whole process of policing. We had police posts dotted all over the island. Each post was manned by 20 to 22 people around the clock. So the police went out to the people, instead of waiting for people to come to them." The police also got the entire community to chip in through the Neighbourhood Watch. "We got residents to form groups and alert the police of any suspicious goings-on," he said.

Jessie Sarkies, whose Armenian paternal granduncles founded the fabled Raffles Hotel in 1887, shared another perspective on how relatively egalitarian Singapore society was. Sarkies was born in 1946, decades after her famous ancestors had died. She said: "If I go and have a cup of coffee at the Raffles, I have to pay for that cup." She could take heart in the fact that her family name lived on in not one, but two places in Singapore – besides the hotel, Sarkies Road, just off Bukit Timah Road, was named after her grandmother Regina Sarkies, who owned land where the road is today.

Sarkies recalled how kind and generous her paternal grandfather Arathoon Sarkies was, right up till his death. Rendered bankrupt by a profligate son-in-law, the old man had taken a *sampan* (a small wooden boat) out to sea, around the Riau Archipelago, to jump into the waters and kill himself. His granddaughter said: "He took off his Rolex watch and his felt hat and gave it to the *sampan* man. The *sampan* man said, 'Tuan Besar, why are you giving me all this?' And he replied, 'Where I am going, I don't need these. I want you to have them'." With that, her grandfather jumped into the sea, but the *sampan* man jumped in after him and pulled him back into the boat. Alas, after they came ashore, the old man died.

The boatman who tried to save Arathoon Sarkies was likely an Orang Laut (Malay for "people of the sea"), who were Singapore's first settlers. **Haji Abu Bakar Bin Abdul Halim**, who was steeped in Malay folklore, said the Orang Laut were from the islands surrounding Singapore, such as Lingga, Inderagiri and the Riau Archipelago. "The Orang Laut eat, drink and sleep in their boats which are built beautifully by the Bugis," said Abu Bakar. "Those from

Raffles Hotel founders Martin Sarkies (seated) and his younger brother Tigran (standing second from left) seen here with two of their employees. Martin and Tigran's younger brothers Aviet and Arshak were the hotel's two other co-founders, and they were all granduncles of Jessie Sarkies.

Pulau Brani ferry people hither and thither. Those who live near Jardine Steps in Singapore Harbour are fishermen. Some work in tin smelting for The Straits Trading Company." In Singapore, Abu Bakar added, the Orang Laut were mainly from three *kampungs* – Teluk Saga, Selat Sengkeh and Masak Timah. The community's most distinguished member, former cabinet minister, diplomat and newspaper editor Othman Wok, was from Teluk Saga.

Unsung Heroes

Some of Singapore's greatest community heroes are also the least known.

Take P. Govindasamy Pillai, who came from a family of silk weavers in Mayavaram (now known as Mayiladuthurai), Tanjore District in Tamil Nadu. Pillai, who was born in 1887 and died in 1980, came to Singapore in 1899. He set up his own sundry shop at

The businessman and philanthropist P. Govindasamy Pillai, seen here with his wife Packkiriammal at the Sri Srinivasa Perumal Temple in Serangoon Road, 1970s. He had no known vices, not even chewing *betel* nuts or drinking coffee.

Serangoon Road and helped found the Singapore Indian Chamber of Commerce in 1937, but lost everything during World War II. He picked himself up again and by the 1970s, had sponsored the *gopuram*, or entrance tower, to the Sri Srinivasa Perumal Temple on Serangoon Road – to the tune of $425,000.

His daughter Dhanalakshmi recalled: "When he had made his fortune, he still got up at 3 am every day, drank a glass of water by 4 am and went for a walk daily from Race Course Road to Katong Park. Then he would have a bath and meditate. By 6.30 am he was in his shop, going through the bills and accounts and by 8 am he would open the shop... He had no vices, not even chewing betel nuts or drinking coffee!"

Humble as he was, Govindasamy helped set up the Ramakrishna Mission orphanage in Bartley Road in 1952, which cost him more than $300,000. He also built hospital rooms and *chatrams*, or travellers' bungalows, near his birth village in India. He even converted his family's former resident in Thiruvarur to a *kalyana mandapam* (Telugu for "wedding hall"). "He thought that once he had made enough money, he should continue to give to some charities," his daughter said.

Toh Lim Mok, however, did not wait till he made enough money to help all in Singapore. Toh grew up in a 50-member household, all living on the second floors of a few shophouses

The Thaipusam festival procession at the Sri Srinivasa Perumal Temple in 1984. Businessman and philanthropist P. Govindasamy Pillai contributed funds to build the magnificent entrance tower (*gopuram*) of the temple.

in Beach Road. At the age of 17 years old, and while still in secondary school, he joined the Singapore Red Cross as a volunteer because, as he put it, "Since I was young, I felt that it's good if I can help others."

Toh, who was born in 1947 and so would have been 17 in 1964, soon started the first ambulance service to supplement those provided by the Singapore General Hospital. Most remarkably, this service was offered free of charge. "Singaporeans needed this supplementary service especially in the evenings," he said.

Then there was **Keki Medora**, a Parsi woman who grew up in a family of 23 in Mumbai, India, who started a scheme in the 1950s for well-to-do Singapore families to sponsor needy children. Each sponsor paid a subscription of $60 a year per child – or $5 a month. From this monthly sum, $2 was for the child's pocket money, $2 went into his or her savings account in a bank, and $1 was for their Christmas present. Medora recalled: "We raised funds with Loke Wan Tho, the Shaws, Lee Kong Chian. We wrote hundreds of letters and with all their donations, we started Trafalgar Home." Loke was the Cathay cinema magnate; the Shaws his business rivals and Lee Kong Chian's Lee Foundation had sponsored the education of thousands of poor families over the years.

As long as one feels 'I am Singaporean', well, that's the point. Of course, that was the government's problem at Independence…

She said of her fellow volunteers: "We were professional beggars. But the public was really good. They always helped. And so many shopkeepers we approached donated rice and canned food… it was very successful." In 1965, the government awarded her the Public Service Star, two years after she became a Singapore citizen.

Over the years, the late Govindasamy's Perumal Temple has received many donations from people of all walks of life, including huge sums from non-Hindus. Such community spirit has also done much for Yayasan Mendaki, the self-help group set up in 1982 for Singapore's Malay-Muslim community. Syed Esa Almenoar, who helped defuse the Prophet Muhammad riots in 1964, said the setting up of the Malay-Muslim pioneering self-help group Mendaki was significant because the Malay community was in dire need of help then. "The Malays in *kampungs* didn't have shoes to wear. They didn't have books to read. They had no money. When the stomach is empty, it's hard to start a race together."

Most heartening, Syed Esa stressed, was how much non-Malay communities took to supporting Mendaki. "One of the main outstanding features of Mendaki that I have observed is that even the non-Malays contribute to the funds for the Malays, So there is the encouragement from the majority race in Singapore. With this encouragement, there will be nothing to worry about. It will take time, but Mendaki is the first step."

He then mused: "As long as one feels 'I am Singaporean', well, that's the point. Of course, that was the government's problem at Independence – to get the population to live in Singapore and die in Singapore… if you can get that, everything should be all right."

CHAPTER TWO

SCHOOLDAYS

Saved by the Bell

As a boy, **Sin Leong** neither walked nor cycled to school. He was not driven there either. Instead, his mother carried him all the way – on her back. Sin, who later became a renowned chef with a restaurant to his name, recalled that each time before she set out, she took care to wrap a red rag around his head. This was because of the superstition that children's faces should be shielded from strangers. The cloth she used was from the *hong tou jin* (red headgear) that she wore on her own head, a trademark feature of the Samsui women. The street on which these women lived, Nankin Street, was one of Singapore's first. It was also known as Black Cloth Street, after the all-black garb of the Samsui women who lived there.

As a boy, Sin Leong neither walked nor cycled to school. He was not driven there either. Instead, his mother carried him all the way – on her back.

These hardy women from Samsui district in Guangdong, China, built much of Singapore's infrastructure, brick by brick, from the 1930s till the 1980s. How heavy could Sin be to his mother then, when her day job was hauling soil, stones and other construction material on building sites from dawn to dusk.

Recalling this in February 2007, Sin stressed that there was nothing unusual about his piggyback rides with his mother. "It was not a matter of age or whether you could walk by yourself," he said in Cantonese. "This was the traditional school-going ritual then." Fortunately, his alma mater – a private, informal one in the Chinese medium in a shophouse on Hokkien Street – was but a few hundred metres away from their lodgings.

Their piggyback ritual also had nothing to do with his family not being able to afford transport. Retired schools inspector **Alice Cheang Wye Lan**, whose family was well to do, recalled their servant giving her a piggyback ride to school on her first day there. Unlike Sin, her head was not covered in cloth. But she was asked to hold a sprig of *chong* (Cantonese for spring onion) in her left hand and a sprig of *kan chow* (Cantonese for Chinese celery) in her right. Cheang recalled: "When I asked my teacher why I had to carry these, she said *chong* signified "chong meng" (Cantonese for "clever") and *kan chow* signified "kan lek tok shuee" (Cantonese for "study hard"). "When my grandson started school, I was wondering whether to give him all these things or not," she added.

Samsui women like Sin Leong's mother were the backbone of Singapore's construction industry in the nation's formative years.

Cheang, who was born in 1903, began her formal education in an "old-style Chinese school" at the age of seven in 1910 but joined Raffles Girls' School from Standard VI to IX, leaving school in 1922.

After her puzzling first school day, she learned to ride the tram from her Craig Road home to her school, where the Bras Basah Circle Line MRT station is today. "I caught the tram from Tanjong Pagar Road and went up to Bras Basah Road. My school was next to Raffles Institution."

"The tram had no walls; if it rained, you got wet," she added. "When we wanted to get down, we just called to the driver to stop." Each ride cost 2 to 3 cents, the price of a plate of *char kway teow* (fried rice noodles) in those days. From 1 October 1925, trolley buses replaced these trams. By then, Cheang was well on her way to becoming a teacher.

Her schoolday began at 8 am and ended at 1 pm. For engineer **Noel Arthur Pereira**, who was born a few years after Cheang, classes began at 9 am. He would, however, sometimes reach his school only around noon. His teachers would not berate him for arriving so late because they knew that for him, going to school was a daily adventure fraught with danger.

Pereira's family used to live on Moulmein Road but his father's work as a shipping executive led them to settle on Pulau Bukom. Recalling the island as "full of granite quarries", he said, "At that time, you couldn't move around at night because there were tigers roaming

Whenever Alice Cheang Wye Lan rode an electric tram in the 1900s, such as this one down Bras Basah Road, she hoped the heavens would not open as the tram had no side walls to keep the rain out.

around. We used to hear them roaring. And in the morning, you could see their pad marks around the house." Pad marks or no pad marks, he would wake up by 4.30 am to make it to the jetty in time to catch the ferry to mainland Singapore. Being in school on time was not his only struggle; getting home for a good night's sleep was a hit-and-miss affair. "We sometimes got back after midnight because we had to come back by tug boat and there were sometimes strong currents," he said. "So it took quite a while to get back."

Noel Arthur Pereira's family used to live on Pulau Bukom. "You couldn't move around at night because there were tigers roaming around. We used to hear them roaring. And in the morning, you could see their pad marks around the house."

Journalist **Khoo Teng Soon**, who was an Anglo-Chinese School boy from a wealthy family, had no such hurdles. Yet he found it a royal pain to wake up in time for classes every morning. As there was no television when he was a boy to occupy his time, he admitted "there was no problem going to sleep early."

"Whether I liked it or not," he said, "I had to wake up at 7 o'clock and have my bath while my mother prepared either a fried egg to eat with rice or a couple of soft-boiled eggs to eat with bread."

Unlike Khoo, **Carmee Lim**, who later became principal of Raffles Girls' School, was always on time for classes. That was because she lived in her school, Yang Zheng Primary, as her father was a teacher there. But it was poverty, not privilege, that had them living and learning in the same place. Lim, who was her family's first graduate, continued living under Yang Zheng's roof even after she was awarded a $75-scholarship to attend Stamford School. After classes, to help her family get by, she would tutor her neighbours' children for $10 a month – a princely sum, as a plate of chicken *biryani* cost 25 cents then.

Winsome Carmee Lim, seen here at her school Yang Zheng Primary in 1951, did not go home after classes because she and her family lived in the school grounds.

Marks Were Like Gold Bullion

It was not such a stretch for Lim to juggle tutoring and homework because in those days, students were relatively "relaxed" about their studies, compared to the cramming – or mugging, as Singaporeans call it – that has been a mainstay of student culture since then Deputy Prime Minister and Minister for Education Goh Keng Swee introduced streaming in the 1970s. Lim, who was born in 1939 and was the longest-serving principal of Raffles Girls' School – from 1988 to 1999 – recalled: "My O-Levels were relaxed. We worked hard but not like what they do now… we just went for the exams. We still played games."

When she garnered a Grade I, the highest possible score in her school-leaving exams, she recalled her father saying "That's very good". "And that was it," she added. "No monetary rewards, no promises, because we did not have any money."

Despite such a sanguine attitude towards studies in general, students of yesteryear strove to better themselves, knowing full well that securing good academic results was their ticket to a better life. **Sukarti Binte Asmoin**, for one, enrolled in night classes after a full day in school just to master the English language. She said: "I found learning English a very uphill task. I did not know any English words except 'Yes' and 'No'. So when I was in Primary 6, I enrolled in English classes in a Chinese school in my village, which had night classes."

She recalled further: "One of my teachers was a Mr Dragon; he was such a nice teacher and I really caught up fast with my English because of him."

The extent to which many dedicated teachers inspired their students should not be underestimated. Teacher **Mrs Goh Heng Chong née Teo Moh Tet**, a former student of

Methodist Girls' School and whose last principal was Ellice Handy, author of *My Favourite Recipes*, Singapore's first cookbook on local cuisine, said: "We could go to her house and do lessons. We got influenced by her and wanted to study."

And study they did, amid various privations. Veterinarian and former civil servant **Ngiam Tong Tau**, who grew up with his four siblings in a *kampung* in Serangoon, recalled: "We used to study by this small kerosene lamp... all of us would sit around the table, we shared one lamp to study." Their father, who died when Ngiam was three, did not see the latter become the director of the Primary Production Department in 1984 and then chief executive officer of its successor, the Agri-Food & Veterinary Authority of Singapore, in 2000.

The people who egged former civil servant **Soh Siew Cheong** on to do his best in school were not his parents, but his schoolmates. Soh grew up in Chinatown where he watched most of his mates join secret society gangs known as 08, 24, 369 or The Boxer Rebellion. He said: "I've seen a few of my childhood friends slashed to death with *parangs*. The only way out was not to join them but to study hard." *Parang* is Malay for machete.

Fortunately, Soh added, he had a "far-sighted" father who pulled him out of his private Chinese vernacular school and sent him to St Joseph's Institution. "He wanted me to do well in life," he mused, adding that in his time, those who mastered the English language had a better chance of being employed by the few multinational companies such as Royal Dutch Shell and Standard Oil that were entering Singapore from the late 1960s.

Soh said, however, that there was much to commend studying in a *sishu* (a traditional Chinese private school), as Sin Leong had. *Sishu* students learnt by rote and the knowledge drilled into them by relentless recitation stuck. Soh surmised: "As you grow up, you are able to realise the beauty of the message in the culture that the Chinese developed over the years. And that, in a way, sort of shapes your thinking, your approach to life."

Still, studying your socks off was seldom enough if you had teachers like **Eugene Wijeysingha**, who taught at Raffles Institution and was its principal from 1986 to 1994. He was, by his own admission, "very stringent" in his marking, so much so that at a gathering of Raffles Institution's class of 1960, former Prime Minister Goh Chok Tong said of Wijeysingha, "Getting marks from him was like buying gold bullion."

Wijeysingha's way with marking did not endear him less to his students. Once, when rain prevented them from track and field activities, Wijeysingha remembered how *bomohs* (Malay for shamans) would plant a broomstick in the sodden ground with a chilli and onion tied to it. That, they believed, would stop downpours immediately. He recalled: "I remember walking out and planting this broomstick with the chilli and onion on it. It was recorded afterwards in *The Rafflesian Times*: 'The Rafflesian Magician stopped the rain by planting a broomstick'."

There were, of course, countless other students for whom the prospect of studying hard was boring at best. Among them was gangster-turned-pastor **Neivelle Tan**. Tan actually aced his studies easily but that led him to be lazy as schoolwork did not challenge him enough. It did not help that he had an unusual name which few knew how to pronounce – most took

Raffles Institution principal Eugene Wijeysingha speaking at the 163rd Founders Day celebrations of Raffles Institution and Raffles Junior College in 1986. He was so strict in marking examination papers that his former pupil Goh Chok Tong, Singapore's second prime minister, said getting marks from him was "like buying gold bullion".

Goh Chok Tong (centre), Singapore's second Prime Minister, was a swimming champion in his days at Raffles Institution. He is seen here with his mates Tan Im Huat (on Goh's right) and Douglas Munro (on his left) with their trophies from the individual championships.

to taunting him as "Nei-vel-lie", "Nei-ville", "Nei-val" or, most annoyingly, "Neighbour" and "Navel". Tan, whose name was pronounced "Neville" said: "They would point to the stomach and say, 'What's your name – Navel? Are you born on the navel?' or something like that."

Bored and goaded repeatedly, Tan soon became a loose cannon. In Standard 5, he started playing truant. By Secondary 1, his school had expelled him. He explained: "I was kicked out because I threatened one of the teachers even after being given the last warning. She caught me playing truant and not doing my homework." Prior to his expulsion, he had punctured the tyre of her car, "put something dirty" in her drawer, scattered thumbtacks on her seat and also stained it. The last straw was when he told her, "If you do not give me a passing mark, I will…" – and left it at that. That did it. Tan's formal education had ended; he became a full-blown gangster and eventually wound up in jail for some time.

Despite having to leave school early, Tan had actually started his school life toeing the line with his teachers – even at the risk of soiling his trousers. He recalled: "Unless your teacher says, 'Yes, you may go to the toilet', you are not supposed to go. So, always, we would be wondering, 'Would it be too late?' These were the worries."

Crying Like Life Was Going to End

A child's main worry, by far, would be his or her first day in school. Neivelle Tan remembered this day when he was six: "I was very scared – I had to be among strangers, then when I came into class for the first time, it was a real marketplace. Children were crying, wetting their pants. Parents were running in and out. Teachers were screaming."

"I didn't cry," he added, "but I just couldn't understand why these children were crying like their life was going to end."

Many students from poor families, however, had to be content with just black tea, taken straight without sugar or milk, much less any bread to go with it.

One wonders, then, what they would have made of "The Opening of the Pen" ritual which Sin's teacher observed at the start of each year at his Chinese school. Sin Leong said: "The teacher would bite into a live chicken's comb. Blood would flow from it and he would dip a new pen brush into the blood and dot that onto the four sides of The Three Word Sutra book – Heaven, Earth, Man and Harmony."

Recess brought much-needed respite. Tan's mother would pack him a simple snack of buttered bread and milk or water, while Khoo Teng Soon sometimes got to enjoy fish slices between his buttered bread.

Many students from poor families, however, had to be content with just black tea, taken straight without sugar or milk, much less any bread to go with it. Their plight moved social worker **Khatijun Nissa Siraj** such that she took it upon herself to write to the Social Welfare Department to do something about it. She recalled: "At that time, we were getting milk powder for children from Unicef (the United Nations Children's Education Fund). I wrote to the Department and asked them if they could give me, say, 200 lb of milk powder. There were these families with many children though the husband's salary was small… at least the kids get milk to drink instead of *teh-o*." *Teh-o* is tea with sugar but no milk.

A rare instance when schoolchildren were given a special treat was when they went on an excursion to the bottling plant of the aerated water company, Fraser & Neave (F&N). **Tan Wee Him**, the one-time erstwhile aviation correspondent of *The Straits Times*, recalled: "Schoolboys were thrilled to be going to the F&N bottling plant for the first time. You could drink as many bottles as you liked. The teachers normally did not stop us and you got to try different flavours. And it was a thrill in those days to actually get beautiful bottle caps."

For some, just going to school improved their parents' lot. When award-winning writer and editor **Haji Muhammad Ariff Bin Ahmad** attended the Tanglin Besar School in Ellis Road in the 1930s, his headmaster, whom he addressed as Cikgu Saparwan, asked Haji Muhammad's father to cut all his schoolmates' hair, for 5 cents a head. Muhammad Ariff said: "My father had this makeshift shop under the school staircase. The students did not pay my father directly, but gave what they owed to their respective teachers." Back then, he added, teachers had to coerce their students into cutting their hair and fingernails – and even brushing their teeth. "Every Monday and Thursday, our hair and nails would be checked. We had to squat in a line along the school drain and brush our teeth, using coal instead of toothpaste. We brushed our teeth only in school."

"Every Monday and Thursday, our hair and nails would be checked. We had to squat in a line along the school drain and brush our teeth, using coal instead of toothpaste. We brushed our teeth only in school."

During the Japanese Occupation of Singapore (1942–45), lots of teeth went unbrushed as the education of schoolchildren was, in general, disrupted badly. The extent of young lives lost to war hit home hard when surviving children went back to school after the war. There were simply not enough students to fill existing classrooms. **Chan Kai Yau**, a former director of education, recalled how the age range within each class then was very large – there were at least 10 to 12 years between some of the students. He added: "I was in the very young group. So when I compared myself to those who were much older, I would say, 'Well, when I reach that age, perhaps I will do some of the things that they were doing'."

These classes of mixed-age groups did not have enough exercise books, as there was a shortage of paper, and much else besides, after the war. "So," Chan explained, "we cut up exercise book pages that had not been used and stapled these together to make new exercise books."

Nevertheless, the people soon bounced back from the ravages of the Japanese Occupation. By the early 1970s, as a lecturer in the Teachers Training College (TTC) here, Chan found his trainees most reluctant to recycle old exercise books the way he and his classmates had

In the 1950s, it was rare for children to brush their teeth. Haji Muhammad Ariff Bin Ahmad recalled how in those days, teachers had to make children brush their teeth, cut their hair and fingernails regularly.

done. He recalled: "Some of my students were not so happy when I told them, 'When you finish the book you just throw it away; why not use the good paper left? Save some trees'."

Alice Cheang was among Singapore's earliest trainee teachers. "In 1925, I started learning how to teach," she recalled. She opted to do so in the mornings, at a boys' school in Pearl's Hill, then attend teachers' training classes the rest of the day, instead of training full-time at the Teachers Training College.

Her mornings were jampacked. "I would help the principal, Mrs Bishop, look after the registers and bookshop," Cheang said, adding that she was known as a "student teacher". "Then we had a few hours of observing how the good teachers taught. We sat behind the classes during observation, and also walked about to help the students. And once a week I had to teach a class for my principal. She would come in and see how I was teaching the children reading, writing and arithmetic."

Her teaching days were not always as routine as they seemed. For instance, she once had to hunt around Rochor Road for a live squirrel, for her students to observe how it ate, and learn how to treat it decently.

Shaping a Nation

Such quirky moments in class were, however, few and far between as children fell in and tried to make something of themselves. For most, learning languages was an especially hard struggle. **Bryant Hwang Tchuan Thau**, who worked in the Singapore stock market for many years, recalled his father, who was Teochew but spoke to his children in English, urging him and his two siblings to learn Chinese. There was little impetus for him to do so, however, as schools were indifferent towards teaching Mandarin until after the People's Action Party came to power in 1959 and made Mandarin a "main language", along with Malay, English and Tamil. "When I was a child," Hwang noted, "Mandarin was spoken by those who were higher educated – the Mandarins, as Minister Mentor Lee Kuan Yew referred to them." In other words, to the hoi polloi at the time, Mandarin was the preserve of a scholarly elite.

With such a relative disinterest in Mandarin and other languages such as Tamil, the English-educated found it hard to master other tongues. Teacher **Mangalesvary Ambiavagar** recalled how Singapore's founding prime minister himself would harangue school principals in ensuring that their students were bilingual. "Mr Lee Kuan Yew used to give talks to principals because he wasn't convinced that others could do the job properly. He would tell them, 'Second language must improve. I am watching the results'."

But bilingualism cut both ways in the Singapore education system.

After students in Chinese middle schools rebelled against the then colonial government's policy of requiring them to sit exams in English only, student numbers in Chinese vernacular schools began dropping significantly from the 1960s. By the late 1970s, most schools in which Chinese was the main medium of instruction began closing down due to a lack of students. The government was thus concerned about the career prospects of teachers in these schools.

So the Ministry of Education (MOE) decided to shore up their careers by retraining them to teach their subjects in English instead.

Dr Lau Wai Har, Director of the Institute of Education from 1976 to 1979, who had to train these teachers, rued how many among them eventually quit teaching altogether. She frequently told MOE officials that it was folly to make these Chinese-medium teachers teach in English. She said: "The teachers who completed the training told me, 'It's no use; I still can't do it'."

Their challenge was not simply the lack of confidence, she stressed. "These retrained teachers couldn't speak English well as they didn't have a strong foundation in the language," she said. "So when they were teaching in their schools, the students would laugh at the standard of their English or would believe that these teachers didn't have enough knowledge since they couldn't speak English well."

Eventually, MOE relented somewhat, allowing such teachers, many among whom were top-class in the teaching of mathematics and science, to switch to teaching the Chinese language instead.

Marie Ethel Bong, Principal of Katong Convent from 1971 to 1985, noted that education was "one of the key ways of developing a nation quickly". "We had to get the children quickly into schools," she recalled, "and make sure that there was a unified system in the schools." She added, pointedly: "The way education had... been left to grow on its

These children from Joo Avenue Integrated Primary School in 1964 dressed in ethnic costumes in a showcase of Singapore's vibrant multi-culturalism. The government had always been clear in its aim to integrate students of all races in the schools.

own previously was very unsatisfactory for building a nation."

That task itself could take some countries a lifetime to overcome. The first thing the government had to tackle was, as Bong put it, "the big problem" of building different ethnic communities and language streams into an integrated citizenry.

Mrs Marie Ethel Bong, who was Principal of Katong Convent from 1971 till 1985, saw first-hand what a cornerstone education was in shaping Singapore as a nation.

One immediate way to rally everyone around the idea of Singapore being one nation with one people was for everyone to honour the national flag, sing the national anthem "Majulah Singapura" – composed by Zubir Said – and recite the National Pledge daily. Teacher **Christabelle Alvis** recalled that her students "liked to listen to the national anthem" but were less enthusiastic about singing it. She said: "When Majulah Singapura was played on cassette tape, you could see that they were more attentive and standing up. But when they sang it, it wasn't done with gusto. So we used to make them sing it over and over and over, as in 'you don't go home until you have sung this properly'."

Her students were lackadaisical about reciting the National Pledge, which was officially introduced on 24 August 1966 in government and government-aided schools as part of a daily pledge-taking ceremony. Alvis said anyone could tell from the way they stood while reciting it that "they were quite bored". She and her fellow teachers were determined that their charges should honour the words that defined who Singaporeans were and what they believed. "So on rainy days, when we wouldn't meet at assembly, we would take The Pledge in the classroom. We pinned the Singapore flag to the blackboard and everyone would stand up and say The Pledge.

> The first thing the government had to tackle was "the big problem" of building different ethnic communities and language streams into an integrated citizenry.

"This was a good time for us to hear The Pledge really being said and we could then also correct them and make them see the seriousness of it all." She and her fellow teachers also took care to teach students how to raise the national flag "in a dignified way, slowly" so that "it didn't fall down in the evenings".

Another, perhaps subtler, way to help all of Singapore's communities come together was through the National Library's mobile libraries – first introduced in 1960 – which contained books galore in the nation's four main languages – Malay, English, Chinese and Tamil. Bong's sister, **Hedwig Elizabeth Aroozoo Anuar**, recalled: "The Ministry of Culture used our mobile libraries... going around the rural areas... to the community centres and all that

Mrs Hedwig Anuar (far left), the first local to head the National Library, is seen here pointing out something interesting to Minister of Culture S. Rajaratnam at the presentation ceremony of the Gibson-Hill Collection to the National Library in 1965.

Mobile libraries, such as the one here in 1960, travelled to community centres and the rural fringes of Singapore to help all in the fledgling nation bond over books.

kind of thing. That helped build national consciousness." So too did regular messaging on national radio and television, in the press – and lots of talks by librarians in schools. Anuar, who was the National Library's first Singaporean director from 1965 until 1988, said: "I gave so many talks at schools that, half the time, I'd probably be out of the office."

To align everyone in the same direction quickly, the government made a member of parliament the president of the Singapore Teachers' Union. In this way, the government brooked neither dissent nor experimental approaches towards its education policies; there was simply no time to tarry in trying to shape a nation that could depend only on the wits of its people.

Bong agreed: "The government's heavy-handedness was necessary to try and solve the little problems within the schools… individual grievances and so on. It played a part quietly in the personal grievances of principals and teachers." She knew the teaching profession deeply; her father, Percival Frank Aroozoo, was the first Asian principal of Gan Eng Seng School from 1938 till 1955. She herself began teaching in 1951, and was awarded the Efficiency Medal in 1979.

Bong noted that before the government restructured the education system from the 1960s, the system had been left to meander in disparate ways, and soon went to seed. After all, it would not help a mostly Caucasian colonial government to educate the indigenous peoples of Singapore lest they have ideas and try to rise above their stations – and likely question, perhaps even challenge, the policies of their colonial masters. Even at an institution as vaunted as Raffles Girls' School in the 1920s, Alice Cheang recalled not having a single teacher who was Chinese, and only a few other Chinese girls as schoolmates. Most teachers were either Caucasians or Eurasians. The former specialised in subjects such as literature, while the latter taught needlework and singing. Each class had about 30 students, sitting at desks in rows.

By the 1950s, when the people of Singapore were picking up the pieces after the war, there were more locals teaching in schools. Most were non-graduates, said Eugene Wijeysingha. In fact, he said, the non-graduate teachers "formed the backbone" of schools then. They were, he added, very active in sports because with sports, they could find common ground with their fellow teachers who, like Wijeysingha, were graduates. "We ran into them, they ran into us," is how he explained their bonding on and off the sports field.

Kasinather Sauntharararajah said there were few local women who were teachers when he trained as a teacher in Singapore from 1950 to 1953. Sauntharararajah, better known as K.S. Rajah, who later became a lawyer and judge, said: "A very interesting thing was that they were expected to be not only good teachers but also sportsmen who would… teach the children games." He added that the government schools then simply preferred recruiting men as teachers, although only women taught in all-girls' schools.

What Great Teachers Are

In those days, teachers were among the better earners in the workforce. Carmee Lim recalled her starting pay in the 1950s was $500, excluding her living allowance, compared to a fresh lawyer's pay, which then averaged around $750. In fact, Eugene Wijeysingha taught English, geography, history and general paper for $750 a month in the 1960s, a sum which included a living allowance of $150. Being resourceful, he also taught night classes at Beatty Secondary School for another $140 a month.

Not all good teachers were with the MOE. French-Canadian Catholic priest **Brother Vincent**, whose birth name was Guy Joseph Janvier Barbe, trained as a missionary in London and came to Singapore in 1940. During the Japanese Occupation, he became a prisoner-of-war and while in Changi Prison, established a makeshift school for boys who had lost their fathers in battle. In 1948, he founded Boys' Town home for wayward boys, housed in an abandoned building in Bukit Timah. In 1973, the home became the Assumption School where Brother Vincent held the position of director until February 1987.

While Boys' Town was for setting naughty boys on the straight and narrow path again, Brother Vincent stressed: "I tell every boy that comes here, 'If you want to come here, you must fill up an application and sign your willingness to stay here. We are not going to force you to be with us. We are not a prison. If you want to go, there is the door and the gate is open'. So the boy says, 'Wow, I thought my parents are punishing me by sending me to Boys' Town. How come Boys' Town is like that?' So they change their attitude."

Such a keen grasp of human psychology saved many a boy, including one Tan Ah Kiang, who became unruly after his mother died suddenly in a car accident. Brother Vincent recalled: "At the beginning, after his mother died, he was very sullen. After some time, he said, 'I want to be baptised'... and he said, 'I want to be called Vincent'." So he became known as Vincent Tan Ah Kiang and, Brother Vincent was glad to note, a very successful salesperson later.

Brother Vincent added that the toughest boys to crack were those from rich families who had fallen into bad company. "They were the toughest actually as they were the most demanding," he mused. "And to bring them to the level of others, you have to make them swallow hard... It takes us quite some time to reduce them to have another sense of value, of people, of money, of what life is all about, and what is right – and what wrong."

In the early years of independent Singapore, few among Singapore's best students could pursue tertiary education, either because they had no money for the tuition fees to begin with, or were from families who needed them to get a job as soon as possible.

Ambassador-at-large **Professor Tommy Koh Thong Bee** was one of the few who could attend university. He was, in fact, among the pioneering batch of 22 law students at the University of Malaya in Singapore. His entry into law school was sweetened further by what he called "an extraordinary gift" from his father, an urbane salesperson who could speak English, Malay, French and German. It was he who taught Koh to love books. What, then, was that extraordinary gift? "He opened an account for me at the City Book Store in

The City Book Store in Collyer Quay, 1950. This was where Ambassador-at-large Tommy Koh's father opened an account for him so that he could buy any book he wanted there.

Collyer Quay," Koh said. "And he told the people at this bookstore that I could take any book I wanted and charge it to his account."

Well into the 1960s, the University of Malaya in Singapore had mostly expatriate teachers. Former librarian **Vilasini Perumbulavil** recalled her "very jolly" history lecturer Kennedy G. Tregonning, who would pronounce Bukit Timah, where the university was located at the time, as "Boo-det Tee-mah" in his "marked Australian accent", while John Burton Sanderson Haldane, a distinguished Scottish scientist and polymath then visiting from his base in India, went about the campus "in a Punjabi shirt and a loincloth".

Eccentrics aside, the lot of undergraduates on the campus had some defining moments, most notably during the first few weeks of a freshman's life. Vilasini remembered that S.T. Ratnam in particular – the brother of distinguished surgeon and fertility expert S.S. Ratnam – was "famous for ragging". Nevertheless, however bad the ragging was, those involved understood its underlying purpose. She explained: "It is to take away all your airs. And to make you feel that you are really an undergraduate. It's a bit of bullying… but a little bit is okay, not too much. I used to hear some people had it very bad." Among other things, she said, some seniors would pour buckets of urine over freshmen.

Many among them had no hope of studying abroad without financial support of some sort from the government or international foundations such as Ford or Rockefeller. Few, if any, among them would have turned down a prestigious scholarship for further studies. But that was exactly what **Tan Gee Paw** did.

Tan Gee Paw drafted Singapore's Water Master Plan in 1972 and was Chairman of the Public Utilities Board from 2001 to 2017.

A day before he was due to sign a bond at the Public Service Commission (PSC) to do marine engineering on the coveted Colombo Plan scholarship, he did some soul-searching at Clifford Pier. "I sat on the parapet of the pier and looked out at the ships," he recalled. "And I thought, 'I don't think I want to spend my life inside those ships'." The following day, he told an official at the PSC that he had decided to turn down its scholarship offer. The official almost had a fit. Tan recalled further: "He said, 'How can you turn down the Colombo Plan scholarship and so late – at the last minute? Who's going to take your place?'" He proceeded to try to browbeat Tan into reversing his decision, but the latter stood his ground.

Tan had not made his decision lightly. He was from a family who could barely afford a train ticket to Kuala Lumpur, which was where he eventually wound up, after enrolling at the University of Malaya campus there to study civil engineering. Luckily, there were no hard feelings between him and the PSC as it eventually awarded him a bursary to help cover his tuition and expenses in Kuala Lumpur.

Unfortunately, in his final year, Tan had to attend classes and sit his examinations in a straitjacket-like weighted suit after suffering a slipped disc. He was often in agony and it would take him hours to "uncurl" his body from the confines of that suit. His mother, fretting for his well-being, asked him to quit his studies and return to Singapore but he stuck it out, graduating with a First Class Honours in Engineering in 1967. He went on to craft Singapore's Water Master Plan in 1972 and was later Chairman of the Public Utilities Board.

What lies ahead for education in Singapore? And to what extent has the lot of teachers improved in the past 50 years or so?

Marie Bong said: "Respect for the teaching profession has got to be built up. And the only way it can be done is for teachers to have confidence in themselves and see themselves as professionals, as people making a valuable contribution to society, as having the respect of others." So the current "confrontational situation" between teachers on the one hand and parents and the public on the other is, to her, "just mass against mass". Better, she thought, for everyone to think of teachers "as individuals, as professionals", not faceless nobodies who serve society.

> "Respect for the teaching profession has got to be built up. And the only way it can be done is for teachers to have confidence in themselves and see themselves as professionals, as people making a valuable contribution to society, as having the respect of others."

The path to that, perhaps, is to revisit what makes great teachers great in the first place. According to Eugene Wijeysingha, "A great teacher would be one who enjoys the company of young people, who likes to share in their adventures because at the end of the day, it's a matter of whether a child wants to learn from a particular teacher." He added: "A child will learn from a particular teacher if the child likes the teacher. If a child is able to feel that this teacher is interested in him as a total person, interested in his total welfare, then the child will be more inclined to relate to the teacher, to learn from such a person."

Words to live by.

CHAPTER THREE

PASTIMES
Happy Days

Evenings on Read Bridge, located at Clarke Quay, belonged to the Chinese storytellers. As dusk fell, these men – for only men were itinerant storytellers then – would lug low wooden stools, kerosene lamps and soapboxes to the bridge. They would then regale their listeners with yarns of yore as the Singapore River rippled languidly around them.

Journalist **Tan Wee Him** recalled the storytellers' audience being "the coolies who carried sacks of rice and rubber" from *sampans* (small wooden boats) on the river to the godowns on its bank. Tan said: "They would sit on those wooden stools and listen to the storyteller's stories and after that, they just put coins into the soapbox in front of him." Impecunious and illiterate, the labourers' only pastime was listening to tale after tale, as the night enveloped them.

Gangster-turned-pastor **Neivelle Tan**'s father would, similarly, read his children bedtime stories on the five-foot-way of their home on Pennefather Road, in the East Coast of Singapore. Tan, whose uncle was the Malayan independence leader Tan Cheng Lock (also the founder and first president of the Malayan Chinese Association and after whom Jalan Tun Tan Cheng Lock in Kuala Lumpur was named) said: "The custom was to sit at the five-foot-way in front of the house. We would drag up some milk boxes and sit in front of him there and ask him to tell us stories.

"He would invariably tell us one of his long stories, and capture our attention to the part where it's most interesting. Then he would say. 'Okay, I have to stop, I will tell you tomorrow.' We would be anxiously waiting to know what happened."

Other families, especially those who were better off, enjoyed storytelling on the radio. Guitar maestro **Alex Abisheganaden**, dubbed "Father of the Guitar", recalled that a radio then was "bigger than a table" and had to have an outdoor aerial, which was fiddly to adjust, especially in bad weather. "When we finally had an indoor aerial," he said, "it was a wonderful thing."

For much of the 20th century in Singapore, there was precious little to do after dark. **Soh Siew Cheong**, who was born in 1942, said shops closed by 5 pm. When night fell in Chinatown where he grew up, its residents would "come out into the streets, visit each other, sit around at five-foot-ways, smoking or playing the *erhu*". The *erhu* is a Chinese two-stringed

A Chinese storyteller of yore regaling his audience of mostly humble workmen on cool Singapore evenings, 1950. Street storytelling was a popular form of entertainment in Singapore up till the 1960s, and the stories were told in different Chinese dialects.

All-rounder musician Alex Abisheganaden (centre, on double bass) was dubbed Singapore's 'Father of the Guitar". Here he is in a jam session with the Goh Soon Tioe Orchestra, also known as The Skiffle Group. With him are (from left to right) Samuel Miao, Lim Chin Beng, Lee Boon Siong, Errol Pang and Goh Heng Leong.

> For much of the 20th century in Singapore, there was precious little to do after dark. When night fell in Chinatown where he grew up, its residents would "come out into the streets, visit each other, sit around at five-foot-ways, smoking or playing the *erhu*".

instrument that, when played, emits keening wails. "During Mooncake Festival and other festivals," he added, "they would dance in the streets." He said the Cantonese community, in particular, was big on organising social activities. They would, among other things, stage Cantonese operas by the roadside in the evenings.

Earlier in the day, he said, the Cantonese also had the habit of throwing coins onto the road outside the temples where they prayed. "We'd rush over and pick a few of these, then dash back into our own territory," he recalled. "Otherwise, if we were caught, we'd surely be beaten up." Soh and his playmates were dicing with danger because areas in Chinatown then were controlled by different clans. For instance, Chin Chew Street and China Street were under the Hokkiens, while Upper Chin Chew, Upper Nankin and Hong Kong streets were Teochew territory. "We never crossed boundaries," Soh stressed, "except during the Seventh Month." With Chinatown a hotbed for gangsterism, one paid for transgressions with one's life.

Too much tipple often invited the Grim Reaper to take lives too. Tan the journalist noted that Stamford Canal along Orchard Road used to be open and rank-smelling from waste – the Urban Redevelopment Authority covered it up only in the 1980s. Before that, tipsy drivers died after hurtling straight into the water-filled canal. Other drunkards fell into open drains, with some breaking their bones.

Even the absence of drains could not keep drunks out of danger, as Tan the journalist learnt when he watched labourers drowning their woes at a small, government-run toddy stall on Ord Road, behind where Liang Court is today. Toddy, a highly alcoholic drink made from the sap of the palm tree, was 20 cents a glass then. Tan said: "It was a cheap luxury for a lot of poor people who wanted to have a drink and forget their agonies."

"And," he added, "when they had one too many, you'd find them drunk, loitering around the whole area. And some would be on the road. So if you drove to that area, you'd have to manoeuvre your car away from actual bodies on the road."

Journalist **Khoo Teng Soon**, who was Tan's colleague, was based in Kuala Lumpur then and so rarely saw such spectacles. But even if he had seen all the drunks rolling about River Valley Road, that would not have deterred him from drinking. He had been put off liquor much earlier in life. "My old man was a drinker," he said. "I would accompany him to bars from a very young age, but I took a long time to start drinking myself." Khoo amused himself instead with the nibbles that went with stiff drinks then, such as gingko nuts, *kacang* (Malay for groundnuts), pickles and *kana* (Hokkien for preserved black olives). He recalled further that in the 1930s, a bottle of brandy cost $2...Whisky cost slightly less than brandy, and beer was 15 cents a bottle.

Singapore's Three Worlds

Khoo Teng Soon's father likely quaffed the night away at one of the many cabarets within one of Singapore's three famous "Worlds", namely Great World on Kim Seng Road, Happy World (later renamed Gay World) in Kallang and New World, which was at the junction of Jalan Besar and Kitchener Road. Besides cabarets, each "World" also had theatres, restaurants and amusement arcades, complete with ferris wheels and booth after booth of carnival games.

Newsman and ex-professional boxer **Lim Kee Chan** said that Gay World, in particular, was notable for hosting basketball matches.

It wasn't all play and no work. Tan the journalist spent so much of his teenhood shooting light bulbs and drinking glasses at the air rifle range in Great World's games arcade that he became a top marksman in the Special Constabulary of the Singapore Police Force's Volunteer Wing. He recalled: "An arcade in those days was a dolled-up garage and if you hit the bull's eye, you got to take home a teddy bear. After every shot, you had to reload your gun with pellets."

The three "Worlds" also leased out their premises for businessmen to launch and sell products such as fizzy drinks, biscuits and Crocodile-brand shirts, to members of the public. The latter eagerly awaited such trade fairs, which were held a few times a year, because they were then so starved of affordable entertainment.

The entrance to Happy World (later renamed Gay World), the last of Singapore's three "worlds", or amusement parks, opened on 6 May 1937. Newsman and ex-professional boxer Lim Kee Chan recalled watching many basketball matches here.

This was Fitzpatrick's supermarket in Orchard Road in 1962, where journalist Tan Wee Him encountered Singapore's first automated doors, which he said were the talk of the town then.

Novelty was so rare that the odd innovation or two was a national event. Tan Wee Him the journalist remembered how fascinated Singaporeans were with the country's first escalator – at the old Jackie's Bowl, where Orchard Cineleisure is today – and the first automated doors, at Fitzpatrick's along Orchard Road, where The Paragon is today. He said of the automated doors, "You stepped on the rubberised floor, which was actually the sensor, and the door automatically opened. It was something very exciting then to a lot of people."

Novelty was so rare that the odd innovation or two was a national event. Tan Wee Him the journalist remembered how fascinated Singaporeans were with the country's first escalator – at the old Jackie's Bowl, where Orchard Cineleisure is today.

But the most reliable source of novelty, by far, was the picturehouse. Great World was opposite Khoo's office at Times House on Kim Seng Road when he was the editor-in-chief of *The Straits Times*. Great World housed the Shaw Brothers' cinemas, Sky and Globe. Sky showed newly released movies while Globe screened reruns. At one point, Sky introduced Cinerama, the precursor to today's Imax mega-screen. But Tan the journalist said that Cinerama was not popular. "It died an early death as people found it very difficult to watch a movie that had two joints in the middle of the screen."

Next to the Sky cinema was Great World's cabaret, featuring women "taxi dancers", or professional dancers for hire, who would whirl about with paying customers to the rhythms of *ronggeng*, a lively Javanese dance. Abisheganaden remembered bopping with these dancers "the whole night long" in his teens. He said: "I would buy long coupons... you could have as many dances as you wanted as long as you had coupons to exchange for dancers."

He also went to tea dances from 3 pm to 6 pm at the three "Worlds" when he was "12 going on 16". **Lucy Chen née Lim Seok Hui** – her father was Lim Chong Pang and her grandfather Lim Nee Soon, after whom the former Chong Pang Village (now part of Yishun) and Nee Soon Estate (now known as Yishun) are named – recalled "group dating dances" at an open-air dance theatre in Pasir Panjang. Their group dates also included tennis matches.

Abisheganaden's brother, Paul Abisheganaden, was a talented violinist who played with the Syonan Kokaido Orchestra during the Japanese Occupation.

Long-time Katong Convent principal, **Marie Ethel Bong**, who grew up during World War II, recalled that after the war, she and her schoolmates went to symphonic concerts at Victoria Theatre – for free. "We used to bring our literature books and queue up with these, waiting to go in. As they were free, we got into the habit of going for these concerts. We sat on top-up seats, with cane bottoms."

How Can You Show Dracula With No Fangs?

However, relatively few people in Singapore appreciated cultural pursuits such as symphonic concerts. Whenever working people had cash to spare, they made a beeline for the cinema. **Richard @ Ricky Uy**, a seasoned film distributor and cinema business veteran, explained: "The film business was one of the first to go up when the economy goes up. It's one of the last to go down when the economy goes down. Somehow or other, no matter how bad things are, people will say, 'All right, I think I'll take an hour or two off and I could just go out and watch this movie, forget everything for a while."

"After all," he quipped, "movies are about dreams."

Singapore dance pioneer, choreographer and writer **Richard Tan Swee Guan**, who was a teenager in the 1960s, recalled movie houses as "the 'in' thing". He said: "I remember… when this [Hindi] movie called *Sangam* was played at Galaxy. [It ran for] 63 days and people were still packing [it in for] every show."

That was, perhaps, how overworked film projectors sometimes burst into flames. Tan, a film fan, recalled: "The projector somehow got stuck and the film got burned. The faces on-screen suddenly had holes in them and everything melted and became one lump. The audience would go 'Oi! Oi! *Bakar*! *Bakar*! *Tidur*! *Tidur*! Projector *tidur*!' "*Bakar*" and "*tidur*" mean "on fire" and "sleeping" in Malay respectively. Hecklers aside, his aunt would "drag" him to Hindustani movies at the Odeon cinema in Katong, which gave him an unexpected boon. "I did not know what was being spoken so I read the English subtitles," he said. "I guess that's how I learnt to read very fast in English."

And while Hong Kong had a significantly larger population than Singapore, Uy said that Singaporeans' appetite for movie-going was so healthy that the bookings for movie releases in Singapore were comparable with that of Hong Kong's. "In fact," he said, "when I was booking in Hong Kong, I would book it for Singapore as well, knowing that it was going to follow through."

Fortunately, the one thing Singapore did not mirror was the attitude of Hong Kong's Board of Film Censors. While the Singapore censors were careful to clamp down on anything that had gratuitous violence or obscenities or was otherwise profane, their Hong Kong counterparts went even further. Uy recalled: "When we wanted to play a Dracula film, they asked us to remove Dracula's teeth from the poster. We said, 'We simply can't have Dracula without the teeth... You can ban the film, we'd rather not play it. But how can you advertise Dracula with no teeth?"

That question would likely have stymied cinema poster painter **Lee See Sin** as well. Lee's occupational hazard was, well, his occupation. He had to climb four storeys of scaffolding – nothing more than wooden poles held together with strips of rattan – to paint film posters which, in those days, were the size of billboards. He did not even have a hard hat, let alone a safety harness attached to his torso. "It was quite windy up there and when the wind blew, the scaffolding would wobble. It was quite scary but as I was young, this didn't bother me and I wasn't afraid of heights."

Singaporeans loved movies so much that they would flock to them even if they had to watch these under open skies. Lim Kee Chan recalled attending such movie sessions at a huge house with a big compound near Seaview Hotel in Katong. He said: "On Saturdays, they would show a movie there and you paid 10 cents to watch it. You stood for two hours or however long it took for the movie to play. That is when you got all the communities in one spot – Malays, Chinese and so on." By the 1970s, movie-lovers could watch blockbusters in the comfort of their car – at Singapore's first and only drive-in cinema in Jurong, run by Cathay Organisation.

Singapore's first and only drive-in cinema opened on Yuan Ching Road, Jurong, in 1971. It could accommodate 900 cars at any one time, but closed down in 1985 due to dismal attendance.

Persian businessman Mirza Namazie built Capitol Theatre in the 1930s, which had the largest seating capacity for a theatre in the Far East at the time.

The Singaporean's love of the silver screen blossomed from an early age. Teacher **Mrs Goh Heng Chong née Teo Moh Tet** remembered that when she was in primary school in the 1930s, she and her cousins were allowed to go to the movies – as long as their mothers accompanied them. "I watched my first colour picture at Capitol Theatre," she said, referring to the swanky cinema bankrolled by Persian millionaire Mirza Namazie, which opened on 22 May 1930.

Goh recalled watching shows at the older Alhambra Theatre too, which was on Beach Road along with Marlborough Theatre. Singapore's first enclosed cinema, however, was Paris Cinematograph, built in 1904 by jewellers Levy Hermanos. It opened in the Malay Theatre at 320 Victoria Street and had electric ceiling fans, which was quite a talking point then as the world's first such fan was invented in 1882, and Singapore had electricity only from 1878 onwards, or less than 30 years before the Paris Cinematograph opened.

Singaporeans born before 1950 would likely remember Pavilion cinema on Orchard Road. Previously known as the Palladium which opened in 1914 and screened mainly European films, the cinema was the first to introduce Sunday morning shows – the first being *Our Daily Bread* – in 1935. A special treat for children in those days was to watch *Tom and Jerry* cartoons there for 50 cents each on Sundays. The Pavilion later made way for the Specialists' Shopping Centre, which in turn was replaced by Orchard Central mall.

Cathay cinema opened in 1939 in Cathay Building – then the first skyscraper in Singapore and the tallest building in Southeast Asia. It screened movies with local flavour as its film production arm was famous for, among other things, P. Ramlee releases. Then, in

The fabled Alhambra Theatre in Beach Road, 1947. It was one of Singapore's first picturehouses. Trips there often ended with a *satay* feast at the stalls on its fringes.

Cathay cinema opened in 1939 in Cathay Building – then the first skyscraper in Singapore and the tallest building in Southeast Asia. It screened movies with local flavour as its film production arm was famous for, among other things, P. Ramlee releases.

1959, Hong Kong's Shaw Brothers opened Lido Cinema on Orchard Road. As the Shaws made lots of Chinese movies, Lido bumped up the buffet of on-screen offerings even more.

Former librarian **Vilasini Perumbulavil** said she and her friends would watch movies that were based on their literature texts in school, including the plays of William Shakespeare, Ben Jonson and George Bernard Shaw.

And for Peranakan theatre productions, the audience would invariably be part of the performance. Richard Tan the film buff said: "When the play was going on, the audience would *campur mulut* (interject) with their comments... when those on stage were about to expose the bad guy, you could hear the audience getting into the act, saying, 'Yeah! Yeah! Get him!'"

He added: "They were quite verbal, not like our audiences today where everybody is still. The *bibiks*, especially, were very loud and not shy when they talked." *Bibiks* are Peranakan women of a certain age, who are known to be feisty and loud.

Le Jazz Hot!

As Singapore's economy took shape from the mid-1970s, with incoming multinational companies bringing better-paying jobs for Singaporeans, the local taste for music became even more sophisticated. Why, even **Vernon Christopher Cornelius**, lead singer of local band The Quests and Singapore's answer to Cliff Richard, found himself rejecting the pop-rock music he used to love for jazz. "I had many bitter arguments with friends about that," he recalled.

In 1961, the year Cliff Richard and his band The Shadows played in Singapore, the place for jazz lovers was Golden Venus Bar Restaurant and Night Club in Orchard Hotel at Orange Grove Road. By the 1970s, The Jockey Pub at Shaw Centre on Scotts Road was the spot for an afternoon of jazz on weekends. In the 1980s, the coolest cats would be found at Somerset's Bar in Raffles City's Westin Hotel (now the Swissotel at Stamford). Today, the syncopated beats attract crowds at pubs such as Blu Jaz in Bali Lane, off Arab Street.

One of the hotspots for jazz from the late 1970s was Club 392, named after the street number of the building in which it was housed, on the site where Palais Renaissance shopping mall is today. As fans of jazz are often of a certain age, patrons of Club 392 often did a double take when they learnt that its bandleader was **Jeremy Ian Monteiro**. Monteiro was merely 16 when he was appointed to his position. He had secured the job after his mother, a private nurse, persuaded her patient Mr Isaac, who was Club 392's owner, to employ her son. Monteiro got the job after just one audition.

Singer Vernon Cornelius (far right), also known as Singapore's Cliff Richard, is seen here with his groundbreaking band The Quests in the 1960s.

Jeremy Monteiro seen here conducting the Jazz Association Singapore Orchestra for the "Oktoberfest Big Band Bonanza" at the Tanglin Community Club in 2018. Singapore's foremost jazz musician was awarded the Cultural Medallion in 2002.

Monteiro would later distinguish himself as Singapore's pre-eminent jazzman. He was awarded the Cultural Medallion, Singapore's highest arts honour, in 2002. But at the tender age of 16, even his sheer talent could not save him from life's harsher realities. He said: "At age 16½, it was very difficult for me because the other musicians in the band were in their 30s and 40s… And at that time, I was very puny. I still looked like a small boy, albeit one in charge of a band."

He almost took a tumble after he hauled one of his bandmates up for always being late for work. "I told him, 'You have to stop coming late because the boss told me we need to start on time.' He was very upset and I guess he had a reason to be so – this young boy telling this 40-year-old to come to work on time. So one day, he wanted to beat me up behind Orchard Towers. Luckily, one of my other musicians saw this guy kind of pushing me around and said to him, 'What's wrong with you? You want to bully a small guy, a young guy?'"

Monteiro then mused: "That was a sobering experience. And I guess I learnt to be more tactful when I gave instructions."

Even though his other bandmates kept their cool, playing at Club 392 was sometimes a hairy experience. That was because the club, which Monteiro described as a "hive of activity", was the meeting point for New Zealand's Maori soldiers – who would sometimes fight each other while in the club. "They were kind of a crazy bunch," he said. "Once, one of them picked up a stool to throw at another Maori guy, who ducked. The stool came straight towards the stage. I ducked, but my bass player, Louis Mendoza, didn't see it coming and so the stool slammed into him. He wasn't badly hurt but he was quite shocked."

Among the many local talents his band had accompanied were Rahim Hamid, who would croon in the style of American jazz pianist and vocalist Nat King Cole; Rahim Hamid's daughter, singer and actress Rahimah Rahim; and jazz trumpeter Tony Castillo, whom the acclaimed American jazz musician Louis Armstrong, no less, called his equal. Castillo would later appear on *The Ed Sullivan Show*, the American TV programme which shot English rock band The Beatles and the "King of Rock and Roll" Elvis Presley to global stardom. Monteiro said that Castillo, however, later lost his way and, as Monteiro put it, "spoiled his career quite badly".

A star attraction in Singapore that nonetheless threatened to damage its reputation internationally was seedy Bugis Street.

A star attraction in Singapore that nonetheless threatened to damage its reputation internationally was seedy Bugis Street. From the late 1960s to the late 1970s, amid America's raging war with Vietnam, Singapore became a rest-and-relax pit stop for American GIs – and the bizarre bazaar that was Bugis Street became their haunt. Its alcohol-fuelled thrills included parades of prostitutes soliciting for business and, most famously, open-air cabarets put on by transvestites, who would pose for photographers or disrobe and sit on their patrons' laps.

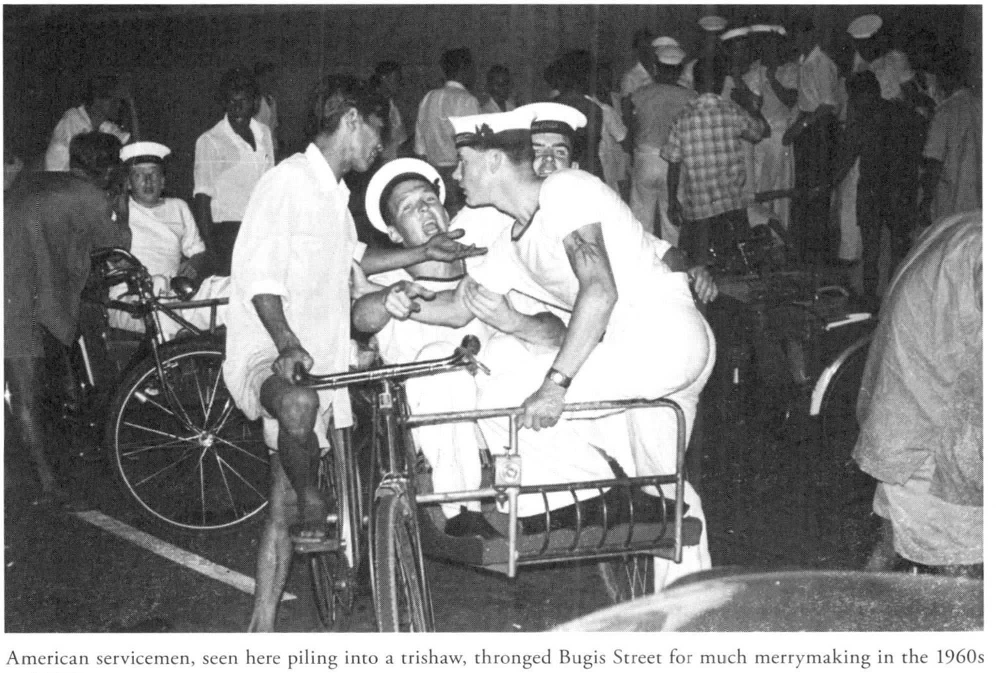

American servicemen, seen here piling into a trishaw, thronged Bugis Street for much merrymaking in the 1960s and 1970s.

Beauty businesswoman **Jean Yip**, who was born in 1958 and grew up in a shophouse overlooking the street, likened it to Thailand's red-light city of Pattaya and felt that the government was right to redevelop Bugis Street in the mid-1980s into Bugis Junction, so as not to taint Singapore's blossoming into a first world country. Recalling a trip to Pattaya with members of the Spa Association of Singapore, Yip added: "I was sharing with my sisters, 'this was like last time Bugis Street. I see already, I am very scared... I have three kids. I don't think I would like to put my kids in the Bugis Street area."

What, exactly, was so scary about Bugis Street? Yip, whose grandmother Hoong Xi ran the famous Yip Kee chicken porridge-cum-*zi char* (cooked food) stall there, recalled its sleazy surrounds. In the 1960s and 1970s, the street's hawkers would start laying out tables and chairs on the street by 4 pm every day, thus barring vehicles from entering. "By 6 o'clock," she said, "it's turned into another place... because of the Vietnam War, a lot of these *ang mohs* [white men] didn't know when they would die... after 10 pm, you don't see Chinese anymore, it's all *ang mohs*, a totally different place.

"You will start to see all these transvestites appearing, don't know if they're women or men. They wear clothes as if going for Pattaya show. Then there were the prostitutes."

By this time, her grandmother would shoo them to bed, forbidding them to gawk at the ladies of the night. But curiosity got the better of Yip and her siblings. "Every time we wanted to see what was happening because we wanted to know more. We would peep from our second floor shophouse." The prostitutes, she learnt, tended to be older women. The transvestites were "very flamboyant" and "would sit at any table". "But," Yip added, "Grandma said we cannot talk to them. So we didn't know about their lives, and we didn't care what they did."

Darting about amid the tables were shoeshine boys, who would shine the GIs' shoes for $5 or $10 a pop. These boys would also bring board games to play with the American soldiers and sailors.

Joys Without Money

Most Singaporeans with young children eschewed nightlife temptations, setting aside what they could for rainy days. And most children of struggling parents knew better than to ask them for pocket money. Instead, as government proofreader **Subramaniam s/o Munian** put it: "I found happiness in simple things which did not cost money." That meant swimming in the sea, playing football and rounders, and

As Subramaniam s/o Munian put it: "I found happiness in simple things which did not cost money." That meant swimming in the sea, playing football and rounders, and watching free movies at the Tanjong Pagar Police Station. His "most favourite" pastime, however, was catching crabs.

Like Subramaniam s/o Munian did in his salad days, these schoolboys enjoyed pitting their pet spiders against one another at Fort Canning Park in the 1980s.

watching free movies at the Tanjong Pagar Police Station. His "most favourite" pastime, however, was catching crabs, which his mother would then cook into a curry. He would catch between 10 and 15 crabs at a time, enough for him, his brother and their mother to have their fill.

Subramaniam and his friends would also catch fighting spiders at Fort Canning Park and then pit these against one another. They would have loved fighting fish too, but a pair cost 10 cents, at a time when you could buy three bowls of plain rice porridge for 5 cents.

Being in want brought out the best in many children. They hunted around for anything that they could improvise into something they could call their own. **Eugene Wijeysingha**, who was a teacher at Raffles Institution and later its principal from 1986 to 1994, said: "We made tops out of guava wood. I'd chop a portion of this solid wood, about six inches, use a knife to get a rough shape of the top and then take a piece of glass and shaved the wood off so the thing looked more like a top with its pointed part.

"And then I put a nail through its pointed part to balance the top... the top had to be well-balanced because if it was lopsided, it wouldn't spin. Once you had that top, it became your prized possession."

As enterprising as the children were, there really was not much for anyone to do in their spare time then. Subramaniam recalled that there were very few shopping complexes. As a schoolboy, his idea of bliss was borrowing books from the first United States Information

Services (USIS, now known as the United States Information Agency) Library in the Asia Insurance Building in Finlayson Green. From August 1960, the library even had books in Malay.

Near Liang Court was Fort Canning Park, where people would gather in the evenings. Journalist Tan Wee Him said: "We would sit on the grass and after 6 pm, different uniformed bands performed. Some people flew kites, kicked balls around. There were ice cream sellers and *kacang putih* men." The latter sold an assortment of sugared or salted nuts and beans. "It was a very wholesome family gathering for us, and there was no need to pay a single cent for it, not even for parking," he said.

Today, weekends at the Botanic Gardens, which since 2017 has been a UNESCO World Heritage Site, approximate those halcyon days at Fort Canning Park. Just as wholesome were family days by the sea in eastern Singapore, from Katong Park to Changi Beach. While silver-spooned child **Lucy Chen née Lim Seok Hui** lived by the sea, and delighted in digging about the beach for *balitong* (top shell) and *seehum* (cockles) she did not learn to swim, thanks to her over-protective father. "My father tried to teach us but he was just holding us; we would be balanced on top of his hand. How can you swim that way?"

A stone's throw from Fort Canning Park was the National Theatre, at River Valley Road. Tan the journalist remembered that it was iconic but, alas, not built for purpose. He said: "It was not meant for any kind of performing because it was like a semi-open theatre with a huge roof that went right to the back and which opened up on all sides. During a heavy downpour, the tail end of the theatre was not well covered by the extended roof, the sides and insides of the theatre would get wet. On top of that, during musical performances, the musicians would have to compete with sounding horns from passing vehicles along Clemenceau Avenue and River Valley Road."

For all its flaws, the National Theatre chalked up many memorable shows. Its inaugural performance was by Dame Margot Fonteyn, the legendary British ballerina, who delighted audiences worldwide from 1934 till 1979. National Day rallies were held there as well. The theatre was finally shuttered on 16 January 1984 as it was not structurally safe anymore.

The one auditorium in Singapore that is still standing after more than a century is Victoria Theatre, which then Governor John Anderson opened on 18 October 1905, and whose first show was a production of *The Pirates of Penzance*. The Palladian-style theatre was built to commemorate the rule of Britain's Queen Victoria, who reigned from 20 June 1837 until her death on 22 January 1901. The theatre was also where Minister for Culture S. Rajaratnam launched Television Singapura, the nation's first television broadcasting station, on 15 February 1963.

It would take most Singaporeans many years after that to save up for a TV set. So residents in a neighbourhood would often pile into the living rooms of households lucky enough to own TVs or congregate at community centres with these picture boxes.

Those without TVs were not missing out on much, though; even the international news they watched was outdated then, said former Radio and Television of Singapore broadcaster

Music lovers enjoying the performance of a police band outside the iconic National Theatre, with its distinctive facade featuring five vertical diamond-shaped bays, in 1974.

Ee Boon Lee. "If there was a Beirut bombing, we would only get the film two to three days later as the film was flown here. By the time it reached Singapore, it was so outdated. But we still had to use it. So we would compile such films into a newsreel." Newsreels were, at least, something everyone could watch. Breakdowns in transmission were all too frequent in the early years of TV in Singapore, with the dreaded graphic "We apologise for this breakdown. Normal service will resume as soon as possible" before the inevitable white noise and "snow" appeared on-screen.

Journalist Tan Wee Him recalls that the open-air feature of the National Theatre, which hosted the 1965 Malaysian Solidarity Convention, would soak its audiences whenever there were heavy downpours. The unique open-air plan of the theatre also offered free entertainment to those perched on the hillside behind.

Excited Singaporeans waiting outside Victoria Theatre on 15 February 1963 to catch their first glimpse of black-and-white television images at the launch of Television Singapura there by Minister for Culture S Rajaratnam.

Singapore's pioneering newsreaders include Vernon Palmer, Claude Doral and Steven Lee. The very act of reading the news was, for Ee, "a very challenging thing". But he questioned the wisdom of telling newsreaders how to do their job, as some of their bosses would. Ee said: "Sometimes the more you tell the newsreaders, "Hey, be careful how you read the words, be faithful to the sentence, it's to be read this way, they would go 'Yeah, yeah.' If you left them alone, they would have done far better. But you can't help it; you're very conscious of the need to... it's a very tough job." The first news broadcast was at 7 am and the last was at 11 pm, after which Ee and his colleagues would heave sighs of relief.

Those who could not afford TV sets for entertainment learnt to pool what they had with their friends for picnics under the coconut trees in Singapore's many open spaces back then. Lim Kee Chan the ex-boxer said that he and his friends would sit around campfires, strumming the latest hits on their guitars and just larking about. "There were a lot of cakes to eat, all the goodies, and then a lot of games and sketches," he recalled. "You got a few of them who volunteered laughs, that sort of thing... it was just good fun. It was nice to see everybody happy."

Memories are made of these.

CHAPTER FOUR

THE JAPANESE OCCUPATION
Three Years, Seven Months

A week before the Fall of Singapore on 15 February 1942, an open coffin saved **Victor Thevathasan**'s life.

He was among the last 10 students at King Edward VII College in Bukit Timah to study for the Licentiate in Medicine and Surgery. They attended classes throughout the Imperial Japanese Army (IJA)'s aerial bombings of Singapore, which began at 4 am in Chinatown on 8 December 1941. That same day, the Japanese also attacked Pearl Harbour in Hawaii. The marauders continued bombing Singapore until the British surrendered two months later, on the first day of Chinese New Year.

British soldiers combing through the rubble of a bombed-out building in Singapore for survivors at the onset of the Japanese Occupation in 1942.

Thevathasan said of these aerial attacks: "During our lectures, Japanese fighting planes used to machine-gun our college and we used to dive under the table for protection." One among his friends, Yoong Tat Sin, was killed by shrapnel. When Thevathasan and his surviving college mates were about to bury Yoong in a slit trench on the college grounds, a Japanese fighter pilot spotted them from above and began raining bullets on them.

"During our lectures, Japanese fighting planes used to machine-gun our college and we used to dive under the table for protection."

Thevathasan lived to tell the tale because just before the pilot fired, one of his friends had asked him to run into the college building for nails to fasten the lid of Yoong's coffin. "I would have gone back to the slit trench," he said, "but all this shelling just happened... I suppose I was not meant to die."

But 10 of his friends were killed. "Sadly, the artillery fire was accurate and the first salvo hit the College of Medicine building," he recalled. "The second salvo hit the trench and 10 of the students around it were killed instantaneously. A few others were wounded and managed to run to safety." One ran into the building covered in blood. "It turned out that another student who was killed instantly had fallen on him and the latter's blood had flown onto him," Thevathasan said. A war memorial now stands at the trench site.

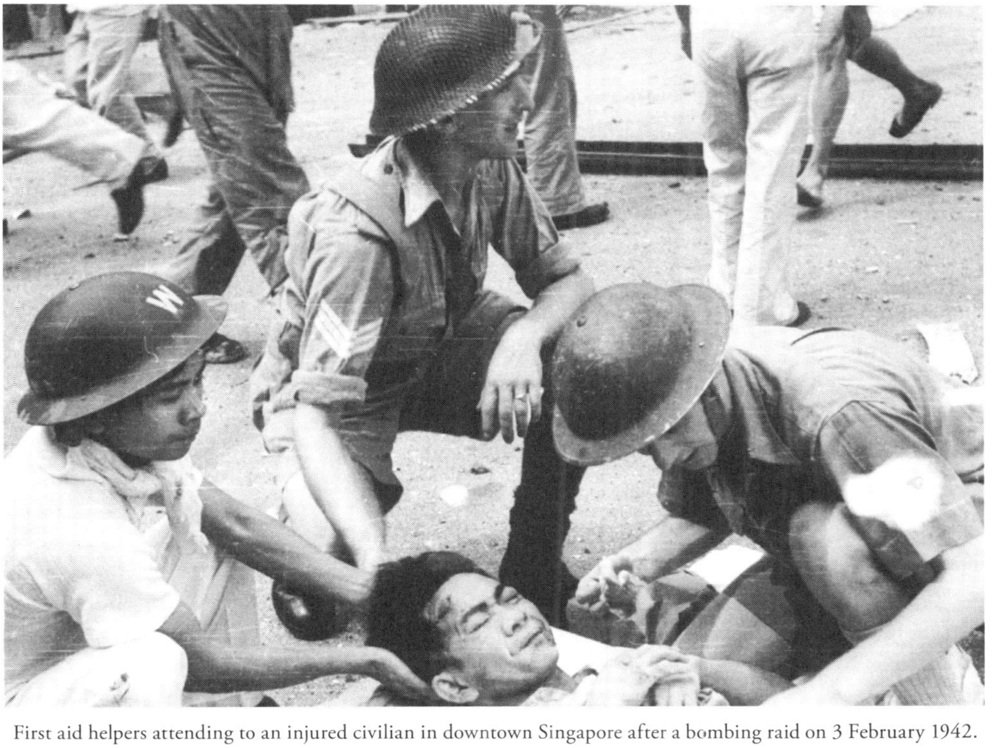

First aid helpers attending to an injured civilian in downtown Singapore after a bombing raid on 3 February 1942.

Journalist **Khoo Teng Soon** also had a close shave during the air raids. Khoo was then reporting for *The Malaya Tribune*, whose office was at the corner of Anson Road and Enggor Street. "We had a couple of direct hits," he said. "What saved us were these rolls of newsprint which we converted into air raid shelters. The density of the newsprint managed to absorb the shock of the blast."

When the IJA came marching into Singapore from 8 February 1942, some locals were initially stoked at the prospect of fighting them. **Heng Chiang Ki**, who was a student then, recalled: "The youths got pretty excited when the war was actually on because prior to that, there had been a lot of civil defence drills such as the Air Raid Precaution, but not any real action."

On the evening of Sunday, 15 February 1942, Britain's commanding officer in Malaya and Singapore, Lieutenant-General Arthur E. Percival, surrendered to his Japanese counterpart, General Tomoyuki Yamashita.

From his home atop Emerald Hill, author **Felix Chia**, who was a teenager then, and his cousin watched Britain's flag being lowered at Government House nearby. Chia recalled his cousin saying, "Well, the Union Jack is going down and I am confident that it will fly again one day."

The French-Canadian Roman Catholic priest **Brother Vincent**, who was born Guy Joseph Janvier Barbe, said that the people of Singapore had "expected war to break out", even though British propaganda insisted otherwise. But, he stressed, "at no time did we think we were going to lose the war." Brother Vincent, who founded the youth rehabilitation hostel Boys' Town in 1948 added: "We had a fleet, an air force, troops from Australia, Britain and India and all along we were under the impression that the Japanese were not well-equipped."

Heart surgeon **Yong Nen Khiong**, who was 12 years old during the Japanese invasion, said all the British propaganda then about Singapore being the "impregnable fortress" and the "Gibraltar of the East" was "rubbish". "Their guns were pointing the wrong way – out to sea – and the Japanese came from the Causeway," he said. "Two of the Britons' mightiest war ships, the *Repulse* and the *Prince of Wales*, were sunk. Why? Because there was no air cover. Everybody in Singapore was completely aghast."

Britain's then Prime Minister Winston Churchill, too, was stupefied. He called the defeat "the worst disaster and largest capitulation" in British military history. Brother Vincent said: "The air support for the British was really very poor. They had a few Brewster Buffalo fighters, Blenheim bombers. The Japanese were not afraid of those as they had terrific air superiority all the way."

To add salt to Britain's wounded pride. Yong said: "I can tell you that our hearts sank with the warships because we knew there was no hope after this." (Both ships were actually attacked and sunk by successive waves of Japanese bombers).

Japanese soldiers coming ashore at Sarimbun Beach in northwest Singapore on 8 February 1942. This marked the first stage of Japan's assault on Singapore.

Imperial Japanese Army soldiers led by General Tomoyuki Yamashita (3rd from right), who was known as the Tiger of Malaya, are seen here right after Lieutenant-General Arthur Ernest Percival (2nd from right) surrendered Singapore on 15 February 1942.

The aftermath of a British battleship bombed by the Japanese off Kuantan in the east coast of Malaya in December 1941.

Japanese troops marching into Raffles Square on 16 February 1942, following the surrender of the British forces the day before.

Friend or Foe?

Retired civil servant **Lee Liang Hye**, however, remembered some locals rejoicing when Singapore fell to the Japanese. Lee, who was 18 then, said: "We had seen how the Japanese soldiers fought in the spirit of the samurai, with complete loyalty to the Emperor.

"And the very fact that, though outnumbered in men and equipment, they were able to defeat the so-called invincible British Army and its Singapore naval base made us, in a sense, admire the Japanese as fighting machines."

Also, he noted, the Japanese had initially waged a successful propaganda war too, promising the Asians whose lands they invaded the concept of "Greater East Asia Co-Prosperity Sphere" in which they would all be equal and have a share in Asia's wealth.

But as the Japanese Occupation dragged on, Lee said: "We could see that they were bleeding the countries in Southeast Asia of all their resources, taking these back to Japan… the Japanese did not keep their promise of being brothers of similar status. Instead, they ill-treated us."

Ismail Bin Zain recalled how brutish the Japanese were right from the start. "Right after the British surrendered, there were some Japanese in my *kampung*. They tried to rape young women; to avoid these, some of the women hid above the ceilings of their homes."

Haji Aziz Bin Rahim Khan Surattee, who repaired Nissan trucks during the Japanese Occupation, remembered just how manic the troops were: "They couldn't stand anyone riding a bicycle; they would take the bicycle away. They couldn't stand anyone wearing a watch; they would take that away. They would go into *kampungs*, looking for chickens, and take these away."

Worse, he added, "they were also looking for girls and on the day the British surrendered, four Japanese soldiers came and raped my next-door neighbour, a Chinese girl… she died a few days later." Aziz could only gawk as other soldiers bathed, buck-naked, from a public standpipe near his home in Mergui Road. "They felt no shame," he said. "They did whatever they wanted."

He then mused: "We had thought they were not so bad. But within the first three days of the surrender, some who looted the Harbour Board godown were beheaded and their heads exhibited at road junctions." He went past "four or five" of these heads at Selegie Road and Stamford Road, near Capitol Theatre. Later, after a quintet of Chinese, Malays and Indians tried to steal a machine at Lorong 3 Geylang, he chanced upon their wizened heads on Kallang Bridge.

Rudy William Mosbergen, the first Principal of Raffles Junior College (1982–87), said beheadings were the IJA's way of getting everyone in line. "The Japanese wanted to restore law and order quickly and they didn't want any nonsense. So they chopped off all their heads and nobody dared to do anything after that."

Nurse **Sheila Bruhn-Allan**, who was a teenager during the Japanese Occupation, witnessed something far worse. Just after the Fall of Singapore, she was walking behind her father down New Bridge Road, past hordes of IJA soldiers. "I was looking at all the people there, dead and dying... you got the smell of the dead, rotten bodies and smoke. And I came across a Chinese lady with a baby in her arms, and the baby was crying," she recalled. "And I thought, 'Ah, poor baby is hungry'." She darted towards them, hoping to pick up the infant and take it to one of the many first aid posts set up nearby.

But before she could reach them, a Japanese sentry took hold of the baby. "I thought, 'Ha, he's going to take the baby to the first aid station'," she said. "But do you know what he did? He threw the baby up in the air and let it fall on the point of his bayonet blade. I could see the blood running down... I thought my mind was playing tricks."

From then on, whenever she heard a baby cry, she would have nightmares of "a baby on the point of a blade, its blood running down". The trauma did not, however, stop her from becoming a children's nurse some years later. It was, she said, "to atone for the one that I didn't pick up that time".

Aziz saw blood flow freely too from the onset of the Occupation. He recalled corpses from the bombings "stacked up" at the Clerical Union badminton hall in Rangoon Road, where his primary school was. "Some of them had no hands, no legs," he said. "Some of them also had no heads. Blood was flowing from the hall into the drains surrounding the area." Such bloodshed, he added, terrified everyone else into staying indoors whenever they could, leaving the streets of Singapore "deserted" at night.

The "Chop" That Saved Lives

There was, however, no way to hide from the IJA's mass screening exercise known as Sook Ching (which means "purge through cleansing" in Chinese), during which time Chinese men aged between 18 and 50 were herded into 20 designated mass screening centres across the island, including Amber Road, Jalan Besar and River Valley Road.

Felix Chia, who had watched the Union Jack being lowered over Government House, was among those rounded up, despite being only 13 years old then. Japanese soldiers barged into his home, shoved him around with their bayonet butts and forced him to head to the North Bridge Road screening point. There, some bald soldiers liked his look – Chia's mother had shorn his head as clean as theirs – and they spared his life.

Chia recalled: "Able-bodied men were herded into the compound of the mosque at North Bridge Road by the thousands. It was cramped and the interrogation they conducted was crazy. It was a case of 'All clerks, put your hands out.' 'All cooks, put your hands out.'

"If they didn't like your face, they would just pull you aside and through an interpreter, find out what you did. Were you a collaborator, a volunteer? Did you help the British? Did you send money to China for the war effort? And for no rhyme or reason, they would just kick and push you up a lorry. Once they pushed you up a lorry, it was the end; you would be driven to Bedok or elsewhere, shot and buried."

The father of **Robert Iau Kuo Kwong** almost met that fate. Iau said: "He was asked to go up the truck, but he positioned himself near the gate and struck up a conversation with a Japanese guard there. By a sheer stroke of luck, the guard had been posted to Shanghai

A Japanese boy named Masaji saved Chia Cheong Fook from being executed by Japanese soldiers in Singapore during Operation Sook Ching. Chia later became a permanent secretary in the Ministry of Foreign Affairs.

before. We are Shanghainese and my father spoke Shanghainese to him. The guard suddenly became very, very distressed, opened the gate and told my father to get the hell out of there." Iau later became well known for his contributions towards the development of information technology and the arts in Singapore.

Chia Cheong Fook, a former Permanent Secretary of the Ministry of Foreign Affairs, was just as quick-witted as Iau's father. Chia and his Anglo-Chinese School (ACS) mates were queueing up for Sook Ching near Arab Street when one of them spotted a Japanese friend among the soldiers. Chia said: "His name was Masaji. I did not know him from Adam, but I called 'Masaji! Masaji!' as if I knew him. And then he looked back and saw us."

Masaji took them aside and stamped their forearms with a square "chop" (or rubber stamp) bearing the Chinese words "hui bing" (Military soldier). "That chop was very precious," Chia said. "It meant that you were cleared... for a couple of weeks, we were careful to bathe around the chop."

Yong Nen Khiong's ACS friends were not so lucky. "One of my teachers was in the Volunteer Force; he and the houseboy of the Oldham Hall boarding school were taken to Changi Beach and machine-gunned." Iau lived in Siglap then, about 2.4 km from Bedok. About a week after his father's narrow escape, he said he heard "machine guns going through the night... they were killing these fellows".

Sook Ching was an Imperial Japanese Army witch hunt of all able-bodied Chinese men in Singapore. Thousands of such men reported to screening stations such as this one in North Bridge Road between 21 February and 4 March 1942, only to be carted away in lorryloads to their deaths.

> "The Sook Ching exercise was an attempt to weed out those whom the Japanese considered bad hats – secret society members or those who wore spectacles, whom the Japanese saw as intellectuals."

Rudy Mosbergen said the Japanese targeted Singapore's Chinese community because first, many among them sent money to those fighting the Japanese in China and second, they had boycotted made-in-Japan goods before the war broke out. "The Sook Ching exercise was an attempt to weed out those whom the Japanese considered bad hats – secret society members or those who wore spectacles, whom the Japanese saw as intellectuals."

Fellow principal **Marie Ethel Bong**, who was in secondary school during the Occupation, rued how even the weakest folk were hauled up for Sook Ching. "Sick people were carried there in camp beds. Old people too... they were rounded up and shot." Depending on who you believe, a total of either 5,000 Chinese menfolk (as the Japanese claimed) or 50,000 of them (as the Chinese claimed) perished during Sook Ching.

Fortunately, Mosbergen pointed out, the Chinese in Singapore had not attacked any of the 10,000 or so Japanese residents living in Singapore before the Occupation. Most of these residents worked as barbers, dentists and fishermen and lived along Middle Road, Prinsep Street and Waterloo Street. The Chinese in Singapore did, however, boycott Japanese businesses such as the once-popular K Baba in Middle Road shortly before, and during, the Occupation.

The Hell of Daily Life

Months after Sook Ching, the Chinese still lived in fear of Japanese reprisals. It did not help that the IJA liked to rough up the locals on a whim. Bong said: "If you passed a sentry, you had to bow to him or else he'd slap or kick you." She noted, however, that the IJA did station fewer sentries in the streets midway through the Occupation.

"The Japanese propaganda said that rice would be cheap," recalled **Haji Mohamed Sidek Bin Siraj**, a civil servant-turned-Haj pilgrimage officer, who was 30 years old when Singapore fell to the IJA. "But when they came to Singapore, they started kicking us. They started slapping us. Slapping and kicking were no different whether you were Chinese, Malay or Indian."

Retired civil servant **Joseph Anthony Desker**, who was aged 21 in 1942, had it worse. He was working as a grasscutter around St Patrick's School when a soldier caught him smoking. "He slapped me around," Desker recalled. "I was cheesed off and walked off the job." Later, he cut grass elsewhere, only to find himself having to ditch his $1.50-a-month job altogether. "I was made to carry heavy logs," he said. "I fell down the slope and could have killed myself. Instead of getting some help, the Japanese took a chunk of granite and whacked me with it. I said, 'No more, thanks, I'm going home'."

Such defiance was almost unheard of because the IJA considered those whom they disliked as guilty until proven innocent. Tan Thoon Lip, who was the first Asian registrar of the Supreme Court of Singapore, endured almost a year of torture – for three bars of soap. His friend **Tan Guan Chuan** said: "He'd asked Wee Sin Choh, the boss of Cheong Koon Seng, to get him three cakes of soap because at that time, it was difficult to get consumer goods. Thoon Lip was going to pay for them. But Sin Choh said, 'Why worry about three cakes of soap?'"

Lieutenant-Colonel Masayuki Oishi was part of the Imperial Japanese Army's deeply feared military police known as the Kempeitai. During the Japanese Occupation, the Kempeitai arrested those suspected of being anti-Japanese.

Why worry, indeed. When the Japanese tortured Wee, he blurted out the "soap story". In Tan Thoon Lip's 1946 memoir, *Kempeitai Kindness*, he recounted his suffering at the hands of the Kempeitai, the Japanese military police. Among other things, they kicked him around like a football for hours.

Just being questioned by the Kempeitai could turn anyone to jelly.

Lawyer, district judge and former opposition political leader **Joshua Benjamin Jeyaretnam**, better known as J.B. Jeyaretnam, once had to spend an afternoon with the Kempeitai for a case involving the theft of tyres. At the time, Jeyaretnam was an interpreter in the wartime Transport Department, which issued tyres for government vehicles. One night, someone broke into the department and took away a lot of tyres. Jeyaretnam's colleagues alerted the Kempeitai and, before he knew it, the Kempeitai had called him and three other colleagues in for questioning.

Jeyaretnam described the Japanese military police headquarters on Stamford Road, where the present YMCA headquarters is, as "gruesome". And while his interrogators did not lay a hand on him, he prayed fervently for the ordeal to end. "All the time," he said, "I was stealing glances at the clock to see whether 5 o'clock was approaching, and wondered what was going to happen to me because 5 o'clock was the time for ending.

"Then, shortly before 5 o'clock, they said, 'All right, I think that's all. You may go.' Woof! I nearly let out a shout of delight, but didn't." He added: "Inside me, I said, 'God.' I think it was probably the first time I was driven to thank God although my awareness of God and his power to protect and to care was beginning to dawn on me."

Lee Liang Hye, the former civil servant, recalled that the IJA's cruelty had many locals wishing for colonial rule again, even if the British considered them "second-class citizens".

The Young Men's Christian Association Building in Stamford Road in the 1930s. The Imperial Japanese Army seized the building during the Japanese Occupation and turned it into the Kempeitai's interrogation and torture headquarters.

A father and daughter seen here subsisting on porridge and peanuts during the Japanese Occupation. Food rationing was enforced, and many people suffered from malnutrition or died of starvation.

Robert Iau remembered that when Geylang English School, where the IJA dumped ammunition seized from the British, blew up one day, "for a while, there was some hysterical reaction that the British had returned."

In March 1942, barely a month after the start of the Japanese Occupation, everyone in Singapore who was not Japanese faced fresh hell – food rationing.

In March 1942, barely a month after the start of the Japanese Occupation, everyone in Singapore who was not Japanese faced fresh hell – food rationing. **Zamroude Za'aba**, a part-time newsreader for Radio Malaya in 1941, said: "Each person was allowed to buy 12 kg of rice a month. But from 1943, this was reduced to 8.5 kg a month. Then, just before the Japanese surrendered in 1945, the rations went down to 5 kg for a man, 3.5 kg for a woman and 2.5 kg for a child."

Those whom the Japanese hired for work breathed a little easier – but only just. Among them was Haji Mohamed Sidek. He said: "Those who worked for the wartime Japanese administration, got 2 kg of rice per person. We also got tapioca from Johor."

Nadesan Ganesan, who worked under Japanese engineers at the Singapore Traction Company, said he got his rations once a week – and "it was enough for two days". Like many other resourceful folk, he and his family grew papayas, brinjals and long beans in their garden to supplement their meagre sundries.

Interned foreign women in Sime Road Camp queueing up for their rations during the Japanese Occupation in 1942.

Khoo Teng Soon, who worked in Domei (now Kyodo News), the Japanese wartime information department, in the Cathay Building, got a free daily lunch of rice porridge with sweet potato. "We could take that home," he said.

Felix Chia, however, took more than porridge home. The Japanese administrators made him a food clerk. Together with a Malay peon, every day at 3 pm in Tanglin Road, Chia would put fresh pork, just-caught fish, eggs and vegetables into baskets brought to them by cooks from Japanese households. Chia said: "The food was for the executives, from the CEO right down to the smallest guy."

"Of course," he added, "I always put aside something for myself." Chia smuggled out the food in his *tingkat*, a three-tiered tiffin carrier; he would come to work with his lunch of rice, salt fish and vegetables in the carrier, wash it after his meal and fill it with his stolen produce. Once home, he added, his mother would share the spoils with their neighbours, especially those who were infirm.

Not everyone was as magnanimous as the Chias. Most times, it was every man for himself. Lee, the retired civil servant, recalled: "The war became an arena in which human nature was split... I learnt how, under pressure, people will change. Under normal circumstances, people can be friendly and good to you. But, under pressure, they might turn against you to achieve some private interest.

"So the war was a kind of catalyst, creating the circumstances in which human nature, at its worst and at its best, showed itself."

And so, in good times and bad, each day dragged on, as dreadful as the last. Retired businessman **Toh Mah Keong**, one of the very first persons whom the Oral History Department (now Oral History Centre) interviewed in 1979, said everyone's movements, in general, were very slow. "There were no buses, and the rickshaw pullers were not pulling," he said, adding that the people formed special groups to bury corpses strewn about the streets.

Ganesan, who was Chairman of the Football Association of Singapore from 1976 until 1982, summed it up thus: "During the Japanese Occupation, this place was dead, grim. I pitied the elders; they were used to good things and then they were deprived."

For Better or Worse

There is, perhaps, no deprivation greater than being separated from your loved ones. On 29 October 1943, **Elizabeth Choy** learnt that the Kempeitai had arrested her husband, Choy Khun Heng. At the time, the Choys ran a canteen at Miyako Byoin (the former Mental Hospital at Woodbridge). Among the patients there were British prisoners-of-war (POWs).

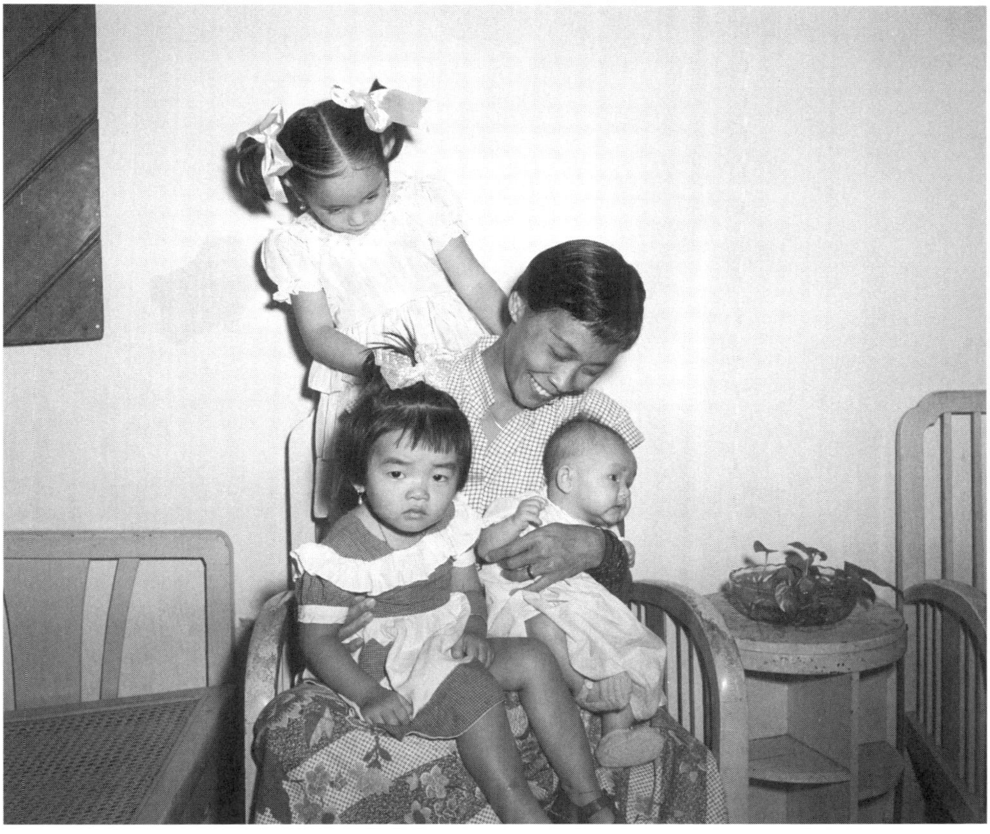

Mrs Elizabeth Choy seen here with her children in 1953, 10 years after she was detained and tortured by the Kempeitai for 193 days.

The Choys were soon, through these patients, smuggling food, medicine, messages and even radio sets to other POWs in Changi Prison.

The Kempeitai arrested Choy Khun Heng on 29 October 1943, after Operation Jaywick, in which British-Australian commandos sunk seven Japanese ships off Singapore Harbour in late September that year. The Japanese believed that Changi Prison internees had transmitted messages about the whereabouts of these ships to the Allied Forces, using a radio supplied by the Choys. On 10 October 1943, the IJA rounded up 57 POWs and beat them up so badly that 15 died. The soldiers never found any radio among the POWs' belongings, and the tragedy became known as The Massacre of the Double Tenth, or The Double Tenth Incident.

The Kempeitai then lured Mrs Choy to their headquarters in the YMCA building in Stamford Road (where the present YMCA headquarters is). They said she would be able to see her husband there. Instead, Britain's *Daily Telegraph* reported in 2006 that when she arrived, they threw her into a "bug-infested" cell with 20 other detainees.

When the Kempeitai accused her of collaborating with the British, she steadfastly denied that. They then demanded to know where a British bank manager, Duncan Wallace, had hidden the bank's money. "I said I didn't know," Mrs Choy recalled. "They said I was a

British-Australian commandos of the Allied Z Special Unit after the completion of Operation Jaywick, during which Japanese ships were sunk off Singapore Harbour on 26 September 1943.

friend of the British and so Wallace must have told me. I told them it was rumoured that, days before the British surrendered, the British had burnt all the bank notes. But the Japanese insisted that the British had hidden the money somewhere instead."

And so the Kempeitai were persistent. "They asked me over and over again," she said. "And I told them I didn't know over and over again. They then threatened to take me to Johor and execute me." Mrs Choy was made of sterner stuff. "I said, 'If you have to execute me for telling the truth, I can't help it. Go ahead'." The Japanese flung her back into her crowded, cockroach-ridden cell.

There was more to come. "One day," she said, "they put some very rough wooden blocks on the floor, tied me up and made me kneel on these blocks. And they stripped me. I was topless. They tied me to the wood so I could neither go forward, backwards or sideways.

"They then gave me electric shocks. And they made my husband kneel beside me and watch me being tortured. They said, 'Now, both of you confess, we'll let you go. If not, we'll execute both of you.'

"My husband said, 'I've nothing to tell you.' They continued to torture me. Tears were streaming down my face and my nose was running... later, I was taken elsewhere, still bound by rope. And halfway I collapsed... I don't know what happened to me after that." For the rest of her life, *The Daily Telegraph* noted, Mrs Choy flinched whenever she saw an electric switch.

> Britain later declared Mrs Elizabeth Choy a war heroine and awarded her the Order of the British Empire. She continued giving back to society, as Singapore's first woman legislator in 1951, and then as the principal of the Singapore School for the Blind.

The Kempeitai detained her for a total of 193 days, during which time she was tortured many more times. In between, she and her fellow detainees tried to cheer one another up through sign language whenever their wardens were not looking. On her 194th day in the YMCA building, the military police told her, "You can go." "They gave me my handbag, all my things. And I just walked out, looking left and right and everywhere. It was so strange."

Her ordeal did not, however, end with her release. "They let me go, but kept my husband back in Outram Jail. That was the worst time. Nobody dared to talk to me after I got out because nobody wanted to be involved." She added: "Everybody sort of wanted to shun you because they thought, 'If I was regarded as one of their friends, there might be danger or something, we'd be observed and followed'." She then mused: "I suppose I could understand. I suppose all of us would do the same." Her husband, whom the Japanese administration had sentenced to 12 years' imprisonment, was released only after the Japanese surrendered.

Britain later declared Mrs Choy a war heroine, invited her to recuperate in London – which she did, alone, for four years – and awarded her the Order of the British Empire. She continued giving back to society, as Singapore's first woman legislator in 1951, and then as the principal of the Singapore School for the Blind. On 14 September 2006, Mrs Choy died at the age of 95, from pancreatic cancer. Her husband had died in 1985, aged 73.

Throughout the war, other couples found it in themselves to love, laugh and hope. On 18 January 1944, Joseph Anthony Desker married his sweetheart Betty Fernandez at St Joseph's Church in Victoria Street. The bride clutched a bouquet of frangipani and their Malay friends, who had wheat flour, baked them a wedding cake. After the priest pronounced them man and wife, they went home to a dinner of *nasi goreng* (Malay for fried rice) – in a taxi powered by charcoal.

Desker said: "Petrol was so hard to come by, but Singaporeans are really ingenious. They fitted a charcoal burner in the back of the car – the charcoal was literally burning there to move the engine." As there were few taxis then, charcoal-burning or otherwise, the newlyweds had to share their cab – with three topless Chinese gentlemen. "They were shirtless," Desker recalled. "There we were, in this charcoal burner taxi, amid half-naked Chinese men."

A week later, the newlyweds were on the train to Bahau in Negeri Sembilan – one of two settlements for Eurasians and Chinese Roman Catholics in Malaya thought up by Mamoru Shinozaki to ease the food shortage in Singapore. The other settlement was Endau in Johor, for the remaining members of Singapore's Chinese community. Shinozaki was, by turns, a spy for Japan, an advisor to the IJA's defence chief in Singapore, the chief education officer and the chief welfare officer. Khoo Teng Soon said Shinozaki got on famously with the chief of the Japanese administration in Singapore and, during Sook Ching, used that goodwill to save the lives of many Chinese men by issuing them "protection cards".

Shinozaki attended Khoo's wedding on 13 April 1945 and signed Khoo's wedding certificate. Khoo said of him: "I knew him from his time as the patron of the Syonan Sports Association. He was a very, very nice person. Mamoru did a lot to save the local population, especially the Chinese. He had a lot of influence on the civil administrator."

The Endau and Bahau settlement projects to solve Singapore's food shortage woes had different outcomes. While Yong Nen Khiong and other settlers in coastal Endau thrived amid plentiful seafood, the settlers in Bahau were literally sent to their deaths, as malaria was endemic there.

Khoo recalled Shinozaki's initial efforts to convince everyone in Singapore that the settlements made sense: "He had volunteers to help in growing food like tapioca; their activities were organised by the sports association. He held one or two press conferences a week, in which he would explain the Endau and Bahau policies." This was all well and good, but then Shinozaki did not have to live in either of these settlements.

Burying the Living

In late January 1944, Joseph Anthony Desker and his wife arrived in Bahau with a suitcase of personal belongings and just $500 between them. They were the last batch of Eurasians in Singapore moving to Bahau. "It was a bad day because it had rained the previous night

This is a painting of a hut in which Dr John Bertram van Cuylenburg and his wife lived in Bahau, Negeri Sembilan. With food shortages in Singapore, the Japanese relocated Singapore's Eurasian community to Bahau, where most of them died because malaria was endemic there. Mrs van Cuylenburg painted this in 1945.

in a road of potholes," he recalled. "It was muddy and slippery. Some of us did fall." Like everyone else, the Deskers were allotted a space in an open-ended longhouse, which was "primitive" and swarming with malaria-carrying mosquitoes.

Desker said the Japanese "deliberately sent us there" much against the advice of Dr Charles Paglar, the leader of the Eurasian community in Singapore – and, curiously, a firm friend of Shinozaki. Desker added: "When the Japanese told him they wanted the Eurasians to settle in Bahau, he said, 'Look at the map – it is a highly malarial place. You will kill all the people who go there'." But the Japanese would not listen. Desker recalled: "Death became such a common thing in Bahau that we got used to it. It practically meant nothing to us. No emotion. Nothing at all."

The menfolk there rostered themselves to act as pallbearers and gravediggers. Worst of all, he said, they ferried the dying to the morgue long before the latter drew their last breath. "We went down to Simon de Souza's hut. When we got there, we found him still breathing. Nevertheless, we were told 'Get him to the morgue.' "We said, 'He is still alive.' And they said, 'Never mind. Take him. He will die anytime now.' De Souza did, indeed, die upon arrival at the morgue. "I tell you, it was terrible," said Desker. In the end, only two out of every 30 people survived Bahau.

Thankfully, Desker did not have to bury his wife Betty, who lay dangerously ill for two months in Kuala Pilah Hospital nearby. He said: "There was no opportunity for me to go and see her. I didn't know if she was alive or dead. Whenever I could afford it, I would send eggs to her through a truck driver."

Back in Singapore, and after much reluctance, **Othman Wok** decided to work for the Japanese; he was desperate for more rice rations to feed his parents and himself. "At first, I refused to work for the Japanese," said Othman, who was later Singapore's Minister for Social Affairs and, subsequently, an ambassador. "I went to sea to become a fisherman," he added. "But when times became harder, my father persuaded me to go to the Japanese school to learn Japanese. I did so for three months." After that, he joined the wartime administration's Butai (a company linked to the Japanese military) housed within the Singapore General Hospital's College of Medicine Building on Outram Road. "I became a lab assistant in the anti-plague lab."

That sounds innocuous enough, but what he did not know was that the Butai was actually breeding plague-infested fleas to carpet-bomb the mainland Chinese. The doctors and research scientists of the Butai did so by first combing the fur of hundreds of rats for fleas. These rats would then be infected with the bubonic plague, also known as The Black Death, which killed thousands of Europeans in The Middle Ages. The harvested fleas would later be fed the dying rats' blood and guts. Othman's job was to collect rats from all over Singapore every single day. "We went out in big lorries with thousands of rat traps," he said. "The rats were brought to the lab and, one by one, were put in chloroform." Othman and his colleagues would then search the half-conscious critters for fleas.

The plague-infested fleas would later be thrown together and bred in the lab. He added: "Once every three to four months, millions of these live fleas would be taken in big glass jars to Thailand by train. "I didn't know what happened to these fleas till the end of the war... I read a sheet of newspaper datelined Chungking which said the Japanese were indulging in biological warfare. Dive bombers dumped jars full of these fleas on Chungking." According to a 2009 Japanese research report, such wartime warfare killed more than 12,300 folk in Jilin, Zhejiang and other parts of mainland China.

Rice or no rice, Othman chucked the job after one-and-a-half years.

Sheep Among Wolves

Yet it would be simplistic to tar every IJA lackey with the same brush. Amid the wanton violence, there were moments of grace – and even mirth.

Eugene Wijeysingha, Principal of Raffles Institution from 1986 to 1994, recalled his family sharing their meals with Japanese soldiers. They were then living in Bukit Mertajam, on mainland Penang. He mused: "These Japanese administrators and soldiers came to our home and were able to share a meal with us and have a drink. That helped to build a certain relationship in which we felt comfortable with them and they felt comfortable with us."

His family's hospitality apparently moved one particular soldier deeply. "Hiyashi was being posted to the Burma front, and he ran all the way from the railway station to our home just to tell us that. He wished us and then ran back to the train."

Khoo Teng Soon was going about his work in the wartime information department when his colleague Pierre Carrier, who was Eurasian, asked him: "Well, shall we toss a coin? Who is going to do the bloody Jap communique?" The thing was, a Japanese could not stand being called a "Jap" any more than a Chinese would tolerate being called a "chink" or an Italian a "wop". Carrier's Japanese supervisor walked in just as he uttered that racial slur. Khoo said: "I looked at Carrier, Carrier looked at me. We were both trembling in our pants when he walked in."

Their supervisor paced about the room for what seemed like five minutes, said Khoo. "Then he went up to Carrier and said in English, 'Mr Carrier, what did you say just now?' And Carrier said, 'Well, I am sorry, sir, I used the term 'Jap'." The supervisor replied: "You will never, never, never, never again use that term." Then he let Carrier and Khoo off. So Khoo kept his $300-a-month job till the end of the war.

Marie Bong's family once risked the IJA's wrath, too. She said: "One soldier came along and wanted my mother, of all persons, to wash his dirty, smelly shirt. And she didn't understand him, so she said, 'No, no, no.' He drew his sword, mind you, and we all rushed to protect her. And then one of my uncles quickly took his shirt and washed it."

My Father, the Chinese Top Gun

For **Merrilyn Fong Wai Lye**, a pilot's jacket, not a shirt, symbolised the Japanese Occupation. The jacket belonged to her father, Peter Fong Soo Yee, who was one among The Flying Tigers, the name given to the ethnic Chinese fighter pilots trained by Americans to fight for China during World War II.

Captain Ho Weng Toh seen here in Wuhan, China, at the end of World War II in 1945. Captain Ho was a member of the heroic Flying Tigers, a special squadron which defended China against the Japanese in the war.

Her father, a first-generation Malayan, took his sister Judy's bicycle and sold it to fund his trip to China to join its airforce. His daughter said that, years later, she remembered "a very romantic picture of Dad looking like Top Gun in his leather hat and flying jacket. At that time, Top Gun was a hit movie and I said, 'Oh, my God, my Dad was the Chinese Top Gun'."

Mr Fong was not the only local Flying Tiger; his compatriot **Captain Ho Weng Toh** was part of the same cause. Ho recalled: "The Americans needed China very badly to fight the Japanese because the latter had bombed Pearl Harbour and the Americans were very angry.

The Flying Tigers in the 1930s. The squadron comprised ethnic Chinese fighter pilots, who were trained by the Americans to fight for China against the Japanese.

"So the Chinese sent us to be trained in the American way of flying, so we went to the American flying school. Then when we came back, we had a unit – the Chinese-American Composite Wing of the 14th US Army Airforce... we were also known as The Flying Tigers."

Ho and Fong gave the Japanese as good as they got. "We attacked them, they attacked us. We did these sorts of things, so we were quite busy." When the war ended, Ho said he was "very jubilant because my life was intact". "That's the No. 1 thing," he added. "That I was alive, and still well and young." He did not, however, stay a Flying Tiger for long after World War II because the politics in China changed – and he faced the prospect of having to bomb the communists of China. "I didn't have the heart to bomb Chinese people because they were my own people." So, on the pretext of having to help in his father's business, he went on "long leave" – and put his Flying Tiger days behind him for good.

While Ho and Fong were in China training to be Tigers, the invading Japanese took some 30,000 British soldiers prisoner when Singapore fell. Another 33,200 troops – comprising 16,000 Britons, 14,000 Australians and 3,200 Indians – became POWs soon after.

For British POW **Charles George Peall**, who risked life and limb when he was ordered to clear bombed-out houses, the real heroes of the Occupation were the humble local folk. He recalled: "When we were returning to Havelock Camp," he said, "this old Chinese lady came and gave us bread. The Japanese wouldn't allow us to stop so we had to grab whatever we could in two minutes flat. The Japanese would beat her later, but the next day, she would be there again."

Robert Iau, who lived near Changi Jail, heard the POWs sing as they marched back to Changi Prison after a day's hard labour. He said: "They used to sing to keep their morale up, and it's very eerie in the middle of the night to hear people singing all the way to Changi Road."

Peall and his fellow POWs did their best to maintain their sanity throughout more than three years of incarceration and hard graft. **Ian MacLeod**, who was born in Katong in Singapore but sent to England just before World War II broke out, had no news of his parents in Singapore throughout the war. Later, he learnt of his mother's last days from her friends. He said: "I spoke to Phyllis, one of her friends in camp and asked her; 'What do you remember of my mother?'

"She said that Mum took on the job of cleaning out all the drains every day, but at night, she used to sing. She said, 'Every morning, we used to see your mother in a bra made of old rags, sweeping the drain and when dark came, we all sat where we were and listened to your mother sing. And, in the end, all the Japanese guards used to come and listen to her.'" On her deathbed, MacLeod was told, "the Japanese commander sent her a boiled egg which, in those days, was like a full dinner. Of course, she was so ill, she couldn't eat it."

Sheila Bruhn-Allan, who saw a soldier impale a baby on his bayonet, would have savoured that egg. She was interned first at Changi Prison and then at Sime Road Camp from 1 May 1944 and, like her compatriots, was always in agony from hunger pangs. There were 4,000 prisoners at Sime Road – and simply not enough sweet potatoes and other vegetables that they grew there. "We ate anything that could be eaten, never mind if it was safe; it didn't matter as long as you could fill that hole in your stomach. That hunger was pretty devastating at times."

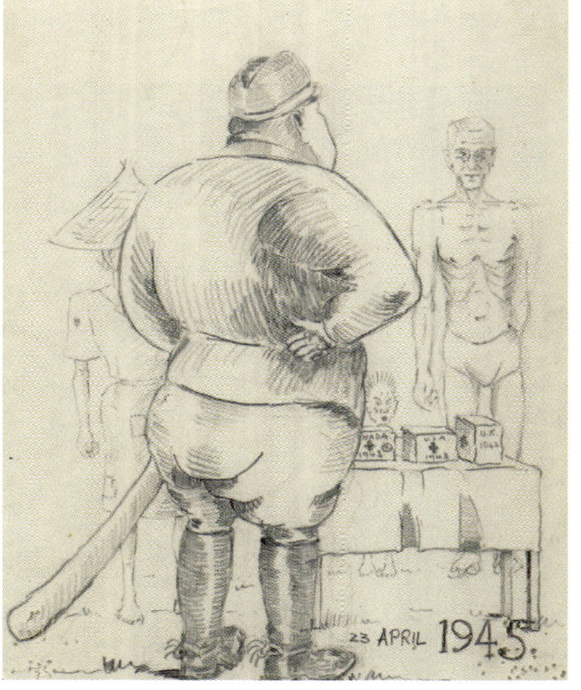

Prisoner-of-war (POW) William R.M. Haxworth drew this sketch in April 1945, which depicts a well-fed Japanese soldier and an emaciated POW. Haxworth was the Chief Investigator at the War Risk Insurance Department in Singapore when he was interned during the Japanese Occupation.

This is Sime Road Camp in 1942, which the Japanese later converted into an internment camp to hold mostly Caucasian civilians.

Four Australian prisoners-of-war at Changi Prison in 1945, who got artificial limbs after being maimed in World War II.

One day, that hunger drove her to eat a rodent. She recalled, "I found a nest of baby mice and a thought went into my head: 'I wonder what they would taste like.' And I opened my mouth and dropped one in. I don't think it was bigger than my little finger, nice and pink. I didn't feel anything. I didn't taste anything. It's as if I swallowed a pill; it just went down." She added that she was "disgusted" with herself afterwards. Then again, she mused, if any POW found worms or rotten banana skins in their patch of community garden, they would cook and eat those. The attitude, she said, was "that was mine, never mind about anybody else. I found the worms in my patch."

Thomas Silcock, the University of Malaya's first Professor of Economics and head of its Economics Department, kept himself sane by writing poems and stories. The rub, he recalled, was how to hide them from the prison wardens. "Some of the POWs were tinsmiths, and I got them to put a false bottom in a tea tin where I kept my sugar," he said. "In this way, I was able to conceal my poems and stories; I wrote them very, very small. But I had to be careful to keep just a bit of sugar in the tin, about three inches." Fortunately, he added, the Japanese rarely emptied anything out.

Amid such subterfuge, he was put in charge of a dozen POWs who had lost their limbs. Silcock said: "They were generally very cheerful and were nice to look after. For the most part, they had got over the immediate shock and were preparing for a different kind of life." Curiously, he added, his maimed comrades liked wrestling one another, bashing others around with their stumps. "It seemed to give them a sense of still being competent," he mused.

The one chore he and other POWs detested was collecting and boiling used bandages. "They had actually to be boiled and boiled on a bamboo stick over a big can, then washed thoroughly, then boiled again and laid out in the sun to be reused. This, of course, was a filthy job."

They Did Not Believe the Emperor

Even the filthiest behaviour had to end. On 6 August 1945, the United States dropped "Little Boy", the first of its two nuclear bombs, on the Japanese city of Hiroshima. Three days later, on 9 August, it dropped its second and larger bomb, "Fat Man", on Hiroshima's neighbour, Nagasaki. Between 129,000 and 226,000 Japanese, mostly civilians, were said to have been killed in the ensuing giant mushroom clouds.

On 15 August 1945, six days after the bombing of Nagasaki, Japan surrendered to the Allied Forces. But in Singapore, Khoo Teng Soon recalled, "the IJA wanted to fight to the last man; they refused to believe that their Emperor had said, 'Surrender'." So, he added, Emperor Hirohito had to send his personal envoy to Singapore to convince them of their country's defeat.

Khoo, whose colleagues then were mostly Japanese and in the propaganda department, had a ringside seat on the aftermath of Hiroshima and Nagasaki. "Hiroshima was not widely reported," he said. "But the Japanese staff were looking very grim; obviously, they knew it was coming to an end."

General Seishirō Itagaki and Admiral Lord Louis Mountbatten signing the documents to end the Japanese Occupation of Singapore on 12 September 1945 at the Municipal Building. General Itagaki was the commander of the Japanese Seventh Area Army, while Admiral Mountbatten was the Supreme Allied Commander, South East Asia Command.

Then, on 14 September 1945, his Japanese bosses suddenly gave him and his other colleagues "three months' pay and 10 katis of rice". "The money was valueless, though," he huffed. "An egg cost $20 then."

The next day, when the Japanese in Singapore surrendered, he and his colleagues were asked to go to a bungalow in River Valley Road. There, the Japanese announced that the war had ended. "That was the term they used – they didn't talk about surrender. 'The war had ended'," Khoo recalled. "The Japanese were crying and we went up to them to say goodbye and all that."

He added that many in the Japanese military, as well as mid-level civilian administrators, committed suicide by slashing their own bellies. "They couldn't accept that the Europeans had asked them to surrender," he said.

The remaining Japanese were later asked by the returning British to interpret on their behalf, and if the Japanese agreed, they would not be interned as POWs. "They didn't expect to be treated the way they were treated," said Khoo. As Shinozaki himself detailed in his 1975 memoir *Syonan: My Story*, the Parsi aerated water magnate Navroji Mistri sent a lorryload of cabbages to the Japanese POW camp in Jurong so that the internees there, mostly women and children, had something to eat.

Freedom, however, hung in the balance for Yong Nen Khiong's father. For the last eight-and-a-half months of the Occupation, Yong, his two brothers and their parents lived in the Japanese-sponsored settlement of Endau, on the east coast of Johor. Yong's father was made manager of the Oversea-Chinese Banking Corporation branch there, and for almost a year, his family enjoyed plenty of seafood and vegetables.

But when the Japanese lost the war, their idyllic world turned topsy-turvy. Yong said: "After the Japanese surrendered, the question was how to get down to Singapore. My father and a few of his friends decided to cycle down." It was a 100-mile journey – and the defeated Japanese threw them into a police station cell at Mersing, near Endau. "They thought my father was an informer."

Yong, his brother and a friend went in search of his father – on foot. "About a few minutes into the jungle, suddenly there were headlights from a whole convoy of lorries going towards the new Syonan Village. So we hailed them for a lift... and when we got onto the lorry, my father was on board. The Japanese had decided to send him back as he was innocent. We thought it a huge stroke of luck." His father later got his whole family home to Singapore by lorry.

Toh Mah Keong and his wife, whom he had wed in a Penang temple in 1945, moved to Singapore in early 1946, shortly after they married a second time at the civil registry in Penang. Then a friend asked them: "Have you got married in church?" So the Tohs decided to register their marriage at Singapore's Registry of Marriages, and walked down the aisle of the church in Canossa Convent in mid-1946. "So there you are," said Toh. "I had a funny way of getting married. Three times."

The Tohs and the Yongs returned to a Singapore whose people had begun to think differently about the British.

Rudy Mosbergen said: "The moral authority they had earlier on was now not there... This expressed itself very sourly in the trade unions that were formed and the political movements that were taking place."

Eurasian dentist **Dr Farleigh Arthur Charles Oehlers**, who was in school during the Occupation, said the privations that he and his family had endured were "a very valuable experience". "It made us appreciate the good things in life, not take them for granted," he mused. "And, of course, it made us see also that the white man wasn't all-powerful as he declared himself to be in the colonial era... I'm sure Independence would have been a long time coming if not for the war."

All things considered, professional boxer-turned-newsman **Lim Kee Chan** recalled: "After the war, everybody couldn't say they had no reason to smile. For no apparent reason, they would smile. But they had every reason to smile. It was good to see people happy."

CHAPTER FIVE

FOOD

Have You Eaten?

Weddings are auspicious occasions, full of love, laughter and feasting. And if you were a Hainanese bride and wanted to be true to your clan's matrimonial traditions, you would present your husband's family with *cheen toei*, which are deep-fried breads as big as basketballs.

These "basketballs" were hollow, just like the cloud-like vanity cakes fried by Caroline Ingalls, the mother of author Laura Ingalls Wilder of the fabled "Little House" series of books. But unlike Ingalls' little puffs, *cheen toei* were exceedingly arduous to make. Pastry master **Wang Cheow Ah** once showed oral history interviewer Jesley Chua how to do so in the early 1990s. Chua watched patiently as he bathed huge balls of dough in hot oil over and over again. She took the photograph you see on this page. The sizzling dough would swell to resemble a *bathura*, the fluffy deep-fried leavened bread from northern India made of white flour, yoghurt, yeast and ghee.

Chinese traditional pastry maker Wang Cheow Ah is seen here frying a *cheen toei*, a Hainanese wedding bread, which is hollow and as big as a basketball, c. 1990s.

A hawker frying *youtiao* in 1980. *Youtiao*, or crullers, are a perennially popular street food in Singapore. Many like to dunk these in congee or hot soya milk for a satisfying snack.

Wang would begin creating each "basketball" by kneading together glutinous rice flour, sugar and water. If he mixed in too little or too much sugar, the dough would be ruined and he would have to start all over again. Once the dough had the right consistency, he would grab a wooden mould, pinch balls off the dough and flatten each dough ball evenly with the mould. "If you didn't even it out," he told Chua, "the ball would be lopsided when you fry it, and become a mess."

After evening out every lump, Wang would gouge a hole in each flattened piece, blow into the hole and then patch it with a scrap of dough. Then came the frying. The cooking oil should not be too hot or too cold, lest the balls burst in the frying pan. Once he got the temperature right, he would fry each ball once and when it puffed up, he would set it aside to rest for two hours before frying it again. Wang would repeat this process a few times the same day – then rest the "basketball" overnight. "If you do not leave the balls overnight to soften and become pliable, not crumbly, they will rupture when you fry them again."

Yes – again. Wang would fry each "basketball" a few times again the next day, resting each between frying until it held its shape satisfactorily. "We fried them a final time just before customers collected them so that the balls were completely round," he said. "We would not give customers flat ones."

Wang's dedication to his craft was almost a labour of love – and all for a few dollars per dough ball. He had followed his father into the bakery trade, working for many years at the now-defunct confectionery Nam Tong Lee on Purvis Street, which shuttered in 2006.

Hainanese wedding "basketballs" are now very much a thing of the past, but Singaporeans have long loved deep-fried dough fashioned into *youtiao* (crullers), sesame-flecked butterfly

The *kacang putih* seller and his paper cone-wrapped treats, 1985. These vendors used to be a mainstay outside cinemas, but have all but vanished today, even though everyone still enjoys beans and nuts.

buns and *ham cheem peng* (salty buns dusted with five-spice powder). Such delicate snacks, cheaper than chips, were a much-welcomed respite from the meals of most locals. Those craving less greasy treats had recourse to the *kacang putih* man. He went around on foot, selling an assortment of crunchy nuts and beans, which he would hand to customers in pieces of paper shaped into cones. Retired schools inspector **Alice Cheang Wye Lan**, who was born in 1903, remembered sellers like him at the Esplanade, which was then a sprawling clipped lawn, with no flora to perk up the plain. "He carried his partitioned basket of wares on his head, while the lights along the Esplanade were far apart and rather dim," she said.

Such peddler's nibbles sprang from society's need for cheap snacks that could keep the wolf of hunger from one's door. Most families in Singapore were of modest means, especially after World War II, and their meals often consisted of hot white rice, over which they drizzled thick black soya sauce and, for those who could take pork, a dash of liquid lard with nubbins of crackling. A chicken or duck egg was then as prized as caviar. Chinatown-born **Soh Siew Cheong** said: "We looked for empty boxes to build fires. We went to public standpipes for water. We ate plain rice with soya sauce." That was so even though his paternal grandfather owned a restaurant, Hing Hwa Chuan, or Xing Hua Chuan in Mandarin.

A chicken or duck egg was then as prized as caviar.

Those on meagre salaries – bus drivers, rickshaw pullers and odd-job folk – made do with bowls of watery rice porridge, which they glugged with a smear of *taucheong* (yellow bean paste) and shreds of *kiam chye* (salted mustard leaves). The gourmand **Vincent Gabriel**, who kept tabs on Singapore's food scene for more than half a century, recalled that hawkers would sell each of the poorest earners three bowls of rice porridge for 5 cents. He added that much of the rice eaten then, including that sold as porridge, was "broken", with "pebbles and paddy seeds in it". "If the household was eating at 6 pm," he said, "I would have to start sorting the rice from the chaff by 4 pm."

Even snacks were indulgences, to be had only when one could spare the change.

For much of the 19th and 20th centuries, even snacks were indulgences, to be had only when one could spare the change, which was not very often. Children were, at most, allowed to buy ice balls, or compacted shaved ice over

Relishing Teochew porridge in the 1980s. Gourmand Vincent Gabriel recalls how such plain rice porridge was about all humble folk could afford to have, with some salty bean paste and pickled mustard leaves.

An ice ball seller, 1978. Ice balls, or compacted ice over which rose syrup and evaporated milk were drizzled, were a firm favourite of schoolchildren, especially if their parents forbade them from enjoying these for fear they might be risking typhoid.

which the ice-ball seller drizzled syrups in various hues and evaporated milk. Sucking on one, for 5 to 10 cents a pop, took the edge off a scorching afternoon.

Ice balls were, however, a dodgy treat as water-borne cholera outbreaks were not uncommon before the 1970s. Gabriel recalled just how filthy the supply of ice could be, beginning with the sawdust streaked over the blocks of ice. The sawdust kept the blocks from melting until the *kopi kia* (literally coffee shop boy in Hokkien) could hammer these into ice chips. The boy would then chuck the chips into a bucket. "Ice chips would go flying in the washing area of the coffeeshop," he recalled. "The coffeeshop floor was dirty, the bucket was dirty, the sawdust-covered ice was dirty, the hammer was dirty and the boy was dirty."

In those days, when just being able to eat was a blessing, few counted calories or pleaded allergies to fat, sugar, salt, gluten, meat or anything else in today's litany of food taboos. Beauty businesswoman **Jean Yip**, for one, relished fizzy drinks and butter sold by Cold Storage. Yip, the granddaughter of a popular chicken congee seller in Bugis Street, said: "We went to Hailam coffeeshops for Coke and Cold Storage butter. Cold Storage butter was supposed to be good for the throat." Many Hailam, or Hainanese, folk worked for British troops stationed in Singapore, and later took to serving Western cuisine at home and in the coffeeshops that many among them opened after Britain pulled its soldiers out of Singapore in 1971.

Those who seldom ate out sometimes had another thrill – free food! Civil servant turned Haj pilgrimage officer **Haji Mohamed Sidek Bin Siraj** said that, as a boy, he and his playmates did not have to go to school on Fridays. So they would scamper along Rochor Canal, asking those on incoming boats to toss them a banana or sweet potato. These boats were also laden with black rice, spices, palm sugar, and other produce from neighbouring countries. He recalled: "Sometimes, things fell out of their boats. We would simply pick those up; they wouldn't scold us because there was a lot coming in."

For engineer **Noel Arthur Pereira** and his family, getting food for free took a bit more effort. Pereira, whose shipping executive father moved his family from Moulmein Road to

Pulau Bukom, where his office was, said: "We used to gather seaweed and dry it all out." His mother would then turn it into a snack for the family.

Feasting After Fasting

With even free food a case of hit-and-miss, most folk counted the days till festivals or community celebrations, for that meant much feasting. **Maarof Salleh**, a former President of the Singapore Islamic Religious Council, recalled how excited his neighbours in Katong were whenever Hari Raya Aidilfitri was around the corner: At the tail end of Ramadan, the Muslim fasting month, they would ask one another, "How many *ketupat* have you prepared? Have you bought the coconut leaves for the *ketupat*? Where do we want to cook the *ketupat*?" *Ketupat* are cakes of boiled rice made by filling little pouches of woven palm leaves with rice. The pouches are then boiled en masse over a charcoal fire for up to five hours. Two or three families, he added, would join forces to make and cook these rice cakes, which are a lip-smacking savoury treat when eaten with a spicy, tamarind-spiked groundnut sauce.

But even *ketupat* fans left room for the array of traditional *kuih-muih*, or petit fours of glutinous rice or bean flour, coconut milk and *gula melaka*. These were a must every festive season. Maarof recalled *kuih koya* made with mung beans mashed with cane sugar. There were many egg, sugar and wheat flour concoctions too, including *kuih bahulu*, or light-as-love egg sponges redolent of coconut milk. A premium offering, Maarof noted, was

The yearly Hari Raya Puasa festivities, which come after a month of fasting from dawn till sundown, are all the merrier thanks to the array of cookies and other snacks to nosh on, including those stacked in neat rows here at Jalan Sultan, 1989.

A bountiful array of traditional Malay delicacies tempts customers at this food stall in the 1980s.

This vendor at the 1991 Hari Raya Puasa Festival at the National Museum in Stamford Road is slicing into some of her homemade *kuih-muih*, or traditional Malay petit fours.

sugar-encrusted rabbit-shaped agar-agar, called *beleda kering*. Cookies, especially tangy and buttery pineapple tarts, were a perennial delight.

Haji Mohamed Sidek said the Malays came up with so many different dainties that they were sometimes at a loss as to what to call these. "When people began making cakes in the 1920s, they didn't know how to name the cakes... so, for example, the name *kuih bahulu* was a truncation of "belum masak, bau dahulu" (Malay for "you can smell it even before it is baked").

He added that there was usually an ulterior motive to preparing such delights. "During the fasting month, everybody, especially the girls, would make cakes that they would then send to the neighbours – to impress the boys of those households." Knowing how to cook and bake was, he noted, "the qualification needed to be a bride" at the time.

By the 1960s, when women went out to work in earnest, commercial cooks took to selling festive dishes that used to be prepared at home. Every Easter, Vincent Gabriel said, shops in Katong – the hive of Eurasian activity – would proffer oxtail stew, in all its thick, clove-scented glory. To be sure, red meat was reserved for special occasions. Government proofreader **Subramaniam s/o Munian**, whose father died young, mused: "Deepavali was the only time I got to taste mutton. My married sister bought it for us."

For many years, even after Singapore attained independence, few could afford meat as part of their daily meal. A rare exception was anyone who had mastered the art of firing pottery in dragon kilns. One such master was **Chua Eng Cheow** who, in the 1920s, left his hard life in Fengxi Village in Chaozhou, China, for a better future in Singapore. He said that three days before any firing of the kilns, everyone involved had to worship the *Toh Dih Yah* (Teochew for Earth God). "We prayed with tidbits like groundnuts and sesame seeds, chicken and duck," he said. "So every three days, master craftsmen were treated to chicken, duck or pork. In the ordinary days, it was rare to have chicken and duck for a meal."

For others, the long wait for festive feasting was worth it. For instance, salted groundnuts from Menglembu, Perak – better known as "Hand brand *kacang*" – and orange squash or cherry soda – with their auspicious hues – became synonymous with Chinese New Year in Singapore and Malaysia. Gabriel said: "When Chinese New Year comes, I buy myself a bottle of F&N Red Lion Cherryade and drink it. Then I tell my son, 'Chinese New Year has officially begun'."

Give Us This Day Our Daily Rice

These days, a typical school day ends with either tuition classes or games with friends. Not so for the students of early Singapore. Former Director of Education **Chan Kai Yau**, who was born in 1930, said of those lean years: "After school, I used to queue for up to an hour or longer for bread for the day – a loaf which was fairly brown and maybe 300 g or so. That was about all that we were able to get." He and his friends also had to queue up for rice and sugar – but, very rarely, for meat, for there was little of that to be had.

Chan's family was fortunate that they could often afford food made from wheat, which was, and still is, more expensive than rice. **Gnanasundram Thevathasan**, a former Justice of Peace, said: "Bread and other wheat-based foods were a luxury. Rice was the staple. We used rice flour for stringhoppers, *apom*, *putu* and so on." Stringhoppers, or *putu mayam*, are coils of rice vermicelli, eaten with either curry or brown sugar. *Apom* are crepes of rice flour and a dash of fermented coconut liquor, or toddy. *Putu* are steamed, springy little cakes.

For special occasions, such as when a baby cut his or her first tooth, she said rice was prepared in "fancier" ways. This included shaping a mixture of steamed rice flour, mashed green pea, fresh coconut and jaggery into a cake that looked like a curry puff. "In the middle of the filled dough, they would put a tiny piece of coconut in the shape of a tooth," she said, adding that the baby's household would then send these cakes to relatives to inform them that the infant had its first tooth.

To the Indians, the coconut symbolises goodness. At weddings, for example, male nurse **Saravana Perumal** recalled fresh coconuts being cracked open – two for the bride and three for her groom. He said: "A coconut is comparable to the human heart. It must be pure as the inner portion of a coconut is pure. The outer portion, the husk, is soiled so you must be pure in heart."

Tommy Koh Thong Bee said he and his uncle Koh Han Yean tried to vary their family's diet by catching eels in monsoon drains.

Ironically, as scarce as wheat was compared to rice and coconuts, the supply of wheat was actually more plentiful than rice when the Japanese occupied Singapore during World War II. Teacher and writer **Chan Kwee Sung** recalled: "Wheat flour was in abundance, so much so that there were loaves of bread aplenty. There was so much surplus flour that certain households had to make good use of the flour by making noodles themselves. At almost every corner of Chinatown, you would find a *wantan* (dumpling) noodle stall."

But while most people in Singapore were, initially, not exactly starving during the Japanese Occupation, supplies of food dwindled as the war wore on. Ambassador-at-Large **Professor Tommy Koh Thong Bee** said he and his uncle Koh Han Yean tried to vary their family's diet by catching eels in monsoon drains. Koh said: "On the sides of monsoon drains are gaps behind which are the homes of eels. So we introduced a hook with bait into these gaps to catch the eels." He added that, fried with sambal or garlic and soya sauce, their catch was "quite delicious".

Koh and his family were lucky to have any chilli or garlic at all. Lawyer **Nadesan Ganesan** said that during the Japanese Occupation, "there were no potatoes, no onions, no garlic and no chilli powder either, as all these had to be imported. How they made curry, I don't know." Ganesan added that the people's main source of protein then was salt fish, which they had to buy on the black market along with dried prawns, rice – and more of that dreaded wheat flour.

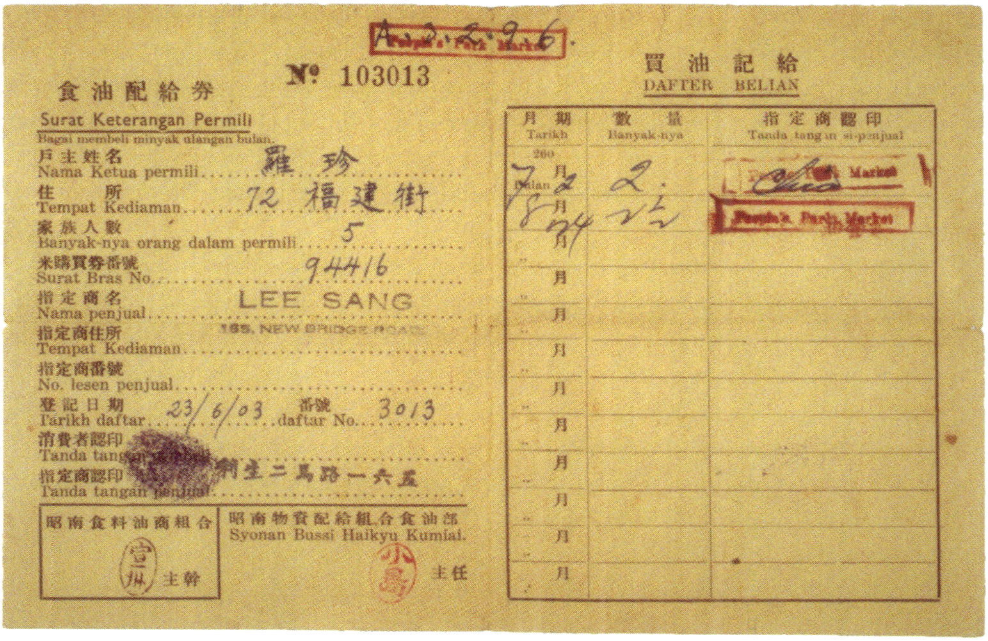

This ration card for cooking oil is from 1943, during the Japanese Occupation of Singapore. Queuing for rations became a way of life. Each time rations were bought, the card would be stamped to record the purchase.

Noel Arthur Pereira, whose mother had gathered seaweed on Pulau Ubin, worked under Japanese engineers at the MacKenzie Road pumping station. He said that most folk did not even have salt because the Japanese hogged most of the salt supply to make chlorine for the water filtration plant. Noting the great shortage of petrol at the time too, he added: "The oil shortage forced us to run our engines with palm oil."

And while sweet potato fries are a hit with hipsters today, Ganesan kept his wartime vow never to touch the tuber again. "Till today, I won't touch these two damn things: tapioca and sweet potato. The worst-tasting was sweet potato."

Those lucky enough to have rice, he mused, were not that fortunate either. With little else to go with their white, polished rice, they soon developed beriberi as their diet was deficient in Vitamin B1. He said: "With beriberi, all the limbs would swell, then burst."

Such a lack of food was egregious because Singapore's wartime food problem was not so much a shortage of supplies as it was uneven distribution. Chef **Sin Leong**, one of the "Four Heavenly Kings" of Singaporean Chinese cuisine, began working as a busboy in Da Dong Restaurant in 1942, the first year of the Japanese Occupation. He said: "All food was rationed, distributed from Da Dong and Hoi Kei restaurants. Representatives from the other restaurants, such as Wing Choon Yuen and Empress, came by trishaw to collect their rations."

All those trips were for feeding those with Japanese banana money to burn. And how they ate! Sin recalled delicacies such as chicken and bird's nest soup; deep-fried chicken livers; mock goose made from crispy tofu skin; and even shark's fin and abalone. There was also a dish called Happy Family, or Singapore's version of haggis, which was pig's stomach stuffed with chopped-up chicken parts. The *piece de resistance*, said Sin, comprised two sets of braised pig's brains, steamed with mushrooms and served in a bowl lined with vegetables. "The dish looked like human brains, and was very fragrant," he recalled. That said, pork was also very hard to procure so, Sin said, restaurant cooks usually made do with wild boar and sea turtle meat.

He added: "The restaurants in wartime did a roaring business because of gamblers." The Japanese invaders had opened casinos within the three amusement parks of New World – where Da Dong Restaurant was – Great World and Happy World (later renamed Gay World). Retired businessman **Toh Mah Keong**, who was among the Oral History Unit's earliest interviewees in 1979, said: "The cabarets were full up. The attitude of the people then was: 'If we have to suffer the effects of war, we might as well go on enjoying our lives'."

The teahouses of Chinatown were crowded, too. Sin recalled: "We ate a lot of *dim sum*. There was no bill then – we went by the number of plates." A plate of two small *bao* (steamed meat buns) was $1 and one of big *bao* was $1.20 in Japanese banana money.

Incidentally, in the late 20th century, when pork was easily available, veterinarian **Ngiam Tong Tau** would shun *bao*. He said: "After I graduated, I was interested to study pig diseases and I asked farmers here to give their dead pigs to me so I could do post-mortems on these. But every time I visited them, they said, 'No pig died.' Now, I knew pigs died. So I soon found out that when the pig died, the farmer would just call a gentleman on a motorbike and sidecar, who would collect the dead pig to make *bak bao*. So for a long time, I did not eat *bak bao*." *Bak bao* is Hokkien for "pork bun".

Grassroots leader **Fong Chiok Kai** remembers less questionable eats, as well as different types of establishments in Chinatown where one could get one's *dim sum* fix. Wealthy Cantonese, he said, thronged the teahouses as they had to start their mornings with *dim sum* and a pot of tea. Fong said: "Cantonese teahouses opened at 4 am and served *dim sum* and tea. The *cha lau*, or tea restaurants, sold tea, dim sum and other cooked food. The *cha teng*, or tea shop, sold tea, coffee, lotus paste tarts, walnut tarts, egg tarts – including preserved egg ones – and other pastries."

Besides being short of pork, Sin said restaurants had to use coconut milk in place of fresh, condensed or evaporated milk. Much of the fresh milk then was reserved for the Japanese, with the bakeries they patronised advertising fresh cream cakes in their windows. Fitter **Soh Guan Bee** recalled: "During the Japanese Occupation, people boiled cow's milk with sugar, stirring constantly so it turned into condensed milk, which they could dilute with water and feed to babies. Condensed milk could last three days to a week, whereas fresh cow's milk spoilt after a day." Refrigerators were rare then and, according to Sin, too pricey for even restaurants to own.

What a world away that was from the 1930s, when Bengali cowherds took their *kerbau* (Malay for buffalos) from house to house every day to sell fresh milk to families.

Kannusamy s/o Pakirisamy, a tutor and longtime resident of Little India, who was born in 1914, said Tamilians, similarly, sold goat's milk door to door. Kannusamy added that the cowherds kept their *kerbau* in Potong Pasir, and bathed them in big ponds nearby. "*Kerbau* that wandered the streets sometimes fell into drains," he recalled, "and four or five Bengalis with big sticks would pull these out of the drains."

Bengali cowherds took their *kerbau* (Malay for buffalos) from house to house every day to sell fresh milk to families.

From 35-Cent Meals to Popiah Parties

The people of Singapore, too, likely felt like they were languishing in ditches after the Japanese surrendered on 12 September 1945. The Allied Forces had liberated Singapore, but there was a shortage of food as trade took time to recover. So the returning British administrators hatched a scheme to provide cheap meals for the masses. In a *Straits Times* report of 14 December 1946, T.P.F. McNeice, the chairman of the post-war planning committee for communal feeding, recalled that when the Social Welfare Department revved to life again in June 1946, it had to act fast to stem hunger in the streets lest, as he put it, Singapore became post-war China "where a man carrying $2,000,000 in his pocket could not make ends meet". Such was the scale of post-war inflation then.

These two men are tucking into a well-balanced meal for only 35 cents each at one of the People's Restaurants in downtown Singapore in 1946. The post-war colonial government set up these restaurants to alleviate the malnutrition people suffered during and just after the Japanese Occupation.

With the support of Singapore's post-war governor Franklin Gimson, from 29 June 1946, McNeice and his team rolled out a chain of People's Restaurants, first at Telok Ayer and then at Handy Road, Maxwell Road and Queen Street. These "restaurants" were actually communal canteens where, for 8 cents, a person could have a freshly cooked lunch of rice, potatoes, salmon, peas, gravy and coffee or Chinese tea.

Gradually, the Social Welfare Department offered a tier of menus, which cost between 10 and 50 cents. Chan Kwee Sung recalled: "Lunch was 30 cents, a big mess tin of rice with a big hunk of meat and various vegetables, lots of gravy and a big mug of steaming tea. The government should be given credit for that, for supplying such cheap lunches, which were prepared by the Social Welfare Department."

On 14 August 1948, *The Straits Times* reported that the People's Restaurants had served 3.5 million meals and had thus "achieved its purpose". These restaurants wound down sometime in 1949.

By 1951, Singapore's post-war fortunes had improved such that a suggestion within the government to revive the People's Restaurants was shot down immediately. The freer flow of foods into Singapore meant that the cost of eating and drinking had dropped considerably. **Lim Kee Chan**, who was a professional boxer in the 1950s, got to enjoy even Western fare at coffeeshops in the early 1950s: "I could get a decent steak for $1 when I was boxing. One of the coffeeshops around Katong sold steak, pork chop and fish and chips...for $1 at the coffeeshop, you could have had a plate of rice, soup and a glass of water to wash everything down."

The second edition of the bestselling Singapore cookbook, *My Favourite Recipes*, by school principal and kitchen doyenne Ellice Handy. This edition was published in 1960 and, in total, there were 11 editions of the cookbook over five decades.

Those with families mostly ate at home, though. **Peter Wee Ban Kheng**, a stalwart of the Peranakan community – who are noted for their delectable cuisine – said: "Most of the time, people ate at home... They did not patronise restaurants so often. They'd only go on weekends or unless there was a wedding or something." This was the custom then, he added, "because people had the time to cook. Today, if you ask people to cook, they'd just say, 'Aiyah. No need. You just go and buy the food'." Workdays after World War II till the late 1980s began at 8 am and ended around 4 pm, so fathers were usually home in time for dinner with the family by 6 pm.

The need to make just about every meal from scratch drove most housewives, especially those who were newly married, to crave easy and quick dishes that satisfied everyone's tastebuds. That

Renowned Singapore cook Madam Chua Jim Neo, the mother of founding prime minister Lee Kuan Yew, is seen here conducting a cooking demonstration for wives of delegates to the Alliance International de Tourism in 1977.

fuelled a demand for cooking teachers. Kitchen mavens such as Chua Jim Neo, whose son was Singapore's founding premier Lee Kuan Yew, her great rival Mrs Leong Yee Soo, school principal Ellice Taylor nee Handy and Chan Sow Lin became household names through their cooking classes and cookbooks, most of which have been reprinted many times since.

The culinary Heavenly King Sin Leong left the restaurant trade in the 1960s to sell salt-baked chicken and beer, and held countless cooking classes for those who wanted his secrets to roasting meat. He was even a food truck pioneer. "For $600, I bought a Hock Lee bus, which was made of wood," he said. "I called it the Sin Leong Seafood Meal Bus. With it, I fried and sold prawns and crabs in Kallang, and taught cooking."

Ever enterprising, Sin graduated from his food truck to his own restaurant in 1976 when he bought a shophouse in Wan Tho Avenue, a road named after his former boss, the cinema magnate Loke Wan Tho. Loke's mother ran The Cathay Restaurant where Sin and his fellow Heavenly Kings of Singapore Chinese cuisine met. The three other Heavenly Kings were Tham Yew Kai, famous for his *pipa* tofu (deep-fried tofu and minced prawn quenelles); Lau Yeok Pui, who made his name with fried glutinous rice and ginger chicken; and Hooi Kok Wai, who was feted for his Fragrant Monk's Bowl (a soupy mix of greens and grains).

The Kings' most famous legacy, however, crowns every Chinese New Year celebration in Singapore, Malaysia and Hong Kong today – *yu sheng*, or raw fish salad. They invented it at The Cathay as a way to jazz up the classic, but staid, festive menus of their day. As famous as they were, Sin said you would never catch any among them sporting a chef's hat. "Chef hats are not suitable for Chinese cuisine because our heads would be very wet and the hats would cut off our circulation," he said.

But, as Wee noted, eating out used to be rare. For many Malays, that meant not restaurants, but picnics of *nasi lemak* (steamed rice infused with coconut milk and fenugreek), curry puffs and other portable goodies, on the beach in the East Coast. For the Chinese, the highlight of eating in were house parties with friends, often featuring *popiah* (Hokkien for, literally, "thin biscuit"), made by wrapping a rice flour crepe over a dollop of stewed root vegetables, chopped egg, chopped groundnuts, pureed garlic and chilli paste. *Straits Times* correspondent **Tan Wee Him**'s family threw his aunt one such party to celebrate her baptism on 24 December 1948. He said: "My pregnant mother was preparing *popiah* for my aunt's gathering of friends at 6:30 pm. Suddenly, I decided to come into the world. Panic stations." She delivered him safely in a nursing home near their Killiney Road dwellings.

Everybody Shares Saliva, Everybody is a Friend

As the workday grew longer and the cost of living inched up, most families took to having most of their meals out. That was because it actually became cheaper for them to eat at hawker stalls than expend time, energy and money on cooking at home.

Hawkers in Singapore started off without pushcarts, said Alice Cheang. "They carried all their wares on a huge, long pole on their shoulders," she recalled. "The *ah kok kei* man

With his livelihood on his shoulders, this wandering hawker is hoping residents around the Jalan Jumat Malay village will flock to him wherever he goes, 1949.

If any of these people on the second floor of a Chinatown shophouse is peckish, all they would have to do is yell their order to the hawker downstairs and unleash the pulley seen in the top right-hand corner of this photograph taken in 1960. The hawker would put the ordered food on the pulley's seat, which the customer would then pull up, recalled Alice Cheang Wye Lan, who grew up with this system.

sold Chinese sponge cakes. Indian men would carry glass pots with taps. The pots contained coffee and you got it just by turning the spigot. There were quite a few of these men about, carrying glass pots on poles. The laksa man also sold his wares from two baskets suspended on a huge pole."

She added that if she was at home on the upper storey of her family's shophouse and felt peckish, all she had to do was "dangle a basket, in which we had put money, down with a long rope and shout out to the passing hawker what we wanted. The hawker would put the food in the basket, which we would then pull up." This way of buying food, she added, was very popular in Chinatown then.

After the war, hawkers went from poles to pushcarts. Vincent Gabriel rued that some of their best dishes vanished along with the poles. These included *tiong kai*, or offcuts and offal of pigs and fowl stewed with *taucheong* into a gelatinous gloop, which Gabriel considered food for the gods. He said: "It was very thick and rich. In the 1960s, this was sold in Katong by a man in a rickshaw because he had lost the use of his legs. When he passed away, the dish disappeared."

Other dishes have stood the test of time, including fish head curry, which Gabriel said was thought up by the folks at Soon Heng in Race Course Road. He added: "Fish heads used to be thought of as fodder for cats and dogs only. Then this Chinese man experimented by cooking fish heads into a sour curry, to rid the heads of the fishy smell. It worked." Curried fish heads, however, took some time to catch on. He said: "At that time, fears about how fresh fish and prawns were got everyone deep-frying such fruits of the sea to a crisp... Only a few brave souls like me would want to try it." Gabriel, for one, grew to like it so much that when a friend asked him what he wanted for his birthday, he said, "I only want one thing – Gomez's fish curry." Mr Gomez sold his famous dish first at Selegie Road, where Peace Centre is today, then at Outram Road.

An itinerant *laksa* hawker setting down two big pots from his carrying pole at Club Street in 1983.

You could tell who the best hawkers were because dishes were named after them. Besides Mr Gomez, Subramaniam s/o Munian remembered "Mr Gupta's *mee goreng*" at Tanjong Pagar. Others enjoyed Yip Kee chicken porridge from the Bugis Street stall run by Jean Yip's paternal grandparents.

A *char kway teow* seller frying his sinfully scrumptious rice noodles with egg, beansprouts, prawns and sometimes cockles, 1965. For takeaways, he would wrap the *char kway teow* in *opeh* (*Areca catechu*) leaves, seen here stacked on the cabinet right behind him.

And if you, like many, believed that hawker food tasted better in yesteryear, Gabriel knew why that was so. He said: "At the end of the day, if there was unsold food, the hawker and his family would stuff themselves with these leftovers. That's why they became famous; the food they sold customers was always fresh. That's something which many hawkers today don't understand."

Their commitment to selling fresh-cooked food was perhaps why many hawkers would ply their customers with more food than they could eat in one sitting. *Satay* sellers, for one, used to bring 50 sticks of *satay* to the table, even if a customer had only ordered 10. Gabriel recalled: "If you ate only 10 sticks, you could return the other 40, which they would then just warm up and serve the next guy. So if you got a second round of *satay*, it would be overdone."

Chinese restaurants had the same gambit, with questionable consequences. "They were real businessmen. They realised that if you were hungry, you'd be tempted to overeat. So they would immediately bring out a whole range of dishes, chicken, fish, tofu and vegetables in little saucers. You paid for only what you ate.

"So some people would just nibble some of the food in the saucer and leave the rest so they need not pay for it." It was, he added, "a good thing that the Ministry of the Environment cracked down on this as it's not hygienic."

Hygiene, however, was not exactly top on everyone's list then. After a meal, many would spit onto tables and floors. That was a hazard as tuberculosis, whose sufferers coughed up blood, used to be rife in Singapore. Gabriel got a shock one day when the customary white towel he was given after meals was stained with blood. He added: "They gave you the towel to wipe your hands after a meal. But people used it to wipe their faces, then their hands, then their armpits and so on."

Gradually, everyone became much more mindful of hygiene, which was perhaps why *satay celup* fell out of favour. At about $3 per person in the 1980s, *satay celup* was an expensive experience of dipping skewered bits of meat, seafood and vegetables into a communal vat of hot, spicy groundnut gravy. Gabriel said: "Some would take a bite of the food and dunk it into the gravy again. There is a Cantonese proverb: 'Everybody shares saliva, everybody is a friend'." The *satay celup* hawker, he added, would collect all the used skewers, wash them quickly in water – and use them again.

There is, however, always something comforting about sharing food with friends. **Sally Chan née Sally Liew**, who was among Changi Airport's pioneering ground staff, recalled a colleague nipping out regularly to buy a packet of *char kway teow* (fried flat rice noodles) for them to share. With no cutlery available, they improvised by folding the chits torn off boarding passes, each of which was the size of a cinema ticket. They would then use these chits to scoop the hot, fried noodles into their mouths. It is much like how National Servicemen used to tear the corners off their styrofoam lunchboxes to use as makeshift spoons.

Retired school principal **Carmee Lim**, too, remembered happy evenings of tucking into a packet of hot, spicy noodles with her friends – fellow hostelites at Eusoff College. "On certain nights," she recalled fondly, "we would have a *mee goreng* supper from the hawker."

Many hawkers' families were in the habit of ordering stir-fries off their stall's menu for supper at around 10 pm daily. Those accustomed to such night-time noshes were stumped when they learnt that others made do with bread; they found that practice too staid for words. Jean Yip, whose grandparents' stall was at Bugis Street, said: "When I first met my husband, he lived in a HDB flat, where they bought bread back for supper. I thought eating bread for supper so ridiculous." She said that was because eating bread seemed to her as run-of-the-mill compared to having *zi char* staples like fried *hor fun* (wide rice noodles) or fried *bee hoon* (rice vermicelli).

In time, Singaporeans grew to crave novel eats. Artist **Amanda Heng Liang Ngim** said: "I remember Singaporeans lining up for Yaohan's *anpan*. We could see it being made." That was in the 1970s or, as she put it, the time of the "Japanese cultural invasion". The Japanese supermarket chain Yaohan first opened in Plaza Singapura and besides *anpan* (Japanese for buns filled with red bean paste) they sold Singapore's first sky blue-coloured ice cream, a mint-and-ice cream soda confection.

Plaza Singapura, which opened in 1974, was but one stop in the foodie haven that was, and still is, Orchard Road. High-, mid- and low-brow eateries peppered this shopping strip, with even the carpark opposite Cold Storage (where The Centrepoint shopping mall is today) being converted into Glutton's Square by 4 pm daily. Most diners there made a beeline for the famous *orh luak*, or fresh oysters flash-fried with egg, tapioca batter and lashings of lard.

Hawker stalls at Glutton's Square in 1970, site of the present Orchard Gateway and 313 Somerset malls. It was a huge open-air carpark that transformed into a higgledy-piggledy hawker haven for foodies from 4 pm daily.

This Indian *rojak* seller at Rasa Singapura Food Centre is arranging his enticing spread of eggs, potatoes, prawns and assorted vegetables dipped in batter, deep-fried and then eaten with a thick, red sweet sauce and slices of cucumber, 1985.

The Magnolia Snack Bar at Cold Storage supermarket, a favourite hangout of teenagers in the 1970s.

Like these boys, many schoolchildren hung out at the now-defunct Scotts Picnic Food Court, a huge and bustling underground food court in the heart of Orchard Road in the 1980s and 1990s.

Journalist **Tan Wee Him**, who had a photographic memory of Orchard Road hotspots, recalled the pull of the Dong Lock Wee cakeshop at the junction of Killiney Road and Orchard Road. "They were famous for their cupcakes, each topped with half a cherry. They were, he added, also very popular caterers in the years before hotels and restaurants started a sideline in catering, too."

Across the road from this cakeshop was Cold Storage supermarket, which from the 1970s was the height of sophistication as it had the Magnolia Snack Bar, where teenagers chugged 80-cent milkshakes and scarfed down $1.80 meals of fish and chips. Upstairs was the decidedly more adult Salad Bowl restaurant, with its Western eats and reasonably priced set lunches. Sweaty schoolchildren swarmed Cozy Corner down the road towards Tanglin for tea and ices. And countless couples courted over meat and potatoes at The Ponderosa Steakhouse in Plaza Singapura.

The relentless redevelopment of Orchard Road over the years has, however, made distant memories of Glutton's Square, Rasa Singapura, Scotts Picnic Food Court and Taman Serasi at the Botanic Gardens.

Those preferring Asian fare had their pick of such eats at Koek Road, between Orchard Point and Orchard Plaza, which boasted congee, Hainanese food and Teck Kee *bao*. Killiney Road, a stone's throw away, was home to Taiwanese porridge restaurants.

The relentless redevelopment of Orchard Road over the years has, however, made distant memories of Glutton's Square, Rasa Singapura, Scotts Picnic Food Court and Taman Serasi at the Botanic Gardens.

Singaporeans have since emerged champions at international cooking and pastry competitions. The French tyre maker Michelin launched its starred restaurant and hawker stall guides in Singapore in July 2016, catapulting local hawker stalls such as Liao Fan Hong Kong Soya Sauce Chicken Rice & Noodle into global consciousness. The hugely popular global MasterChef cooking reality TV show franchise launched its Singapore edition in 2018, with its first winner Zander Ng, a former IT manager. At the time of writing, Singapore is eyeing a spot for its hawker food on UNESCO's intangible cultural heritage list, which includes the Mediterranean diet and Italy's pizza makers.

Gabriel had this to say about the deeper meaning behind Singapore's food heritage: "Because we came from different parts of the world, and we know we would bring the best, we remember only the best and we brought it all together.

"And because people naturally gravitate towards the best, we began to enjoy the best of one another's culture. And that has helped to blend us as a nation."

CHAPTER SIX

NATIONAL TRAGEDIES

Bolts from the Blue

When 50 people are trapped under rubble, every second is vital in pulling them out alive.

But on Saturday, 15 March 1986, when Hotel New World collapsed, **Lim Siam Kim** had to queue to call his boss, the minister for home affairs, to report how bad the tragedy was. In those days, precious few in Singapore could buy a mobile phone. Lim, who was Director of Operations at the Ministry of Home Affairs (MHA), recalled: "The nearest phone was at a petrol kiosk... I was in civilian clothes and had to queue to make the call to Jayakumar." He was referring to Professor S. Jayakumar, then Minister for Home Affairs, who was later Deputy Prime Minister of Singapore.

"Everyone," he added, "was trying to convey the news of the collapse to their loved ones too."

Lim and his colleague **Cheong Quee Wah** had rushed to the site of the collapse after a policeman called to report the tragedy. At the time, quite fortuitously, Jayakumar, Lim, Cheong and Commissioner of Police Goh Yong Hong were in a meeting at MHA headquarters. Lim recalled that Cheong was so rattled by the call that, instead of waiting for MHA's driver to rush them there, Cheong and Lim jumped into Cheong's car and sped there. Upon arrival, they were stunned by what they saw. "There was no building left," Lim recalled. "I could just see its flattened top; it was like a squeezed sandwich. That was a great shock and everyone was running around. The police were already in charge there, but nobody seemed to know what to do when we were there." Cheong added: "It was like a deck of cards just collapsed... it caught us by surprise."

As Director of Operations at the Ministry of Home Affairs on 15 March 1986, Lim Siam Kim led the search-and-rescue mission in the wake of the collapse of Hotel New World that day.

Cheong was the right man on the scene. He chaired MHA's Executive Group, which managed national crises such as hijackings and hostage-

Rescuers used excavators to search for survivors amid the rubble of the collapsed Hotel New World on 16 March 1986. In the end, 17 people were pulled out alive but, sadly, 33 others perished in one of the greatest tragedies in Singapore history.

taking. So searching for, and rescuing, the Hotel New World victims was his responsibility – one which came just 15 days before he was to retire on 1 April 1986.

Cheong's group comprised, among others, representatives from the Ministry of Foreign Affairs, the then Ministry of Communications and the Singapore Civil Defence Force [SCDF]. "Actually," he said of the collapsed hotel, "we didn't know what to do. We just didn't know what to do."

Engineer **How Mun Heng**, who was among the first rescuers on the scene, said: "In the early days of our planning for relief operations, we had only very basic principles and a team who attended to victims rendered homeless due to fire in their flats or the collapse of one or two shophouses.

"There was no prolonged relief operation such as Hotel New World, which was a pretty large building, burying quite a few people." The six-storey building was actually known as Lian Yak, and sat at the junction of Serangoon Road and Owen Road. It crumbled at 11.25 am that fateful Saturday, after years of cracked pillars due to its structurally unsound design, made worse by a hodge-podge of modifications over time. The building was, in fact, bearing a greater load than its beams could take.

In 1975, there had been a forewarning of how ill-fitted the building was. On 19 August that year, carbon monoxide leaked within the hotel, rendering 35 guests unconscious. After that, the hotel changed its name from New Serangoon Hotel to Hotel New World.

Cheong and his team of rescuers knew enough to set up a command centre and relief centres for the victims' despairing relatives to gather for updates. Lim said: "We had to set up a command post at Serangoon Plaza, at the Eagle Piano Company. Its owner, a kindly, elderly man, allowed us to do so."

Cheong said that his team operated out of the piano shop for about a day before the owner of the President Hotel nearby opened an entire floor of the hotel for them. Meanwhile, How said, Bee Huat coffeeshop nearby was designated the first relief centre for the disaster. "The owner provided his stock of drinks to us without charging us or the relatives," he said. "We really have to thank him for that."

Later, the government set up a second relief centre – in the mortuary of the Singapore General Hospital (SGH). That might seem morbid, but made good sense because relatives would have to identify bodies recovered from the rubble.

Pandemonium reigned in the first few hours after the tragedy. How watched cranes, bulldozers and tunnelling equipment rushed in, along with doctors, nurses and paramedics. "It was chaotic," he said. "Crowds were surging. The police had a hard time controlling them."

Architect **John Ting Kang Chung** was in Sarawak when news of the disaster flashed on a television there: "It happened on my birthday. We just couldn't believe what we were seeing on the telly, but it was happening in real time in Singapore… it was like, 'Hang on a minute – is this some sort of movie or not?'"

The crisis was only too real but, amid it, there were big blessings. One, said Cheong, was the presence of two Israeli military experts in Singapore – Colonel Baruch Doron and Colonel Yaacov Kedem. The two retired colonels, who were advisors to the Singapore Civil Defence Force (SCDF), had survived bombings in Lebanon. They told Cheong two things: First, the rescuers must wait for the piles of rubble to stabilise – which took seven hours. And second, a person trapped alive in rubble could go without food or water for a week. That advice, Cheong believed, led to more lives being saved than would otherwise be the case.

The public at large, however, had no inkling that the rescuers were heeding the two Israelis' advice. So, watching the drama on their TV screens, they were perplexed as to why nothing seemed to be happening on site in the first 24 hours. Cheong recalled: "We got a lot of phone calls from people saying, 'How come you are not doing anything?'" Worse, even when the rescue got underway, much of the action took place under the rubble, away from TV cameras. "We were drilling underneath where the TV cameras can't see," Cheong said. "So to the public, it was like two days without movement."

When Colonel Doron and Colonel Kedem finally judged it safe to move in the cranes, SCDF officers drilled – for what seemed interminably – through solid, reinforced concrete. "The poor chaps were all below," Cheong said. "You drilled for hours, you hardly chipped a bit."

He had also faced delays from an unexpected source – a fellow civil servant at the then Building Control Department – when he tried to get hold of the original building plans for Lian Yak. "The guy said, 'It's Saturday afternoon, the office is closed'." he recalled. "I said, 'Go and break down the door or use a torch or whatever to burn it down!'"

One of Singapore's Finest Hours

A huge blessing in those tense hours was the selfless team of engineers who were building Singapore's first Mass Rapid Transit (MRT) line at the time. Lim Siam Kim said: "Colonel Kedem and Colonel Doron advised us to cut parts of the rubble and lift these off the ground. But the guys working on the MRT said, 'Why not try tunnelling?'... It was decided that, 'Why not? They have the experience and the equipment and manpower. So it was decided: Let's go and get the MRT people."

The MRT engineers and contractors were not the only ones who contributed to the search-and-rescue. The Hotel New World tragedy was, in fact, one of Singapore's finest hours as people from all walks of life donated cash, food and drink as well as services in kind as everyone raced against time to pull as many victims from the rubble as possible. Cheong recalled: "So many people wanted to help, there was confusion. The Contractors' Association Committee wanted to help. Korean workers wanted to help. Shipyards offered their cranes... There were calls from Malaysia and other countries, offering to help us."

There were a few foreigners under the crushed concrete and twisted metal as well. Government proofreader **Subramaniam s/o Munian** helped five among them, all Indian nationals, who were injured in the tragedy. "I was involved because there were Indians from India involved," he recalled. "My duty was to look after them, get clearance from Immigration, get lodgings for them, ensure they had their passports, send them to hospital and finally put up reports on all that." He recalled one among these Indians "hanging from the top floor";

Prime Minister Lee Kuan Yew and Home Affairs Minister S. Jayakumar at the nerve centre of the search-and-rescue operations soon after Hotel New World collapsed.

Rescuers bring a survivor to safety from the rubble of the collapsed Hotel New World on 16 March 1986.

he was later saved. As a rescuer, Subramaniam's reporting point was Annapoorna Restaurant on the ground floor of Serangoon Plaza, which housed the famous Mustafa emporium. "We had a roster and I worked from 11 pm till 11 am daily."

By Sunday, the day after the hotel collapsed, folks from the Singapore Fire Brigade, SCDF and the MRT team joined foreign workers in trying to reach the trapped. "From Saturday till Wednesday," Cheong Quee Wah said, "we were there non-stop – when you are in crisis, you work together, no sleep, no nothing, just worked through five days."

Their fervour was such that, at first, they were slogging without any food or drink. "Then the hawkers started to come," he said. "I don't know where they came from. After one day, there was a whole chain of food stalls along the street, offering free food and drinks.

"The voluntary spirit was very good. Otherwise, actually, all of a sudden, how to feed those people?… Towards the end, it was almost like a fun fair below the President Shopping Centre. The whole street was all food stalls."

As heart-warming as the *kampung* spirit was, there was no let-up in the pressure on Cheong to get all 50 victims out fast. "The pressure was to get somebody out alive. Parliament was in session, and ministers were on my back. They were expecting something; they said, 'Dead or alive, get somebody out'."

It did not help that the day after the collapse, the media went to town with the news that the first voice rescuers heard coming from the rubble was apparently that of a girl named Angel. Cheong said: "On Saturday night, there were voices from within the rubble. One girl called Angel was still alive. But she died; we couldn't get to her in time."

The media reports, however, ratcheted up the pressure on Cheong. "When everybody knew she was alive, we were asked, 'How come you don't rescue her?'"

After seven days of frenzied searching, a total of 33 people perished in the tragedy. The remaining 17 were pulled out alive. How Mun Heng recalled the scene at the SGH morgue: "Even under cold-store conditions, the stench was overbearing and the sight was gruesome because some were in bits and pieces.

"The stench at the site was overpowering despite the purification chemicals there... once we unearthed a body, we had to send it to the mortuary quickly because it had deteriorated badly."

Amid this, the police had to keep the victims' distraught relatives and friends at bay – they kept trying to break the cordon around the disaster area – as well as chase away touts from funeral parlours who were, most egregiously, handing out pamphlets advertising their packages.

How said he was "impressed" by the way the authorities concluded the seventh, and final, day of the rescue and relief operation. "They asked everyone to maintain one hour of total silence... and sent sensitive sound detection devices into the rubble.

"Then they told us to clear the site to prevent other disasters as there could be leaking gas pipes there... and there were broken water pipes. Some of the family members collapsed. I think, by and large, they accepted that was the final hour." Bulldozers and cranes then moved in to clear the rubble and level the site.

After the collapse of Hotel New World, the government tightened building regulations considerably and, among other things, set up the Building Control Authority.

Two Plane Crashes and their Aftermath

How Mun Heng said that the authorities' experience with the Hotel New World disaster actually helped when Silkair Flight MI 185 crashed in Indonesia's Musi River on 19 December 1997. All 104 people on board were killed, when the Boeing 737-300 from Jakarta to Singapore crashed near Palembang in southern Sumatra. "Lessons from the collapse of Hotel New World actually benefitted the team in MI 185," How mused. "There were finally standard operating procedures for command, control and communications."

He added: "Officers were trained in emergency behaviour response for family members. Others were trained to handle such operations without undue delay." This was so, he noted, even though the MI 185 operation was handled largely by the Indonesian authorities, working with the Republic of Singapore Navy.

Together with Singapore Airlines and Silkair staff who volunteered to be "buddies" to the victims' families, How set up a holding area at Changi Airport for the relatives to gather for updates on the unfolding tragedy.

Their experience of comforting the families of MI 185 victims stood them in good stead later. On 31 October 2000, Singapore Airlines (SIA) flight SQ 006 crashed into construction

Members of the public paying their last respects at the public memorial held at the Singapore Indoor Stadium on 30 December 1997 for the 104 victims of SilkAir flight MI 185, which crashed near Palembang, Indonesia, on 19 December 1997.

equipment on one of the runways at Taiwan's Chiang Kai-shek Airport. It was a rainy night, and the plane's pilots turned onto the wrong runway, one which had been closed for repairs. The plane broke in two upon impact and its fuel tank exploded, killing 83 among the 179 people on board, including four SIA crew members. The tragedy marred SIA's impeccable safety record up till then.

Fire Fire Everywhere

As How Mun Heng noted earlier in this chapter, before Lian Yak Building collapsed, the most common crises in Singapore were homes on fire and old shophouses caving in from overload. Plastic surgeon **Lee Seng Teik**, a pioneering member of SGH's Department of Plastic, Reconstructive and Aesthetics Surgery for more than 40 years, said that in the 1970s, there were "close to 700 fires" a year. Tighter regulations in the ensuing years, he added, halved such incidents eventually.

Lee, who headed SGH's Plastic Surgery Department and Burns Centre from 1985 till 1998, recalled most vividly Singapore's worst industrial accident on the Liberia-registered tanker *ST Spyros*, which had been docked in Jurong Shipyard for repairs. Most times, there were a total of 167 workers on board the ship during the repairs.

Just after lunch on 12 October 1978, Lee was about to meet a fellow doctor from the United States when SGH staff were alerted: "After 2 pm, we had the very first indication of a disaster... the hospital notified everyone about the possibility of a major disaster, and to get ready."

At 2.15 pm, welder Lim Hock Hoe had been heating a rusty nut on a ship cover to remove it. Unbeknownst to him, vapour from a leaky fuel siphon was swirling about him. Sparks from his blowtorch ignited the fumes and the ensuing explosion tore huge chunks off the tanker and sent some flying into a ship nearby, injuring those on board.

Captain Chitharanjan Kuttan, who was once the comptroller of port, comptroller of marine safety and comptroller of projects for Singapore's port, said that the eventual Commission of Inquiry into *Spyros* found that it had been "a very unsafe ship". "It was a fiddle and fuddle of a carrier," he said. "They were siphoning fuel from the Spyros for machinery."

"Within half an hour," Lee recalled, "came the first casualties. We knew we had a true disaster because the casualties were in truckloads." He stressed: "We were caught in a totally unexpected disaster we had never seen and hopefully would never experience again."

In all, 76 people died from the blast, 57 among them on the day it happened. Most succumbed to burns or from breathing in carbon monoxide and oil fumes. Another 69 were injured much the same way. "We stayed in hospital without going home for three days," Lee said. "We thought it was quite something, we worked non-stop." At the end of it all, Lee "almost fainted" on his way home.

At the time of writing, the *Spyros* tragedy is one of Singapore's worst post-war disasters.

The Greek oil tanker *Spyros* was in Jurong Shipyard when sparks from a welder's blowtorch ignited petrol fumes which caused a blast so bad, huge chunks of the *Spyros* went flying into a nearby ship.

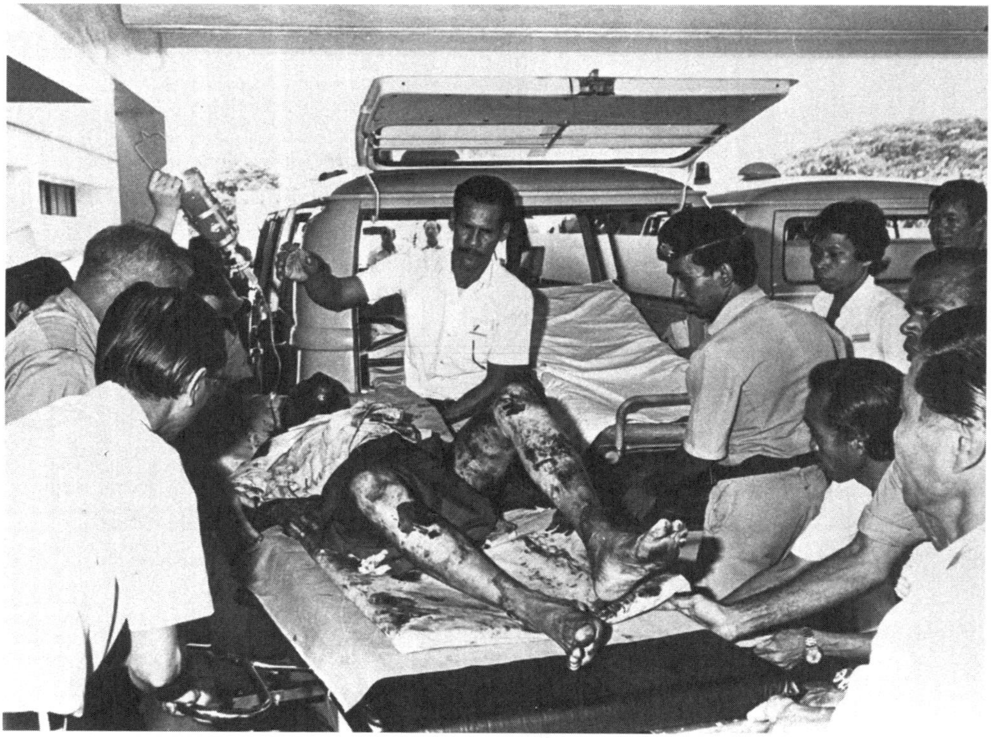

A badly burnt victim of the *Spyros* explosion arrives at the Singapore General Hospital for treatment.

"One of the things we learnt from *Spyros* was the management of disasters. Most often we think of managing disasters, but the managing of relatives in a disaster is equally important."

As was the case with the Hotel New World tragedy, hospital staff also had to contend with near-hysterical relatives and friends of victims, who descended upon SGH in the hope of seeing the victims. "It was so bad, we needed police control," Lee said. "Otherwise, the wards would have found it impossible to function."

Lee then mused: "One of the things we learnt from *Spyros* was the management of disasters. Most often we think of managing disasters, but the managing of relatives in a disaster is equally important."

Singapore's social workers had learnt that lesson several decades earlier, when they worked against time to bring relief to 20,000 people rendered homeless by a massive fire at Bukit Ho Swee. The fire broke out on 25 May 1961. Retired Permanent Secretary **James Koh Cher Siang** remembered it well. He and his pals were waiting for their buses home when flames swept through squatters' homes on the hill, razing an area of 0.4 sq km. Koh said the area was known in Hokkien as *Si Kah Teng*, or "Four-Legged Building", a place that was known for its frequent gangfights.

Koh recalled: "We said, 'How come fire engines were all rushing to Bukit Ho Swee?' And one of my friends said, 'Oh, Bukit Ho Swee, maybe my house is on fire.' So we took a bus there and, indeed, his house had burnt down." Koh was then living in Tiong Bahru. "That was quite far away so we were not affected by the fire, but we could see all the commotion."

Prolific writer **Goh Sin Tub**, who was then working in the Social Welfare Department, had to find a way to house 16,000 of the 20,000 homeless residents of Bukit Ho Swee, as 4,000 among them had managed to find somewhere to stay. That was a tall order, but on top of that, Goh and his team had to put up with "agitators" who were trying to provoke unrest between the government and those who were unhappy with it.

Goh Sin Tub, who was then working in the Social Welfare Department, had to find a way to house 16,000 of the 20,000 homeless residents of Bukit Ho Swee.

They also tried to pull a fast one on Goh. He recalled: "Some of the agitators came to me, politely asking me for permission to use our public address system. They said, 'Well, there are some messages we want to give these people and we'd like to talk to them'."

But Goh was not to be taken in so easily. "I said, 'Look, what messages are these? You pass them on to me and we will relay them to these people.' They refused to do that, so it was suspicious." Goh managed to rebuff the agitators.

Firemen fighting the raging blaze at Bukit Ho Swee on 25 May 1961.

Residents rendered homeless after the Bukit Ho Swee blaze queue up for their daily meals at a government relief centre on 1 June 1961.

It was bad enough that some had accused the government of deliberately torching Bukit Ho Swee. Goh said: "There was even an allegation that the government had set fire to the *attap* huts in Bukit Ho Swee in order to clear out the squatter area.

"But that was soon squashed because there was an investigation into the matter and it was made very clear how the fire had started." The reader should note that although Goh's recollection is that the source of fire involved a cooking utensil, the cause of fire has never been established.

Allegations aside, the magnanimity of Singaporeans came to the fore again, just as it would later with the Hotel New World tragedy. "The HDB [Housing & Development Board], the police, the health authorities, PUB [Public Utilities Board], everybody else in the community came in to help," Goh said. "This was the shining hour in the history of our country." Thanks to everyone's efforts, the Social Welfare Department succeeded in housing all the homeless within three weeks, after they were temporarily put up in classrooms. HDB, for one, found empty flats in estates such as Queenstown to house them. Those who could not be given flats were housed eventually in welfare homes. "Our main success was that we were genuinely sympathetic," he mused. "We went from classroom to classroom attending to their problems. We distributed clothes, food, everything on time."

Singapore's next big fire broke out at 9.55 am on 21 November 1972 in Robinsons department store at Raffles Place. Journalist **Tan Wee Him** was almost trapped there – but luckily, he left the store half an hour before it went up in smoke. Tan recalled: "I had a haircut at The Arcade nearby and then went to Robinsons to look at the train sets for about half an hour. Then I headed to my office. Then, just before lunch, I got a call – there was a fire at Robinsons! I said, 'How can that be? I was there just a while ago!'"

Tan rushed back to Raffles Place – to a "towering inferno". "The flames were shooting up and even the bronze statue at the top of the Robinsons roof had melted." The heat from the raging fire was so intense that he had to take cover behind pillars a short distance away. For almost a week afterwards, Tan would return to the site daily to report on the fire's aftermath. A total of nine people died; they had tried to escape by taking the lift. "It was very sad because all these people were actually the store's old staff," Tan said. "The whole area was eventually hoarded up and there was a giant cavity where the store used to be. The cavity would turn into a mini lake every time it rained." The site is now home to One Raffles Place. It was only after the Robinsons fire that Singaporeans became more aware of the folly of using a building's elevators when there was a fire. Before that, everyone's view of building safety procedures was a relatively neglectful one of "it won't happen to us". Which, perhaps, explains why, as plastic surgeon Lee said, there were close to 700 fires a year in the 1970s.

Tan said that there were actually bomb threats throughout the early 1970s. These kept the authorities very busy indeed. "When I joined ST in 1970, there was a bomb threat almost every other day," he recalled. "It could be a hoax – or the real thing. And we in the newsroom were always called upon to cover bomb disposals by the Army."

Scenes from the shattering aftermath of MacDonald House after it was bombed by two Indonesian saboteurs on 10 March 1965.

These threats were from the Communist Party of Malaya (CPM), which had waged a guerrilla war against the colonial government in Malaya from 1948 till 1960. The CPM then unleashed the second phase of this insurgency on Malaysia and Singapore from 1968 till 1989. As the website of Singapore's Ministry of Home Affairs states, "Singapore continued to face the communist threat after Independence in 1965... the CPM revived its underground networks to carry out assassinations and 'bombing' assignments. The Internal Security Department (ISD) intensified efforts against the CPM and by the late 1970s had eradicated almost the entire communist underground network in Singapore." The CPM finally laid down its arms in 1989, after it signed peace pacts with Malaysia and Thailand.

Tan noted that, most egregiously, those behind such bombing assignments hid these bombs along overhead pedestrian bridges. He huffed: "I believe they wanted to inflict injuries to members of the public to instill fear in the people."

Well before the CPM's revival of its underground sabotage, however, Singapore was beset by Konfrontasi (Malay for Confrontation). *Konfrontasi* refers to the attacks mounted by Indonesia on Singapore and Malaya after the latter two merged with Sabah and Sarawak to form the Federation of Malaysia on 16 September 1963. Indonesia's then president, Sukarno, launched *Konfrontasi* because he felt that the formation of Malaysia was a gambit to prolong colonial rule in the region.

Konfrontasi's deadliest strike in Singapore was at MacDonald House on 10 March 1965, just five months before Singapore attained independence. Indonesian commandos Osman Bin Haji Mohamed Ali and Harun Bin Said set off 11 kg of explosives near the ground floor lift of the building in Orchard Road. The blast, which happened at 3.07 pm, killed three people – secretaries Elizabeth "Suzie" Choo and Juliet Goh, and driver Mohammed Yasin Bin Kesit – and injured 33 others. The pillars of the 10-storey building were badly damaged.

Osman and Harun were arrested, brought to trial and in 1967– the year after *Konfrontasi* ended – were found guilty. Both were hanged in Singapore on 17 October 1968. Their executions kept ties between Singapore and Indonesia tense for some years. The relationship between the two countries became warmer only from May 1973 when, on a state visit to Indonesia, then Prime Minister Lee Kuan Yew scattered flowers over Osman's and Harun's graves.

No Safe Harbour

Neglect lay behind Singapore's next major tragedy, and one that most Singaporeans today still remember – the cable car crisis of 29 January 1983. Like Hotel New World, it happened on a Saturday.

At dusk that day, three tugboats were towing the drillship *Eniwetok* out of the oil wharf in Keppel Harbour. The drillship was 69 m high, while the cableway between nearby Sentosa Island and Mount Faber was 56.5 m high. Suddenly, the tugboats' towline slipped and the *Eniwetok* drifted eastwards, towards the cableway, on which plied 15 bubble-shaped cable cars. The drillship's mast got entangled in the 1.75-metre-long cableway, sending two

A Singapore Armed Forces helicopter lowering a member of the rescue team to the stranded cable car.

One of the wrecked cable cars being hoisted from the water.

cars – one yellow, one blue – crashing into the sea, smashing into one another. The seven people in these cars were killed upon impact. An eighth passenger, a baby, was flung out of another plunging car, landed in the sea and was later saved.

Thirteen other passengers dangled in the air for some three hours before rescuers, led by then Singapore Armed Forces Colonel Lee Hsien Loong, freed them. Lee would become Singapore's third prime minister in 2004.

Cameraman **Mun Chor Seng** saw it all. He and his family had been looking forward to attending a colleague's wedding when all hell broke loose in the harbour. Mun said: "We were all dressed up when my boss rang me and said, 'Mun, you better come back to the office. I said, 'What happened?' And he said, 'The cable cars fell into the sea; we need a big team'." The national television station, then known as the Singapore Broadcasting Corporation, sent a total of four teams to Keppel Harbour. The timing of the tragedy proved a particular headache for them. "It was in the evening, and so the lighting and all that needed to be tackled." But, ever the professional, he added: "It was one of those assignments that you told yourself, 'The show must go on'."

At the time, Chitharanjan Kuttan the ship captain was the harbour's comptroller of the port, comptroller of maritime safety and comptroller of projects. He was, however, on a family holiday in Cameron Highlands when the tragedy occurred. He read about the disaster in the Malaysian newspapers the morning after, "dropped everything" and drove right back to Singapore. Speaking to the Oral History Centre in 2004, Kuttan mused: "There was an oversight in the height regulation. The cables were already there; the shipyard should have been mindful of what its workers were doing… the shipyard should have advised the Eniwetok's pilot." Those who were negligent, he added, could not plead ignorance as the harbour's height regulations were made known to all concerned.

The cable car tragedy led the harbour to tighten its measures against such accidents. Among other things, Kuttan said, it now has a radar control system to ensure that ships that breach height regulations do not veer near the cableway, even by accident.

"Cock the Gun Against My Head"

There was, however, one major Singapore crisis on the high seas that did not end tragically, thanks to the cool-headed Singaporeans in charge of defusing it. On Thursday, 31 January 1974, four guerrillas – two Palestinian and two Japanese – hijacked a boat to Pulau Bukom and bombed the Shell oil company's refinery there, which was one of the world's largest such facilities. The Palestinians were from the Palestinian Front for the Liberation of Palestine (PFLP), who were known for hostage-taking and the bombing of airplanes. Shell's parent company was Dutch and as The Netherlands at the time did not support the Palestinian cause, their attack on Shell's refinery was seen as a tit-for-tat move.

The Japanese, meanwhile, were from the Japanese Red Army, who were protesting the Vietnam War. They were known for suicide bombings, and had joined forces with the

Palestinians to further one another's causes. Before Bukom, they had tried to take seafarers hostage off Karachi in Pakistan.

All this was not immediately known to **Tee Tua Ba**, who was then the officer commanding Singapore's Marine Police and later Commissioner of Police from 1992 till 1997. At first, he said, given the billowing clouds and multiple explosions, he and his compatriots thought someone was bombing Bukom from the air.

In May 2001, Tee recalled: "With the smoke and the explosion, and coincidentally, two defence aircraft flying past on training, some thought that it was an aerial attack and bombing on the island. Nobody on this island knew what was happening. Panic was everywhere." The island's security personnel, and at least one Shell employee, tried to fend off the guerrillas, but were forced to flee when the latter began shooting at them.

The guerrillas then jumped onto the ferry *Laju* (Malay for "speedy"), and took its five-strong crew hostage. Tee and his team, in 10 motorboats, pursued them right into Singapore Harbour. Up to that point, Tee said, he was "under the impression that it was a straightforward, serious criminal case involving armed men on an island". Then again, he added, Bukom seemed "the last place to do an armed robbery". "I was asking myself, 'Could it be drunken seamen on a wild shooting spree?'"

He thought about shooting at the ferry to immobilise it, but decided against doing so in case there were hostages on board – they might be killed in sudden gunfire. "I reluctantly instructed all men to lower their weapons and not be provocative," he said. His judgement proved right as, shortly after they withheld fire, his superiors – the commissioner and assistant commissioner of police – ordered him not to shoot at the hijackers as they had, indeed, hostages.

This is Ulot Bin Idris, who was among the five crew members of the *Laju* ferry (seen in the background) taken hostage by four hijackers on 31 January 1974. Ulot spent seven nights in the ferry's wheel room, unable to bathe or even change his clothes.

S.R. Nathan, Director of the Security and Intelligence Division at the Ministry of Defence, speaking to reporters after he and his team arrived back in Singapore safely on 9 February 1974. He had led a contingent of Singaporeans to Kuwait to resolve the *Laju* crisis. The contingent comprised eight local government officials and four commandos. They took the place of the five crew members who were initially taken hostage by the hijackers, and travelled to Kuwait with the hijackers to guarantee the latter's safe passage out of Singapore.

After *Laju* "majestically entered Singapore Harbour", Tee recalled further, one of the hijackers waved to him, threw a blue plastic container into the sea and gestured to Tee to pick it up. In the container – which resembled an explosive – was a message explaining who the hijackers were, what they were trying to do and their confession to having bombed Bukom. They demanded that Japan's ambassador in Singapore meet them on board the ferry.

The standoff lasted eight days, and Tee was the only person communicating directly with the hijackers. Tan Wee Him the journalist was reporting on the crisis for *The Straits Times* (ST). He recalled: "Thirty to 40 ST newsmen were working on this alone. We didn't go home… one night was spent at Clifford Pier because *Laju* was berthed outside the outer road there. Another night, we camped outside the Marine Police Base at Merdeka Bridge in Kallang, hoping that the hijackers would bring the hostages there.

"And another night," he added, "we would be sleeping in my car outside the Japanese ambassador's home in Gallop Road, near the Botanic Gardens. Yet another night was spent at Paya Lebar Airport. The airport was the best place because it was fully air-conditioned and we could actually sleep on the sofa – whereas when we slept under the Merdeka Bridge, we had to contend with mosquitoes and the elements."

The crux of it was that the government agreed to guarantee the hijackers safe passage to Kuwait on a Japan Airlines plane – with 13 Singaporean officials accompanying them. The 13 men, among whom were Tee, S.R. Nathan, Director of Security and Intelligence at the Ministry of Defence – who later became Singapore's sixth President – and Director of Internal Security Department Yoong Siew Wah, took the places of the five hostages, whom the hijackers freed. The Japan Airlines flight would take off from Paya Lebar Airport.

Tee said the VIP lounge at Paya Lebar Airport was cleared as it might become a "killing field" in case the guerrillas resisted his order to hand over all their weapons before boarding the plane. He recalled: "We were determined that the hijackers should give up their arms upon arrival at the airport VIP lounge, which was planned as a killing field and so had been specifically cleared for the purpose. Through two Singaporean interpreters, Tee told the quartet what they had to do. "I told them that if they didn't believe that I was under that order, they could take their gun and cock it against my head."

Tee recalled further that his interpreters' legs had "almost softened" earlier when they heard what he had been ordered to do. "They said, 'How can they ask you to do this?' I said, 'Don't worry, this is part of the duty.' I had to do it. That was that."

When he asked the hijackers to surrender their arms, he recalled "a flash of suspicion, fear, anger. For a moment in the eyes of the hijackers, they thought that I was out to trick them." Tee grabbed the hand of one among the four guerrillas, causing one among his two interpreters to shout "Allah!". He then told the quartet that if they did not trust him, they could keep one bullet and one Browning automatic pistol and hold it against his temple. "I told them, 'You cannot meet my superior unless you surrender'." Nathan was Tee's boss at the time.

The Palestinian whose hand Tee was grasping suddenly became emotional and, Tee added, "uttered words in Arabic and said it was not necessary for them to keep that one bullet and hold it to my temple. They would give up their arms to me. "I accepted their arms with a sigh of relief."

Ever shrewd, Tee pushed his luck. "The agony was over," he said, "but also within, they still had knives. So I strip-searched them, took out all the knives." He then stressed: "Without arms, we were the 'guarantors', not their hostages." Kuwait's international airport was "a beautiful sight" when their plane arrived, he said, and they disembarked safely, surrounded by officials and military tanks. The hijackers then joined some of their comrades there on a plane to Baghdad.

In an age when international terrorism is on the rise, Tee reflected on the *Laju* hijacking: "It is one of the major cases involving real professional hijackers, well trained in arms, tactics and strategies, and it was one of the cases where we had successfully come to a very peaceful conclusion with them giving up."

"I haven't come across any case throughout the world where they have really given up, without injury and successfully."

And so, thanks to the wisdom and sensitivity with which Tee and his team brokered peace with the guerrillas, Singapore averted what would otherwise have been not only a national tragedy, but also a big blotch of blood in the annals of world history.

CHAPTER SEVEN

MEDICAL SERVICES

Doctor, Doctor!

Life is a race against time. That much was clear to midwife **Sumitera Mohd Letak** after she helped a patient with dangerously high blood pressure who had just given birth. "She was bleeding like hell," Sumitera recalled. "Her baby was gasping away and I had to suck mucus out of her baby's mouth... I had to, by hook or by crook, take them to hospital."

Alas, the mother, baby and midwife were on St John's Island, which is about 6.5 km south of mainland Singapore. What was worse, it was the middle of the night. Sumitera added: "It was low tide, so I had to wake up the whole row of people in the quarters there to give me a helping hand." The roused boatmen put the ailing mother and baby in a big sampan. Sumitera and the woman's husband and mother climbed in too and they rushed to Jardine Steps at Keppel Harbour. Upon their arrival, the ambulance from KK Hospital was nowhere in sight, so she left the woman in the care of her husband and the harbour police.

Sumitera flagged down a taxi and, with the baby in her arms and its grandmother in tow, rushed to KK Hospital. Sadly, the baby died there, but its mother was saved. "She was in hospital for three weeks because her blood pressure did not come down," Sumitera recalled, adding that, fortunately, "the hospital treated her for free".

Sumitera, who was born in 1942, joined Singapore's medical service as a midwife in the 1960s. She was among those in the Public Health Division who went out in "travelling dispensaries" twice a month. These dispensaries were ships kitted out with a pharmacy and medical equipment. With it, she visited Singapore's outlying islets, including Semakau, Sebarok, Sudong and Seraya. The ship would berth itself some distance away from the shore, so she had to "go right up to the island in a motorboat, and then on to the community centre".

Well into the 1960s, healthcare in Singapore was largely rudimentary, and not just on the nation's outlying islands. Renowned gynaecologist **Dr Tow Siang Hwa**, who headed KK Hospital in the 1960s, said that at the time, "women walked into KK Hospital to have their 12th or 15th baby. Maternal complications of the most horrendous kind were a common experience. Maternal deaths from bleeding, from obstetric complications, from obstructed labour and from malpractice outside." Speaking to the Oral History Centre in July 1997, Tow added: "All this is never seen again today."

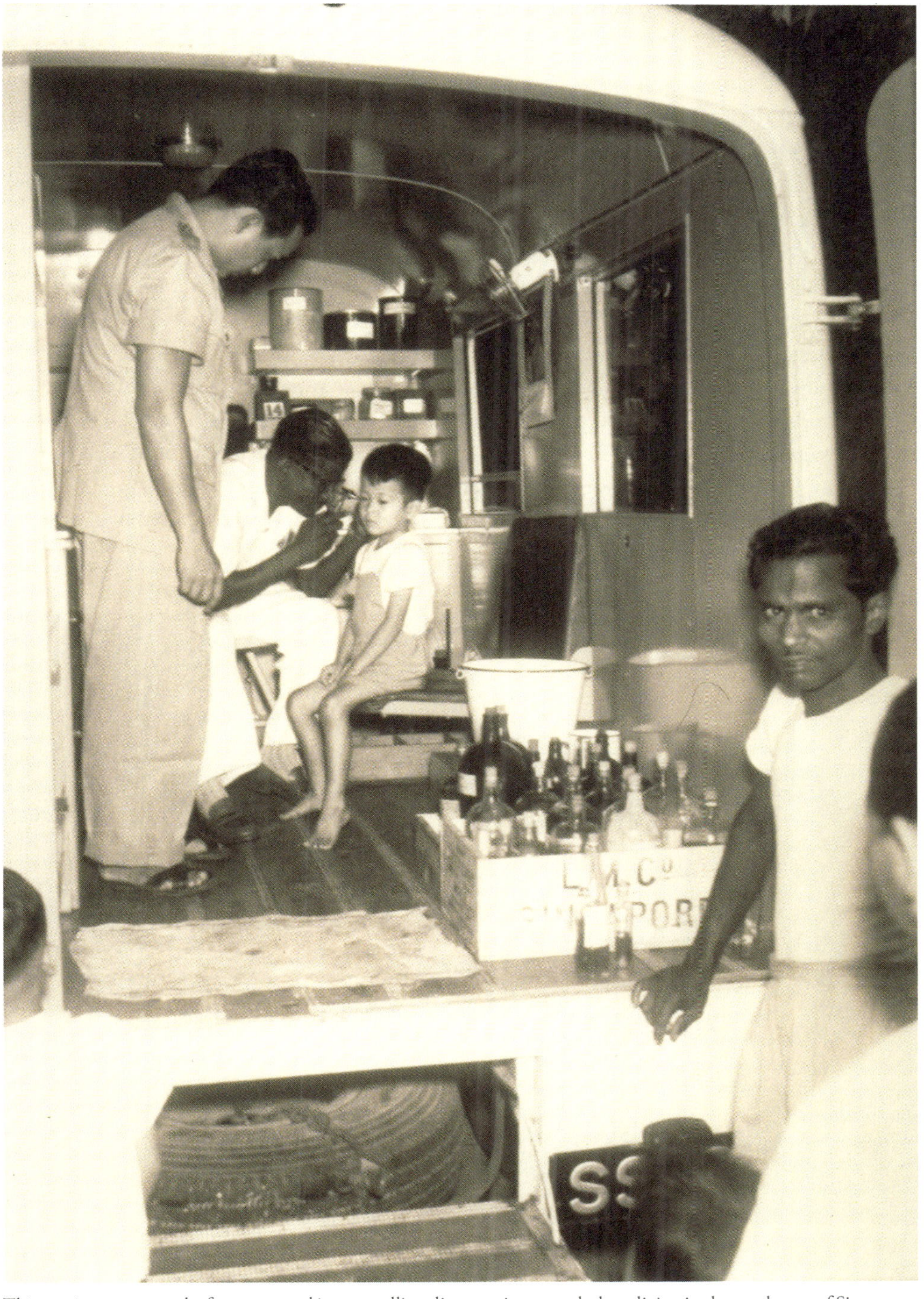

This van is one among the few converted into travelling dispensaries to reach those living in the rural areas of Singapore. When nurse Sumitera Mohd Letak was a midwife in the 1960s, she made her way on a ship that was converted into a travelling dispensary to serve Singapore's smaller islands.

Singapore's colonial administrators had provided free clinics for the needy, but these were few and far between. "The colonial government did give us free medical care at Outram Park outpatient clinic," Chinatown resident **Soh Siew Cheong** recalled. In the 1960s, Tow recalled fewer than 50 medical specialists practising in Singapore. Among those training to be one was **Dr Yong Nen Khiong**. Yong, who became a heart surgeon, recalled his college days at the University of Malaya in Singapore: "My medical cohort had 100 students. I took the bus to college every day... I was doing open heart surgery, practising on dogs."

When Singapore attained self-government in 1959, its leaders had to overcome the most fundamental problems to give the nation a fighting chance to thrive. Founding Prime Minister Lee Kuan Yew listed his Cabinet's priorities as the setting up of defence forces; the provision of affordable public housing for all; the restructuring of the education system; more stringent family planning to curb over-population; and the creation of jobs for the tens of thousands who were unemployed then. Against all these pressing necessities, Lee judged the development of medical services and improvement in healthcare to be, perhaps, fifth or sixth on his list of to-dos. To compound matters, the government was strapped for cash.

So Singaporeans made do, as they always had, with traditional folk medicine or, most often, store-cupboard remedies.

Many swore by traditional Chinese tonics brewed from roots, barks and seeds, such as those being dispensed here in 1983 by Eu Yan Sang (余仁生) medical hall on South Bridge Road. This medical hall was founded by Eu Tong Sen, after whom the street is named, who treated the ailments of the humblest folk. Eu Yan Sang has since grown into a globally renowned brand.

Eugene Wijeysingha, a former Principal of Raffles Institution, recalled that, as a boy, he cut his foot deeply while running around barefoot, playing cops and robbers with his mates. "Blood was dripping and we went to someone's house nearby," he said. "They got a piece of cloth, put coffee powder and sugar on it, and wrapped the cloth round and round my foot. They hadn't cleaned it first. But the wound healed; no tetanus or anything like that."

Housewife **Yau Chung Chii** remembered well the kitchen-table wisdom passed down to her generation. Speaking in Cantonese, Yau said, for example, that pregnant women would avoid lamb, lest it gave their babies epilepsy. Upon giving birth, women would be fed pig's trotters stewed with ginger and black vinegar, a dish thought to be effective in ridding their bodies of gas. She added that, however, some mothers told their doctors that they feared the vinegar would be so acidic that "it would melt their plastic stitches". She added: "The doctors said, 'No such nonsense. But if you believe it, don't eat it'."

The Malays had plant-based pastes and potions for women in confinement. Midwife Sumitera remembered two – *param* and *jamu*. "*Param* was a herbal concoction that you rubbed all over the mother's body. It opened the pores, out of which impurities oozed… if you went near those using *param*, they smelled so sweet, none of that fishy afterbirth smell which was caused by the poor flow of blood."

Jamu was consumed to expel any blood clots after giving birth. "It's a spicy herbal paste; you mixed it with water and drank it. It also helped the womb contract and return to normal size faster."

Besides pre- and post-pregnancy precautions, Yau said, the Chinese believed that foods could either be heaty or chill the body. The trick, then, was to eat everything in moderation. She said most Chinese in her time would shun green Cavendish bananas, grass jelly and cold soya bean milk because these were thought "too cooling" for the body. Foodie **Vincent Gabriel** recalled the Chinese avoiding cucumber for the same reason.

Sumitera never forgot how basic the islanders' lives were even after Singapore became independent. Women and girls among them who were menstruating would fold cloth, into which they crumpled newspaper, to stanch their bleeding. They would not heed Sumitera's advice to use the sanitary pads that she distributed to them regularly. "They said they would keep it and use it only when they travelled to mainland Singapore."

Singaporean Trailblazers

Amid this rough-and-ready approach to personal hygiene, some Singaporean doctors were already blazing trails in caring for patients.

Pathologist **Professor Kanagaratnam Shanmugaratnam**, for one, made sure that anyone in Singapore who had cancer could seek treatment for it without difficulty. Shanmugaratnam, whose son Tharman is a former Deputy Prime Minister of Singapore (and currently Senior Minister), set up a population-based cancer registry in 1968. At the time, he said, "there were hardly any private clinics in Singapore". His fellow doctors, however,

Pathologist Kanagaratnam Shanmugaratnam greeting President Benjamin Henry Sheares at a conference on cancer in Singapore in 1975. Professor Shanmugaratnam, whose son Tharman is a former Deputy Prime Minister (and currently a Senior Minister in the Cabinet), initiated a cancer registry in Singapore in 1968 so that no one with cancer here would have to go without treatment.

were "very supportive" in voluntarily notifying him and his team of anyone who developed cancer. He also scrutinised hospital discharge forms, as he put it, "so we did not miss a case".

Another trailblazer was **Dr Tay Chong Hai**. In 1969, he was among the first Singaporeans to discover a disease that was later named after him. Tay's Syndrome, as it became known, is a disease associated with intellectual impairment, short stature, decreased fertility, brittle hair, and dry, red and scaly skin, making an eight-year-old child look 80 years old.

In 1972, Tay made newspaper headlines when he saved many Singaporeans from over-the-counter pills and tonics that had life-threatening levels of arsenic. These included Sin Lak pills, which killed a woman who had taken them to cure her asthma. He fingered poverty as the root of such drug-related deaths. "It has to do with the cost of living," he mused. "So such over-the-counter drugs are the first line of treatment."

Fortunately, he noted, "Singapore is good with regulating" and so there were fewer deaths than there might have been from such self-medication.

Also, in 1972, Tay became the first doctor to identify Hand, Foot and Mouth Disease (HMFD) in Singapore. His wife, who is also a doctor, alerted him that she was treating many babies with mouth ulcers and rashes on their backs and legs. Jurong was the site of Singapore's first HFMD epidemic in the 1970s, but the disease – caused by the coxsackievirus – soon spread islandwide. In 1974, together with six other doctors, Tay published a paper on the outbreak of the disease in the September issue of the *Singapore Medical Journal*.

At the time of writing, there are still occasional HFMD outbreaks among kindergarten pupils in Singapore. Tay told the Oral History Centre in 2014 that this was because children would experience a dip in immunity when they reach the age of five or six, making their entire cohort susceptible to HFMD.

Tay rued how "panicky" many parents were about HFMD, likely because, he added, the media hyped up each outbreak. "I wanted to say, 'This is like the Ebola virus' or make some silly comment like that," he added, sarcastically.

All Hell Breaks Loose

The yearly panic about HFMD is nothing compared to the terror that seized many Singaporeans when the Severe Acute Respiratory Syndrome (SARS) began infecting their countrymen in March 2003.

The very contagious SARS, which originated in diseased civet cats in China, hit Singapore in March 2003, after air stewardess Esther Mok caught it from an elderly man in Hong Kong, with whom she had shared an elevator. Mok, also known as Patient Zero then, survived SARS but watched her parents, uncle and pastor die from the disease, which spreads through infected droplets.

Tan Tock Seng Hospital (TTSH) in Novena, where Mok had sought treatment, was designated SARS Central, that is, the nerve centre for treating SARS patients, although the disease spread to Singapore General Hospital (SGH), Changi General Hospital and National University Hospital, in that order. Ironically, according to hospital administrator **Liak Teng Lit**, he first got wind of SARS at a dinner thrown by TTSH on 14 March 2003: "My friend Francis Lee had heard a conversation at his table during this dinner that staff of TTSH were falling sick."

Healthcare officers moved as swiftly as the spread of the SARS virus after that and, Liak recalled, on 21 March 2003, the public finally heard about the epidemic. "Basically, all hell broke loose," he recalled.

Bus driver **Ang Chit Poh** said the private bus business plunged such that most drivers switched to other trades for good. Those who remained in the business had to disinfect their buses day after day in the hope that would restore the confidence of passengers who abandoned this transport option. Traditional Chinese medicine practitioner **Tan Siew Mong** recalled the prices of popular herbs and roots going through the roof as, once again, people resorted to folk remedies as their shields against SARS.

Liak, who was then Chief Executive Officer of Alexandra Hospital – the only Singapore hospital whose patients did not die of SARS – recalled how landlords were so fearful, they kicked out nurses who rented their rooms. He recalled: "They had no place to stay." So his staff and the hospital's volunteers cleared a rundown former nursing quarters within the hospital's grounds to house the stranded nurses.

Liak ordered new beds and furnishings for them from IKEA, the Swedish flat-pack furniture giant. Enter hitherto unsung SARS hero Philip Wee, who was then general manager of IKEA in Singapore. "He and his team personally brought and installed the beds in the hospital," Liak said, his voice breaking as he recalled this. "We tried to pay for the beds, but they said, 'Compliments from IKEA for helping the country fight SARS'."

Once the quarters were fully habitable, Liak invited Jennie Chua, then General Manager of Raffles Hotel – and the first woman to have held that post – to, as he put it, "declare Hotel Alexandra open".

Besides IKEA's Wee, Liak was also very impressed with Ho Ching, the Chief Executive Officer of Temasek Holdings and wife of current Prime Minister Lee Hsien Loong. He recalled Ho updating everyone concerned about the SARS situation in various countries "late into the night". "She was also very creative," he recalled. "People were worried about Malaysian motorists coming into Singapore, so she said why not set up a drinks stall with thermo-scanners, so that we could check the motorists for fever while they drank their *liang teh* (cooling tea)?" He added: "My admiration for her went up quite a bit."

For his part, Liak – who would usually not walk around the hospital grounds much – made it a point to stroll through its corridors two or three times a day "to show confidence"

$112 MILLION OFFER?: *Real Madrid wants David Beckham and Man United star is keen* SPORTS A10

The Straits Times

PACIFIC AREA NEWSPAPER OF THE YEAR

Thursday • March 27, 2003 • 108 Pages in five parts • 60 Cents

SARS OUTBREAK

All schools closed till April 6

Action to calm worried parents; June holidays will be shortened; first two patients die

By BERTHA HENSON
NEWS EDITOR

ALL schools in Singapore – from pre-school to junior college – are closed from today to April 6 in the latest move related to the pneumonia-like bug which left two men dead yesterday.

Two days after ordering 861 people to be quarantined at home, the government took another unprecedented step by shutting the schools, affecting the entire school population of 600,000.

The reason: To calm parents who have been worried that schools are a breeding ground for the virus causing severe acute respiratory syndrome, Sars.

"On purely medical grounds, there are currently no strong reasons for closing all schools," the Education Ministry and Health Ministry said yesterday.

"However, principals and ...

OUTDOOR SCREENING: Tents have been erected in front of Tan Tock Seng Hospital's accident and emergency department since Monday. They form a screening centre for suspected Severe Acute Respiratory Syndrome cases at the hospital, which has stopped admitting new patients.

The highly contagious Severe Acute Respiratory Syndrome (SARS) dominated newspaper headlines in Singapore between March and July 2003, including this frontpage story in *The Straits Times* on 27 March 2003. This report documented the unprecedented closure of all pre-schools, and primary, secondary and pre-university schools. During those four fretful months, SARS claimed the lives of 33 of the 238 people infected with the virus in Singapore. (*The Straits Times*, 27 March 2003, p.1)

to all. Things were, nevertheless, tense. He tried to ease it with some black humour. "I said, 'If we die, it's game over. If we live, COEs will be cheap and property prices will crash, so we will be able to buy bungalows on the cheap'."

Liak realised that Singaporeans were in the grip of such fear because they knew next to nothing about SARS, and their imagination was working overtime. So he partnered the South West Community Development Council in a campaign to demystify the coronavirus that causes SARS. They worked with a cartoonist to depict the virus as a silly creature with a crown, and then got members of parliament and ministers to "whack" an effigy of this cartoonish creature. He and his colleagues also exhorted everyone to wash their hands as often as they could. "If you can't do anything, you feel helpless," he mused. "So when you wash your hands, you feel better." This is how Liak and his team boosted community morale during the crisis. Liak, in fact, believed that that rigorous handwashing saved his colleagues' lives. "We actually had four patients with the SARS virus at Alexandra Hospital – they even coughed in the faces of my staff." Not one among them succumbed to the virus, though. Many called them "lucky", but Liak said it was more likely thanks to their vigilance and, yes, hand-washing throughout.

To chef **Sin Leong**, however, there was a limit to the number of precautions one had to take. Sin, who was one of Singapore's Four Heavenly Kings of Chinese cuisine, refused to let his staff wear masks while serving customers at his legendary *dim sum* restaurant, Red Star, in Chin Swee Road. He was adamant about that, despite some of his customers suggesting that his wait staff do so. "I said we'd better not do that," he recalled in Cantonese. "I told my customers that once they entered Red Star restaurant, just think there was no SARS."

He stressed: "Wearing a mask to serve customers would show as though the waiter was a leper. That would scare customers off." Sin took pains to say, however, that he made his staff come half an hour before their shift started every day to have their temperatures checked and "should a worker have a higher temperature than the others, I would ask him to go home and rest."

Wasn't Sin concerned that his customers might bring SARS into his restaurant, though? Sin reasoned: "It was unlikely that when a person was having a fever, he would still come to Red Star Restaurant to eat." His conviction paid off – Red Star made more than $200,000 a month during the SARS period from March till June 2003. "We made more than before SARS," said Sin.

So he had no empathy for restaurateurs who demanded that their landlords lower their rents after their eateries lost up to 30 percent of business when the epidemic was at its peak. Sin huffed: "That was unreasonable. It was a natural disaster; if you had no business, what about me? I had no business too? If you didn't know how to handle it, you had to think of ways to do so."

While everyone in Singapore's healthcare system was reminded repeatedly to don protective masks and gowns, and keep washing their hands, some chafed against the sheer, if necessary, inconvenience of it all. Nurse **Loo Yew Kim**, who began her career at Kwong

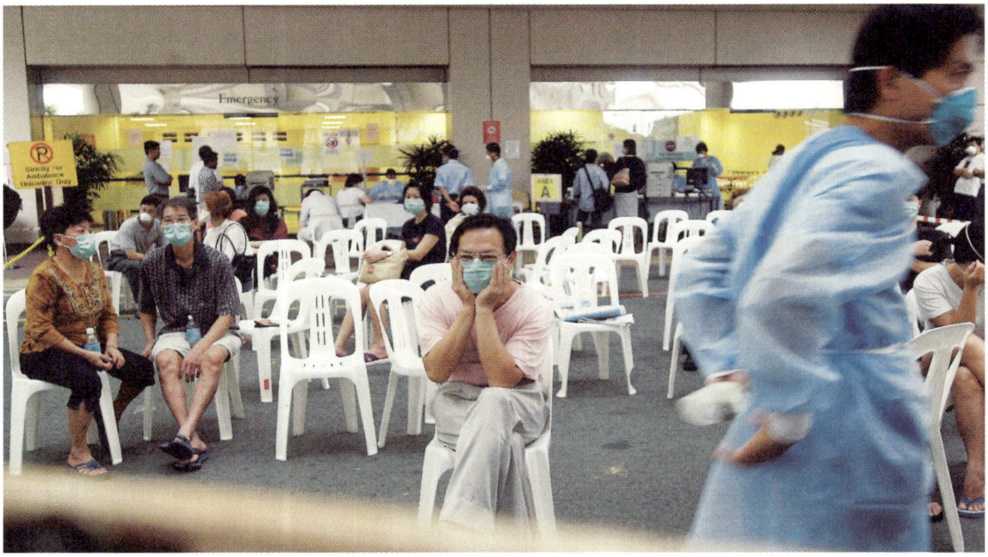

Anxious Singaporeans waiting to be screened for Severe Acute Respiratory Syndrome (SARS) at the Accident & Emergency Department of Tan Tock Seng Hospital in 2003.

Wai Shiu Hospital in 1969 and worked there until she retired more than 40 years later, was at first peeved at the nagging of younger doctors for her and her fellow nurses to wash their hands after every step they took in caring for patients. "I really resented that," she recalled in Mandarin in 2014. "We were by then in our 50s and 60s, so it was not as if we didn't know that we should wash our hands."

Loo and other nurses also fumed at having to don protective gear every minute of every day during the SARS epidemic. "Sweat would be dripping down my face from the mask," she huffed. It was all so inconvenient, she added, that at some points, she would just fling her mask aside as it kept getting in the way of saving lives. "I will never forget the SARS period," she stressed.

That was saying a lot, considering that her daily duties up until then often involved cleaning her elderly patients every time they soiled themselves. They would clamour for her attention, shouting "*Aiya*! Save me!" to her, and were cantankerous to boot. "You need lots of love and patience to do this job," she mused, adding that she would calm them down by enticing them with, "If you want bread, listen to me!" She added: "I was a first-class *amah*." (*Amah* is Hokkien for maid).

In June 2003, SARS was finally contained in Singapore, but not before claiming the lives of 33 among the total of 238 reported SARS patients.

Liak explained that SARS illustrated how much the world had changed due to globalisation. "Germs will always mutate and, often, viruses exchange material with human beings and animals... but in the past, whenever viruses mutated and killed an entire village, it could not spread after that because it had nowhere to go.

"But because transport became globalised, SARS could go from a Guangzhou village [in China] to towns and then cities. That is how dangerous the world has become." Worse, he added, people were now eating more meat, leading to increasingly intensive animal farming, which was cruel, unhealthy and stoked the spread of viruses which, once mutated, would be very hard to curb.

Professor Tan Ser Kiat, who was SGH's chief during SARS, mused: "If a terrorist infected himself with smallpox, the incubation period of the virus would be long enough for him to mingle with everyone else. Smallpox would then spread like wildfire. This is what we are afraid of." That was because, unlike droplet-borne SARS, smallpox is air-borne, meaning "I wouldn't know who has got it until it's too late," he said.

The Goats That Saved Lives

More than most countries, perhaps, Singapore has had an excellent track record of mounting successful health campaigns. Among its biggest wins by far has been the eradication of diseases such as polio, diphtheria and rheumatic heart disease.

Diphtheria, in particular, was as endemic in Singapore as tuberculosis in the early half of the 20th century. The person to thank for its eradication is **Professor Ernest Steven Monteiro**. During the Japanese Occupation, Monteiro was in charge of Middleton Hospital, which was TTSH's infectious diseases wing. The Japanese had taken two of his brothers away, and he never saw them again. He thinks the Japanese spared his life because "they were

Trailblazing doctor Professor Ernest Steven Monteiro had the brainwave to develop an anti-diphtheria serum in goats. With this serum, he and his team eradicated diphtheria in Singapore successfully through a concerted vaccination drive in the 1950s.

Dr Edmund Hugh Monteiro, who is the son of Professor Ernest S. Monteiro, was just as driven as his illustrious father in that he was among the earliest doctors in Singapore to treat HIV/AIDS patients, at a time when they were shunned by most.

By 1977, Dr Edmund Hugh Monteiro recalled that diphtheria and polio were things of the past for Singaporeans.

very short of doctors... and also very health-conscious, especially about infectious diseases such as diphtheria."

At the time, Monteiro was among the very few doctors in Singapore specialising in the study of infectious diseases. He hit upon a solution to cure diphtheria after reading a book in which a doctor had tried to produce an anti-diphtheria serum by injecting the diphtheria organism into a goat named Mephistopheles. In the play *Faust* by German writer Johann Wolfgang von Goethe, Mephistopheles was an agent of Satan.

Monteiro tried that same experiment. After cultivating diphtheria, he extracted its toxins and injected that into the necks of goats. Then, once the goats were producing serum to combat the toxins in them, Monteiro extracted the serum from the goats and injected that into a child with severe diphtheria. The child recovered.

In 1958, Monteiro introduced the oral polio vaccine in Singapore, developed by American medical researcher Albert Sabin. Some 250,000 children were immunised against the disease, which was endemic then. This was despite much opposition from his compatriots in medicine, as the vaccine had not been tested on a large population in the United States. The vaccine, however, proved effective in blocking the poliovirus and Singapore became polio-free.

His son, **Dr Edmund Hugh Monteiro**, who once headed TTSH's Communicable Disease Centre, said that despite his father's diphtheria breakthrough during World War II, the disease was "a growing problem" in Singapore from the mid-1950s. This was, he added, in spite of doctors' pleas to parents to get their children immunised against diphtheria. In the 1960s, he recalled, "only 55 per cent of children had that immunisation". To eradicate the scourge, the younger Monteiro knew the immunisation rate had to be at least 90 percent.

So, in 1962, the government made immunisation against diphtheria compulsory, on pain of paying a $2,000 fine, a sum too high for most families in

One of the many inoculation centres for cholera in 1963. Lawyer Nadesan Ganesan, who was vaccinated against cholera during the Japanese Occupation, remembers that the jab was very painful as the needle was blunt, causing his arm to swell up.

those days. "As far as I can remember," said the younger Monteiro, "no parent has ever been brought to court and fined." Better yet, he noted, once a child turned up at a doctor's for immunisation, he or she would most likely accept being immunised against tetanus, polio and so on. In this way, he said, Singapore soon eradicated diphtheria. He recalled further: "In those days, when they published details about the immunisation programme in *The Straits Times*, immunisation teams would be present for about a week in housing estates.

"And these nurses would actually climb the stairs or go up in lifts and ask parents there, 'Bring your children down for immunisation.' That was the sort of service that was provided – on your doorstep and for free. That set the stage for these childhood diseases to be eradicated." By 1977, he recalled, diphtheria and polio were things of the past for Singaporeans.

Dr Koh Eng Kheng, a doctor in private practice, said the government's anti-diphtheria drive was a fine example of how concerted public health campaigns had to be. Quoting former American president Theodore Roosevelt, he said the success of such campaigns hinged on the government penalising anyone who tried to dodge immunisation. "You cannot soft-pedal these things," Koh said.

Lawyer **Nadesan Ganesan**, a former chairman of the Football Association of Singapore, remembered government nurses vaccinating him against cholera during the Japanese Occupation, another illness that plagued Singapore well into the post-war period and into the 1970s. His experience underscored how relatively scant medical facilities and equipment were in post-World War II Singapore. "There were only two or three nurses vaccinating us, and their needles were blunt to begin with. You could hear the sound 'tok' whenever they poked your arm… because the needle was so blunt, our arms swelled and we were all sick for three days. But we recovered lah and it was good because they helped us not get cholera."

Then, in 1984, measles struck Singapore in a big way. Once again, the government ordered the compulsory immunisation against measles and, once again, measles went the way of diphtheria and polio.

Unbeknownst to Singapore's medical services, it was about to have another terrifying battle on the cards, against which immunisation was powerless – Acquired Immune Deficiency Syndrome (AIDS).

Could Mosquitoes Give Me AIDS?

Edmund Hugh Monteiro remembers Singapore's very first AIDS patient. It was a man admitted to then Toa Payoh Hospital in 1986 for fever and diarrhoea, and shingles to boot. But the hospital transferred him to Monteiro's Communicable Disease Centre when they found that he had a salmonella infection, which the centre handled. Monteiro thought through how the man's immune system could have broken down so badly. He tested the man for AIDS. "And it was positive."

It was not long before the centre's senior staff wanted to transfer out because they feared having to care for AIDS patients. "AIDS was something which they were not used to and it was too terrifying. Some among them were not personally panicking, but their family members were saying, 'You better get out.' So there was, unfortunately, a lot of ignorance as to how the disease was spread." That was triggered by the government designating his centre in 1985 as the lone place in Singapore to treat AIDS patients.

The flurry of fearful queries continued from his staff. "If the mosquito bites an AIDS patient and then bites me, will I get HIV?" was the biggest worry. Monteiro said that what he found "most assuring" about AIDS was that, apart from sexual intercourse with the AIDS patient, "you'd have to stick yourself with a needle" to be infected. "In other words," he said, "you didn't have to be gloved, gowned and masked whenever you went to see the patient." In fact, he noted, it was far easier to be infected with Hepatitis B and C then it was to get AIDS.

The stigma against its patients, however, persisted. Monteiro especially rued the unfeeling attitude of some doctors towards AIDS sufferers. "We talk to people very early in their medical careers, tell them that if they are going to become doctors, sometime in their career, they are going to have to treat a person with AIDS. It's unlikely that you will go through a medical career for 20, 30 years without having to manage a person with AIDS."

There was, he recalled, "one young doctor who wanted to specialise in infectious diseases 'as long as I don't have to manage AIDS patients'. So we closed the door on that person and said, 'You'd better find another discipline if you can'."

First, Do No Harm

The case of that young doctor with an aversion to AIDS patients begs the question: who is a good doctor?

Edmund Hugh Monteiro recalled his father giving him this advice: "You want to do medicine? Okay, two things. One, you never stop learning. Two, you may have to sacrifice your lunch... I think what he meant was that patients can sometimes be overpowering in their demands."

He then cautioned: "You need to put them off at certain stages, and not make it out that medicine is a profession where everyone is to be heroic and self-sacrificing. You need to draw a line, I mean, you will just be burnt out with patients' problems... if I draw a line somewhere, I can actually function better than if I just didn't know what I was supposed to do."

Kanagaratnam Shanmugaratnam the pathologist thought that a doctor's empathy for his patients' predicaments was a hallmark of great medicine. "We inspire them to be interested in the nature of disease because that's how they can be good surgeons or physicians. To understand suffering, to speak freely, to ask us things which require clarification."

He added: "And it's a huge pleasure to be able to solve problems for the medical students. Medicine is not a nine-to-five job; you cannot be a specialist with that kind of mentality. So one has to work long hours, studying in the evenings, keeping up with medicine."

Tan Ser Kiat, the former Chief Executive of SGH, noted that as Singapore's medical services had grown by leaps and bounds within the past 50 years or so, the notion that doctors should be good, business-minded corporate managers too has gained traction.

Tan, who was born in the 1950s, said: "I was brought up in the era where we don't look upon medicine as a business, as a commercial enterprise. We have to tell our consultants that when they prescribe a particular treatment for a patient, watch the prices! You've got to select what works for the patient but at the same time is cheaper than the other options."

The younger Monteiro mused: "The government adopted a very far-sighted and I think correct policy when they realised that they must make every attempt to provide the best healthcare for the population. And in specific terms, to beef up and make sure that there are no misses in terms of childhood immunisation."

As Koh Eng Kheng the doctor noted: "Even up till today, if you don't show all the papers of the children that they have been properly immunised, the child will not get a place in school. So this sort of thing has teeth to it."

First Test-Tube Baby

For many years, proof of immunisation was not a worry for the parents of **Samuel Lee Jian Wei**. That was because try as they might, the Lees could not conceive a child naturally. Fortunately, they were in an age when science had made much progress. On 25 July 1978, Louise Joy Brown, the first baby created from sperm fertilising a human egg in a test tube, was born in Manchester, England.

This unprepossessing man is Samuel Lee Jian Wei, Asia's first test-tube baby. He was born on 19 May 1983, after a clinical trial by Professor S.S. Ratnam and Ng Soon Chye. It was Ratnam who named him Samuel. He is seen here against an enlarged version of *The Straits Times* article of 21 May 1983, chronicling his breakthrough birth.

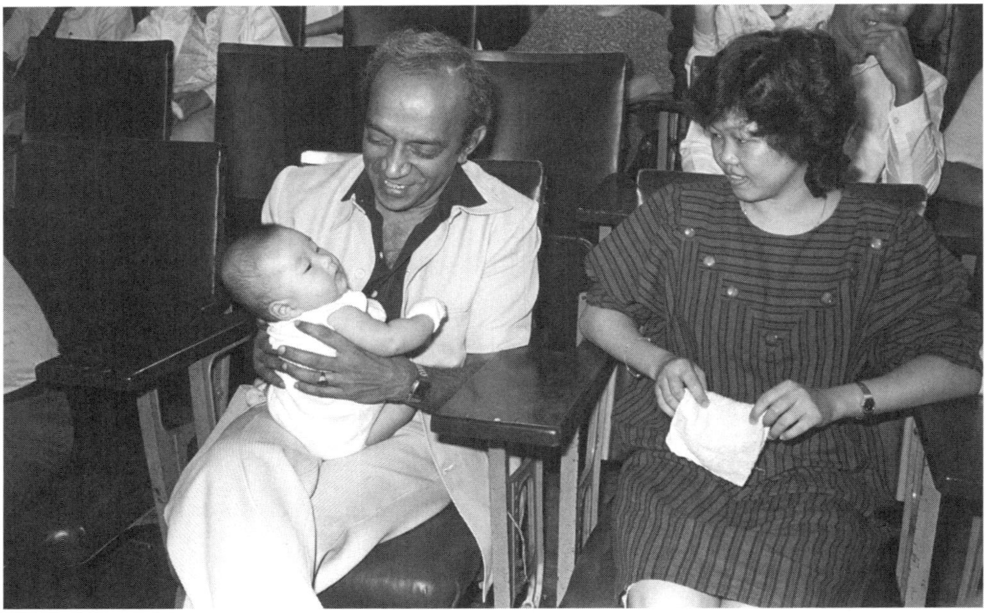

Professor S.S. Ratnam (left) bouncing Samuel Lee Jian Wei, his first test-tube baby, on his lap while the baby's mother Tan Siew Ee looks on. Ratnam was a fertility expert who introduced in-vitro fertilisation (IVF) to Singapore, giving much hope to spouses for whom conception was difficult.

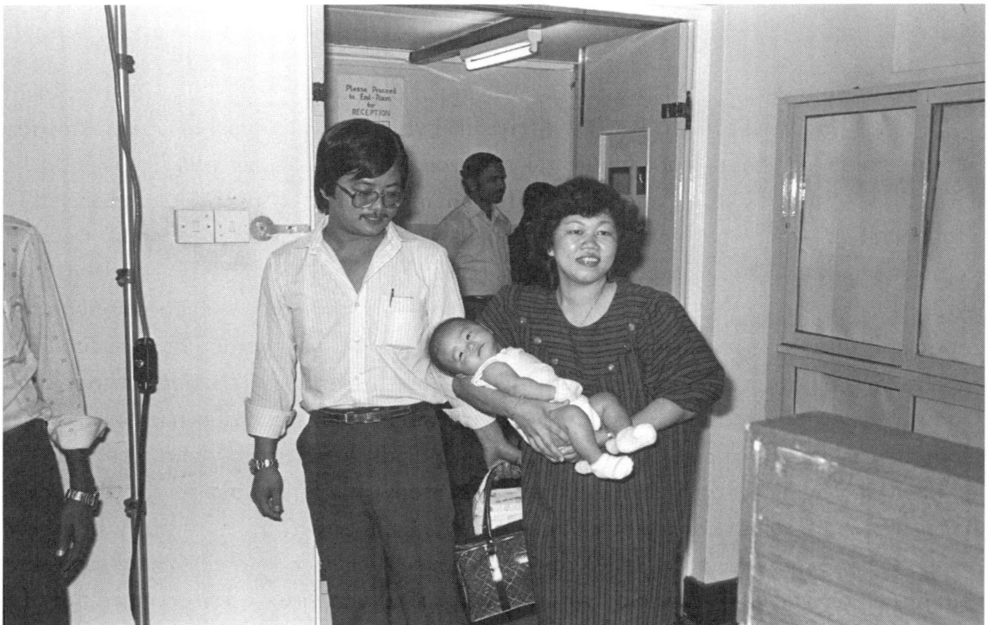

Bouncy Samuel Lee Jian Wei, Asia's first test-tube baby, leaves hospital for home on 17 August 1983 with his father, a security supervisor, and his mother, a secretary.

Back in Singapore, the brilliance of surgeon S.S. Ratnam meant that this artificial method of conception, known as in-vitro fertilisation (IVF), was available to the Lees from the early 1980s.

The brilliance of surgeon S.S. Ratnam meant that this artificial method of conception, known as in-vitro fertilisation (IVF), was available from the early 1980s.

Samuel was born on 19 May 1983 at KK Hospital. He was a triumph for medicine in Singapore and so captured everyone's imagination the moment he came into the world. Samuel recalled: "From the age of three or four, I kept hearing the words 'IVF' and 'test-tube baby'." When he was three years old, a local television programme feted him, and gave him a birthday card with a big "3" on it and a teddy bear to take home. He simply could not shake off everyone's curiosity about how he came to exist. "When I was in kindergarten, even my teacher said, 'Oh, test-tube baby.' Maybe she had watched the TV show... But I know that I was born naturally – just that my Mum conceived me in an unnatural way."

At the age of six, he finally met Ratnam the surgeon who had made his birth a reality. "He asked me some questions, like 'How have you been doing?' He was quite friendly and treated me very nicely... When I was young, I was quite shy, but he made me laugh so I felt very comfortable with him."

Given a choice, though, Samuel would rather not have been Singapore's first test-tube baby. "It's so that I would not get so much unwanted attention," he rued. As recently as 2015, he was in the spotlight again, as his profile was included in Singapore's official SG50 book, *Living the Singapore Story*.

Access to Ratnam's September 1997 interview with the Oral History Centre is restricted, so his views on Samuel and other subjects cannot be reflected here for now. But fellow doctor Tow Siang Hwa, who handpicked Ratnam to succeed him at KK Hospital from 1969, can shed light on how skilful Ratnam was. Speaking in July 1997, Tow recalled: "S.S. Ratnam was my handpicked trainee... He was intelligent and had the makings of a professor." In 1969, when Tow left KK Hospital to start his own practice, he told Ratnam: "Ratnam, I am going to leave, but you will succeed me."

"That was the vision I had, that he would succeed me," Tow mused. "By then, the ship was high and sailing; the groundwork had been done and now it was for him to keep it going. And he sailed the ship well because in no time, he was reaching the highest levels."

Tow, who helmed KK Hospital in the 1960s, had raised the reputation of the nation's medical capabilities earlier. In 1960, his expertise in molar pregnancy – in which an embryo is abnormal, resembling a cluster of grapes, and cannot develop fully – stunned an expert at Leeds University, who encouraged him to submit the discovery for a prestigious lecture in Britain. Before long, inspectors from Britain's Royal College of Obstetrics & Gynaecology recognised KK Hospital as being of the highest medical standards, from the way it ran its operations to how it cared for patients. Tow said: "Now this was a major, major

With much elan, Dr Andrew Chew Guan Khuan helped drive the growth of medical expertise in Singapore, first as a senior government medical officer and then as Chairman of the Public Service Commission from 1998 till 2008.

advance. It meant that obstetrics & gynaecology were on a par with medicine and surgery. So we were able to train our specialists locally.

"So, from that day, instead of having five specialists for the whole population of Singapore, today, in 1997, we have 200 specialists."

A Passport to the World

The urgent need to train, and retain, doctors for Singapore was threatened by a most unexpected event – the Vietnam War. The war, which was fought in Indochina between November 1955 and April 1975, led most in Southeast Asia to fear that the strife would spread to the other countries in the region and topple their governments – just like a line of domino tiles. So many in the region considered migrating to the West to escape such a fate. **Dr Andrew Chew Guan Khuan**, a veteran hospital administrator, recalled that in the 1970s, Singapore had done such a good job of training doctors that "during the Vietnam War, a chartered plane would take 100 or so doctors from the region to register to practise in Australia".

Ironically, Chew noted, anyone who had a Bachelor of Medicine and Bachelor of Surgery (MBBS) degree from Singapore "had acquired a passport to many parts of the world"; that was how well-respected medical training in Singapore had become in only 20 years or so. "A Singapore doctor could easily register to work in England, Australia and New Zealand," he recalled, adding that they might have had to "jump a couple of hurdles" to practise in Canada or the United States.

Singapore's solution to that brain drain was to require that medical students – with or without scholarships – be bonded to serve Singapore for between five and seven years after they had completed their studies. "Whether you are a paying or non-paying student, you had to serve your country," Chew said.

In the nation's drive to train as many bright Singaporeans as feasible in medicine, Chew also recalled how firmly local doctors and hospital administrators took matters into their own hands. Initially, he noted, the government had made the training of specialists a big part of its Healthcare Manpower Development Plan in the 1980s. It set aside $3 million yearly for doctors to take local and overseas courses, and also fly in overseas experts to train everyone in the medical services ecosystem, from physicians to paramedics. Chew said: "The Ministry of Finance gave us the funds because in the early days, one of the Ministry of Trade and Industry's plans was to sell Singapore's medical services."

The government's drive to develop top-quality medical services from the 1980s drew more and more school-leavers to try for places in medical school. "That changed the profession in Singapore from professors handpicking you and setting directions for you, to postgraduate medical students voluntarily sitting professional tests."

"As the postgraduate groups became bigger," he added, "there was always a need to avoid that blue-eyed boy approach. Merit was something we began to take into account so that if you were good, you would not lose out."

Chew, a distinguished public servant who joined the Medical Service in 1956, said that his profession embraced meritocracy such that it began giving out its own scholarships to train in the medical field. In Singapore, the overseeing of scholarships to develop local talent is usually the purview of the Public Service Commission (PSC). But as Chew recalled: "We administered our own scholarships from the World Health Organisation. We never went through the PSC." Happily, he added, "the PSC was quite happy that we had already taken on the task... I think it's a question of trust. If the trust wasn't there, they could have said, 'We will take back the administration of these scholarships from you'." Chew himself was chairman of the PSC from 1998 till 2008.

With that approach, Chew said a good healthcare system eventually evolved in Singapore.

The nation's medical services have continued onwards and upwards since. Well-known heart surgeon **Dr Charles Toh Chai Soon** recalled the dire number of people in Singapore with rheumatic heart disease when he returned from Britain in 1961. The disease, he said, "thrives among those with poor socio-economic status". At the time, 70 among every 100,000 babies in Singapore were born with this congenital heart disease. Fast forward to the 1990s and, Toh mused, "you hardly ever see rheumatic heart disease because we have moved the country so far ahead that it is not so present now."

CHAPTER EIGHT

THE ECONOMIC MIRACLE

The Wonder Years

At 4 pm on Saturday, 7 August 1965, **Subramaniam s/o Munian** was at home with his mother when there was a knock on their door. Subramaniam went to see who it was – and got a shock. At the gate were his two supervisors and a few policemen.

"I thought I had made some mistakes," the government proofreader recalled. "Then my supervisors said that they were taking me to an important job, and not to worry, nothing would happen to me." The policemen escorted Subramaniam and his colleagues to their workplace, the Government Printing Office (GPO) – and locked them in for one-and-a-half days. That was because he was about to check the English and Tamil versions of a special gazette and notices proclaiming that Singapore would leave Malaysia, with which it had merged

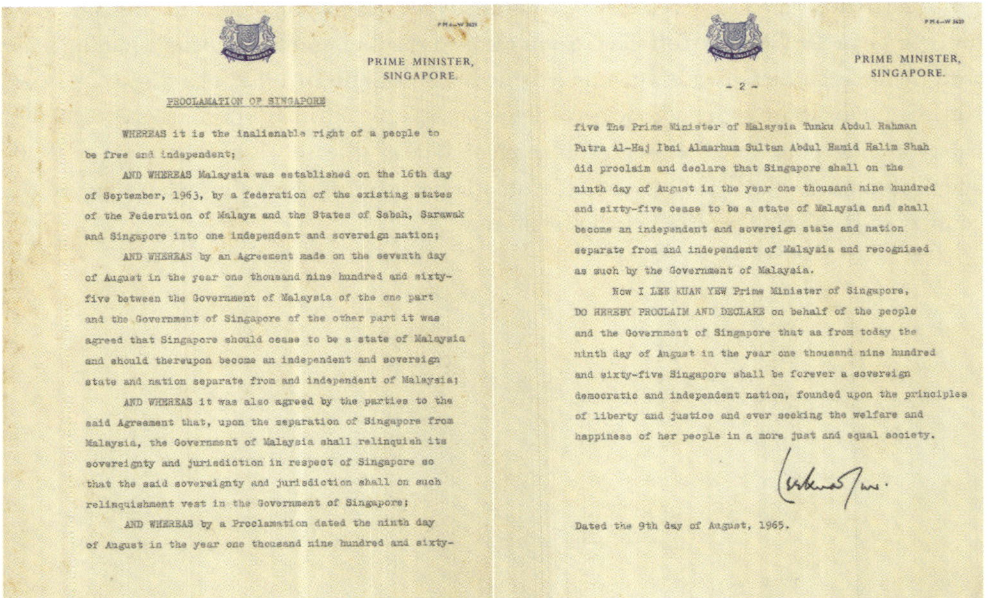

PRIME MINISTER,
SINGAPORE.

PROCLAMATION OF SINGAPORE

WHEREAS it is the inalienable right of a people to be free and independent;

AND WHEREAS Malaysia was established on the 16th day of September, 1963, by a federation of the existing states of the Federation of Malaya and the States of Sabah, Sarawak and Singapore into one independent and sovereign nation;

AND WHEREAS by an Agreement made on the seventh day of August in the year one thousand nine hundred and sixty-five between the Government of Malaysia of the one part and the Government of Singapore of the other part it was agreed that Singapore should cease to be a state of Malaysia and should thereupon become an independent and sovereign state and nation separate from and independent of Malaysia;

AND WHEREAS it was also agreed by the parties to the said Agreement that, upon the separation of Singapore from Malaysia, the Government of Malaysia shall relinquish its sovereignty and jurisdiction in respect of Singapore so that the said sovereignty and jurisdiction shall on such relinquishment vest in the Government of Singapore;

AND WHEREAS by a Proclamation dated the ninth day of August in the year one thousand nine hundred and sixty-

PRIME MINISTER,
SINGAPORE.

\- 2 -

five The Prime Minister of Malaysia Tunku Abdul Rahman Putra Al-Haj Ibni Almarhum Sultan Abdul Hamid Halim Shah did proclaim and declare that Singapore shall on the ninth day of August in the year one thousand nine hundred and sixty-five cease to be a state of Malaysia and shall become an independent and sovereign state and nation separate from and independent of Malaysia and recognised as such by the Government of Malaysia.

Now I LEE KUAN YEW Prime Minister of Singapore, DO HEREBY PROCLAIM AND DECLARE on behalf of the people and the Government of Singapore that as from today the ninth day of August in the year one thousand nine hundred and sixty-five Singapore shall be forever a sovereign democratic and independent nation, founded upon the principles of liberty and justice and ever seeking the welfare and happiness of her people in a more just and equal society.

Dated the 9th day of August, 1965.

Founding Prime Minister Lee Kuan Yew signed the Proclamation of Singapore, marking the fulfilment of he and his comrades' long struggle for independence for their homeland. The proclamation was the formal declaration that Singapore had ceased "to be a state of Malaysia and shall become an independent and sovereign state and nation separate from and independent of Malaysia".

less than 24 months earlier. As the hours ticked by, top officials such as Singapore's Civil Service chief Stanley Stewart and Fong Sip Chee, the Parliamentary Secretary for the Ministry of Culture, dropped in frequently to monitor his progress.

It was an eye-opening experience for Subramaniam: not only was he just 22 years old, he was also rubbing shoulders with VIPs. "Even to go to the toilet," he recalled in his Oral History Centre interview of April 2006, "the police would follow us because they didn't want us to leak the matter."

Singapore's founding Prime Minister Lee Kuan Yew fights back his tears, an unforgettable instance captured for posterity during his televised press conference on 9 August 1965 on Singapore's independence from Malaysia.

Then, at 10 am on Monday, 9 August 1965, national newscaster Steven Lee announced the Separation, as Singapore's break from Malaysia was called, over Radio Singapore. By noon, Singapore's founding Prime Minister Lee Kuan Yew was fielding questions from the press on the split. Former civil servant **Tan Gee Paw**, who was then studying civil engineering at the University of Malaya in Kuala Lumpur, watched a broadcast of Prime Minister Lee's conference on a television with his fellow hostelites. At one point, Lee's eyes brimmed with tears. "For me it is a moment of anguish," Lee said, "because all my life... you see, the whole of my adult life... I have believed in merger and the unity of these two territories. You know, it's a people, connected by geography, economics and ties of kinship... Would you mind if we stop for a while?" Briefly, in what would be a very rare scene in public, Lee lost his composure.

"We saw how he broke down," Tan said. "And I thought, 'I'm now in a foreign country. Home is 250 miles south, I have got to cross the Causeway and that would be home'."

Before Separation, he added, few people in Singapore had thought of their existence in those terms. "You knew that if the train from Singapore crossed the Causeway, it was still *attap* huts and rubber trees all the way to Kuala Lumpur. When you reached KL and went to Bangsar, it was just like Chinatown in Singapore, there was no difference." In 1957, Prime Minister Lee had said that the idea of Singapore going it alone was a "political, economic and geographical absurdity". After all, how long could a land without natural resources, including water, thrive?

Despite such a looming concern, teacher and writer **Chan Kwee Sung** thought Separation, on the whole, was cause for celebration, as did the residents of Chinatown, who set off fireworks at the news. "They were elated by the fact that, at last, they were free of racial prejudice of any kind," he recalled. "When Singapore was part of Malaysia, there were racial riots, aspersions cast. Separation was a measure of relief."

Amid the jubilation, there was much work to be done. Teacher-turned-lawyer **Kasinather Saunthararajah**, better known as K.S. Rajah, said that the act of Separation had been so secret that even the Attorney-General's Chambers – government lawyers – had not been informed prior to the proclamation of Independence. Rajah's boss Ahmad Ibrahim, Singapore's first local attorney-general, had called them into a room first thing in the morning on 9 August 1965 and told them what had happened. "That took us completely by surprise and, of course, Ahmad was as cool as a cucumber. As far as he was concerned, it was just another legal event. And he proceeded to tell us what the legal consequences were and how we should approach the problems." Chief among these, he added, was the pain of having to unpick about two years' worth of legislation, which the government lawyers on both sides of the Causeway had crafted for both to merge as Malaysia on 16 September 1963.

Singapore businessman **Abdul Kader Tyebally**, whose family firm Bombay Trading Company sold rattan, sago, betel nuts and tamarind, had seen his supply of good rattan from Indonesia cut off when the republic waged *Konfrontasi* (Confrontation) – involving armed incursions, bomb attacks and other subversive acts – against Singapore and Malaya to protest their merger in 1963, which Indonesia saw as being against its interest at that time. Now, with Singapore severed from the Malaysian hinterland, Tyebally had mixed feelings. "I thought Singapore would suffer because it was so dependent on Malaysia, even for water and all that…, so I thought business would suffer." He did not, however, make plans to leave the country. "There are millions of people in Singapore," he said. "If they could carry on, I could carry on."

The Best Day in Singapore's Life

The Dutch economist **Albert Winsemius,** however, was upbeat about Separation. When news of the Separation broke, he thought that 9 August 1965 "was probably the best day in the life of Singapore". He told his wife, "You better pack; I expect that in a few days there will be a call for me to go to Singapore because they need a new economic programme."

Up till then, Winsemius had been agonising over how to make the Singapore economy viable while it was part of Malaysia which, for various reasons, he was increasingly distrustful of. Speaking to the Oral History Unit (now Oral History Centre) in 1982, Winsemius said he had foreseen that the 1963 merger with Malaysia would be "a flop". So there he was, after the Merger, "sitting on his hands" in The Hague while politicking stalled progress on his detailed 1960 economic development plan for Singapore. "It was disappointing for the people of Singapore who were working hard without any major results and really badly needing these," he said. "But it was indeed also frustrating for me because I believed firmly in Singapore and we simply did not have enough elbow room to show what we could do. Only after Separation did that happen."

Dutch development economist Albert Winsemius was one of independent Singapore's greatest champions. He called 9 August 1965 "probably the best day in the life of Singapore" and helped its leaders shape Singapore's economy into a miracle beyond anyone's expectations.

Winsemius had helped the Netherlands recover from World War II and also guided Greece, Portugal and the United States to do much the same. He was a clear thinker with a knack for coming up with smart, successful strategies for ailing economies. Independent Singapore's founding fathers, including Prime Minister Lee Kuan Yew and his deputy Goh Keng Swee, trusted Winsemius' prescriptions such that the Dutchman was Singapore's economic advisor from 1959 till 1986.

About a week after Separation, Winsemius and I.F. Tang, an American-born whiz who was later chairman of the Economic Development Board (EDB) and the Jurong Town Corporation, locked themselves in a room and drew up a plan to develop Singapore from 1965 till 1975. Singapore's unemployment rate was then between 10 and 30 percent, compared with 1.9 percent today. Worse, half of those who were jobless were younger than 30 years. They were growing restive and, coupled with their anxieties about the aftermath of Separation, were a ticking time bomb. Winsemius thought the best way to provide as many

> Albert Winsemius said he thought the average Singaporean had "a high aptitude" for manufacturing from just observing them. He marvelled at how small family businesses then did "rather complicated things with little means and also little training".

Dr Goh Keng Swee, the architect of Singapore's economic miracle, is seen here showing his Malaysian ministerial counterpart Dr Lim Swee Aun around the fledgling Jurong Industrial Estate in 1964.

Singaporeans with jobs as soon as possible was to pursue low-wage manufacturing, such as making textiles and garments.

Winsemius said he thought the average Singaporean had "a high aptitude" for manufacturing from just observing them. "I saw them working in the streets, repairing things, making two bicycles from three old ones… repairing axles from motorcars, a tricky thing, with very limited machinery in Kallang Basin." He marvelled at how small family businesses then did "rather complicated things with little means and also little training". So he fully supported Deputy Prime Minister Goh Keng Swee's idea to pursue manufacturing. This led the government to set up Singapore's first industrial estate in swampy Jurong in 1967. Unlike Winsemius, not everyone believed that factories were the nation's ticket to success. So for years, Jurong was called "Goh's Folly". Goh, however, had the last laugh; in 2018, the manufacturing sector contributed 21.4 percent to Singapore's nominal GDP.

One of Singapore's first contracts, Winsemius recalled, was to make Van Heusen shirts; in that, he pointed out, Singapore was doubly lucky because top garment manufacturers like Hong Kong and Taiwan had more orders than they could cope with and were also bound by limits as to how much they could export. So business spilt over to Singapore. The new nation also ventured into making cheap electronics and ship repairing, making the most of the shipyards left by the British.

While such activities were a good start, Winsemius and Tang did not stop there. "We realised that our whole economic set-up was extremely dangerous," said the Dutchman.

"We realised that our main markets were Malaysia and Indonesia – and to such an extent that they could twist our arm." He told Prime Minister Lee that "unless we had economic independence, we would not have political independence".

The way forward, said Winsemius, was to attract multinational companies (MNCs) to set up shop in Singapore too. "I believed cooperation with international firms would work because MNCs had more guts, more expansion capabilities and more capital." EDB, which had been founded in 1961 and was initially overseeing the development of domestic enterprises, was given the remit to bring foreign investors, especially manufacturers, in. The first big win for Singapore came from Winsemius' country, the Netherlands, when Royal Dutch Shell built a S$100-million refinery on Pulau Bukom.

Such concerted industrialisation inspired some Singaporeans to take a chance on new technologies. Among them was egg businessman Teh Lee Thong, who sank S$6,500 into an automated hatchery in the early 1980s.

Service Above Self

Assembly lines need many workers. The surge in job opportunities from the late 1960s, however, ran counter to another of Singapore's most pressing needs – the setting up of a civilian army to shore up Singapore's defence forces. The nation's founding leaders had anticipated that Britain might pull its troops out of Singapore – and sure enough, in 1968, Britain announced that it would withdraw all its soldiers by 1971. That rendered 17,000 more Singaporeans, who had been working as vital support staff, jobless.

In the meantime, explained long-time Chief of Defence Force **Winston Choo Wee Leong**, there were only about 600 local career soldiers, such as himself, to protect Singapore. That is why Dr Goh Keng Swee led the national conscription drive for young Singaporean men aged between 18 and 20 years.

> Chief of Defence Force Winston Choo Wee Leong said that in the late 1960s, there were only about 600 local career soldiers, such as himself, to protect Singapore. That is why Dr Goh Keng Swee led the conscription drive for young Singaporean men aged between 18 and 20 years.

Robert Iau Kuo Kwong, Director of Manpower in the Ministry of Defence (Mindef) in the 1960s, said Singapore literally had to set up its army, navy and airforce from scratch. "We had never fought for ourselves," he pointed out. "But when we got our independence and started to pull in the boys out of school, out of the universities, off the streets, it created a certain amount of dislocation. And on top of that, the armed forces at that time did not have a truly military service, and so everything was a bit hotchpotch."

So, he added, the establishment of Singapore's defence forces took "an enormous amount of coordination" – from setting up camps all over the island, getting suitable trainers, buying lots of military equipment and ensuring that every recruit had a uniform. "Looking back," Iau marvelled, "it's really quite astonishing because not one among us had any experience. We knew nothing about how to do this thing but it was a lot of commonsense and anticipating what was likely to happen and also to take very swift and firm decisions when the time called for it."

Singapore, said Iau and Choo, had a lot of help from Israeli soldiers to establish its defence forces. But platoon commander **Cedric Buher Kleinman** recalled that there was one area which the Israelis were not acquainted with – jungle warfare. "In fact," he added, "they learnt a heck of a lot from us as to how operations in the jungle were carried out. They then introduced a few concepts to us. We never used to move a lot at night in the jungle." But the Israelis taught NSmen how to sharpen their combat skills for their tropical setting.

Often, he added, there was no time for hesitation. "The great big wheel of NS was rolling and it didn't stop for everybody else. We just had to stay ahead of it."

Strictly speaking, from 1967, all men who were fighting fit should have done National Service (NS), never mind if they had just secured places at universities, were midway through their courses or had just graduated. The rub was that all of them were also in great demand in the improving labour market. "It became a little messy," Iau said. "At that time, Singapore was starting to develop and we needed graduates in the market to drive the economy. And they were all… in the army, feeling highly discontented and generally not contributing much."

Iau's solution to freeing up manpower to keep the economy chugging along was not to call up anyone born before 1949 for NS. "That released quite a number of graduating students," he said. "Until today, I still receive heartfelt thanks from some of my friends who just escaped [NS] by the skin of their teeth."

The difficulty in establishing Singapore's defence forces from scratch was compounded by those in the Chinese community who recalled the National Service Riots of 13 May 1954. Students in Chinese-medium secondary schools resisted the call-up as yet another ploy by the British to undermine their educational and career opportunities. They had intended to present a petition to then Governor of Singapore Franklin Gimson, but wound up clashing with riot police. No one died, but 20 students and six policemen were injured.

The riots left such a long shadow that when the government made NS mandatory, Kleinman, who had led A Company – which was the first to train NSmen as army officers – recalled of his recruits: "What struck me at that point in time was not fear, but the way in which the majority of the Chinese cadets viewed military service. They seemed to come across as if they were not there because they wanted to be there, but because they had to be there for NS."

Among the exceptions to this was **Tan Peng Ann**. He started out teaching secondary school students in Pasir Panjang but after two stints of NS – the first was Basic Military Training (BMT) part-time at Beach Road Camp and the second was full-time in 1967 at Ulu Pandan Camp – he signed up as an army regular, retiring as a colonel. Tan said the structure and spirit of the army suited him to a T.

To be sure, some in Singapore who were Chinese-educated and, unlike Tan the soldier, were not the only ones doubtful about their being able to defend Singapore to the death. Businessman **Rajabali Jumabhoy** said his peers were not persuaded that the new nation could thrive. "We were immigrants from India, China and elsewhere. We came to Singapore to earn a living and remit part of our savings to our relatives in our home countries... if you didn't consider Singapore your home country, there could be no loyalty attached to it."

Then again, said Kleinman, even wet-eared recruits like Tan who pledged allegiance to the Singapore flag took a while to get used to the discipline that NS required of them. Meanwhile, their parents were "apprehensive" as to how dangerous simulated combat might be for their sons, on whom they would have to rely as breadwinners.

Kleinman said these parents' minds were soon set at ease when their offspring returned home for breaks, thanks to "the sort of way they'd show respect to their parents and other family members, such as by making their own beds and not being as untidy as they used to be". He pointed out: "It didn't take long for the apprehension to fall away and parents began to realise the need for NS – that you had to provide for the defence forces for our country."

It helped that Mindef introduced policies that showed they understood the concerns of parents and their sons. One such policy was to introduce the Singapore Armed Forces (SAF) scholarship scheme to, as Iau put it, "grow our own graduates from within the army". That, he pointed out, was necessary because NS would otherwise seem like a liability to

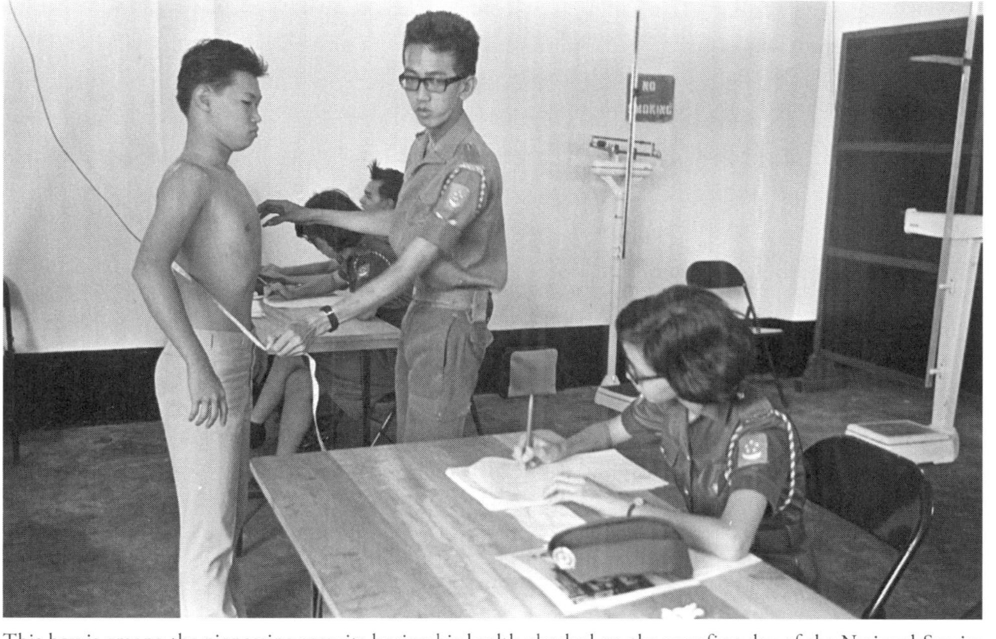

This boy is among the pioneering recruits having his health checked on the very first day of the National Service registration exercise on 28 March 1967. The historic exercise ended on 18 April 1967, and the mandatory health checks were to ensure that every recruit was physically fit for their rigorous military training to come.

many struggling parents who would want their sons to lighten the burden of household bills. Kleinman said: "If the average Chinese lad had the chance to choose what sort of career to pursue, he'd choose everything else. Joining the army would be last." For example, he added, if the man called up for NS was an only son, he might be expected to take over the family business. Kleinman, who used to chair Mindef's Advisory Board for Deferments and Exceptions, explained that in such cases, Mindef might allow such men to do NS part-time, or even defer his service till later. He added: "The government was very conscious of the fact that if we did not do this, certain families would find themselves in dire straits."

Army regular Alfred Goh Kok Kee, recalled his BMT on Pulau Tekong: "We were issued rubber boots, which we would polish, and every weekend, we would carry our Ali Baba backpacks home. Our uniforms were starched to such an extent that these could stand on their own after being ironed."

And while **Maarof Salleh**, a former President of the Islamic Religious Council of Singapore, was not an only son, Mindef approved his request to go home every week, instead of every month, during NS. Otherwise, as he told his superiors, his widowed mother would have to fend for herself and his much younger brother.

Slowly but surely, NS caught on, becoming a rite of passage that most sons of Singapore shared. Army regular **Alfred Goh Kok Kee**, who was aide-de-camp to Singapore President Wee Kim Wee and his successor Ong Teng Cheong, recalled his BMT on Pulau Tekong: "We were issued rubber boots, which we would polish, and every weekend, we would carry our Ali Baba backpacks home. Our uniforms were starched to such an extent that these could stand on their own after being ironed." As he put it: "Some of these things actually made a lot of difference to how we perceived the Army."

The Beautiful Globe

With accommodation all around, Albert Winsemius said Singapore went from having thousands of jobless citizens to having jobs go a-begging within five years. By 1970, Singapore had achieved full employment and its economic prospects were rosy.

That was thanks in part to its introduction of the Asian Dollar Market from 1968. Winsemius, again, helped bring that about although, as he confessed, "I knew nothing of banking". He did, however, have excellent contacts, among whom was his countryman J.D. Van Oenen. Van Oenen worked for the Bank of America in London. Sometime before 1968, Winsemius visited him there. "I explained to him why we wanted more feet to stand on apart from manufacturing and the port. Van Oenen took me to a boardroom. And there was a globe standing there. I will never forget that beautiful globe."

Van Oenen then told Winsemius: "If we put Singapore between the time before the money market in San Francisco closes, then Singapore would take over global financial dealings. And when the Singapore market closes, it would have handed over the dealings to Zurich… then this would be the first time since creation that we will have a 24-hour, round-the-clock service in money and banking." Winsemius returned to Singapore, presented Van Oenen's recommendations to Hon Sui Sen, who at the time was Chairman of EDB and later Minister for Finance. Hon found Van Oenen's strategy sound and so the Asian Dollar Market came into being. That led to Singapore becoming the financial hub for Southeast Asia by 1973.

Alas, in October 1973, oil-producing countries suddenly hiked petroleum prices up from US$3 per barrel to US$5 per barrel and, by January 1974, US$11 per barrel. At the same time, there was a global food shortage from poor harvests. This double whammy, said Singapore's second Prime Minister Goh Chok Tong, sent Singapore's inflation rate up from 6 percent in 1972 to 14 percent in 1974. Speaking at a May Day dinner on 30 April 2001, Prime Minister Goh recalled Singapore's GDP tumbling from 11 percent in 1973 to 4 percent in 1975. But Singapore's founding fathers had nerves of steel and they unleashed a slew of shrewd measures. First, they floated the Singapore dollar, whose value appreciated against the US dollar and made imports cheaper. Then they opened Welcome supermarkets run by the National Trades Union Congress (now Fairprice), which sold household essentials at much reduced prices. They also cracked down on profiteers and raised workers' wages for two years in a row.

The upshot? After oil prices stabilised by end 1974, Goh said, Singapore grew by about 8 percent year on year between 1974 and 1984. The government had bitten the bullet, and emerged fighting fitter than ever.

Winsemius, however, recalled the move to increase wages to cope with the oil and food crises as an instance when Singapore's leaders did not heed his advice. He had actually recommended a wage increase of 14 percent, while the government and employers would accept a hike of only 8 percent. As a compromise, Winsemius said the government agreed on an 11 percent raise across the board. "I should never have compromised," he said. In fact, he considered his caving in "one of the major mistakes I made in Singapore" because he actually thought Singapore workers deserved a 20 percent hike in wages. So, Winsemius mused in 1982, their wages lagged "quite a bit", despite their being in great demand by employers. From 1979, however, the pressure for wages to "catch up", he said, led to a whopping 20 percent yearly hike in wages for three years running.

Recalling all that, he explained: "The moment we gave too low a wage increase, it meant automatically a tight labour market." That was because by then, there were more job vacancies than Singaporeans to fill them, and the relatively low wages all around could not entice them to job-hop. Workers also grew lax from a lack of motivation, and productivity suffered. "We had to give work permits to those coming from abroad," added the Dutchman, who was in general cautious about letting in too many "guest workers", as he called foreign labour. He noted further: "It meant that the employer, especially the manufacturer, had no interest in increasing productivity because he could increase production by simply importing people instead of increasing productivity permanently." In a bid to boost efficiency at work, in 1982, the government launched the national productivity campaign. Its mascot, Teamy the Bee, went by the punchy slogan: "Good, better, best, never let it rest, till your good is better, and your better, best!" Teamy buzzed about year after year till it was retired in 1999.

Going to Work in Bathtubs

For the Singaporeans who had to fulfil the nation's hopes and dreams, the pace was often punishing. **Soh Siew Cheong**, who was among the few local engineers working in the government from 1966, recalled how stressful working life could be. He was assigned to Pasir Panjang Power Station and said his days there were largely peaceful except when the station's alarm "went off like an ambulance siren". "That meant that the whole power system might be in jeopardy," he recalled. "Everyone would be running around and asking, 'What happened? What happened?'

"And it was not uncommon at that time that a few among the operating engineers actually collapsed when the siren sounded because the sudden change in the working environment really shocked them. Those with weak hearts died. It was a professional hazard."

Banking on manufacturing to help Singapore grow meant that *kampungs* had to make way for factories. So the government set about acquiring plots of land in areas best for industrial estates, and paying its occupiers compensation.

Banking on manufacturing to help Singapore grow meant that *kampungs* had to make way for factories. So the government set about acquiring plots of land in areas best for industrial estates, and paying its occupiers compensation. The latter could sometimes be rascals, recalled **Ngiam Tong Tau**, a seasoned civil servant who assisted Deputy Prime Minister Goh Keng Swee in determining how much villagers should be compensated. The government paid such compensation based on the amount of money the villager had spent on planting trees and improving his compound, such as by paving it over with concrete. "So," Ngiam said, "when they found out that the compensation was pretty good, they started planting these little trees before the assessor came... sometimes, overnight, you could see that they had laid a concrete path on their land, with very thin concrete.

"The assessor didn't look at all this and say, 'How well was this built?' So the villagers were laying a lot of concrete." The government soon put a stop to such shenanigans, paying them only for "mature" trees, Ngiam stressed. Even so, he added that he tried his best to be fair in computing the final compensation. In doing so, he irked his boss Goh. "He looked at my numbers, closed his eyes and said, 'Dr Ngiam, do you think you are working for the Social Welfare Department?' And I thought, 'Poor families, they are not going to get much money'." But Goh eventually relented.

Alwee Alkaff remembered such fairness prevailing when the government had to acquire plots of land and properties downtown for urban renewal. Alwee, a trader whose forefathers were the pioneers of early Singapore, managed his family's landed assets. Speaking to the Oral History Unit (now Oral History Centre) in 1982, he said: "For the moment, the government is paying us not badly at all. Because if you own one shophouse, there will likely not be any buyers for it because people tend to buy a stretch of these, pull them down and rebuild on their site. So the best buyer is, in fact, the government."

Before carving out industrial estates, the government had, from 1960, embarked on a concerted drive to build thousands of public flats to house squatters, to rid Singapore of slums and free up land downtown for building office towers and shopping malls. These Housing & Development Board (HDB) flats would also spruce up Singapore's image to incoming investors.

But such en masse building brought on a crisis – heavy flooding across Singapore. Nurse **Mary Hee Sook Yin**, who joined KK Hospital in 1961, remembered the floods of 1969 as being particularly bad. "I had to travel by army truck to work. And some midwives were pushed to KK Hospital in bathtubs."

Tan Gee Paw, the civil engineer who had studied in Kuala Lumpur, was Head of the Drainage Department when the flood crisis peaked in the 1970s. Tan called the bursting of Sungai Kallang's banks at the time "really an eye-opener". "I could see the floodwaters rise all the way up to the roof of the *attap* huts," he recalled. "There were the pig farmers who were squatting on top of these huts. The army had to be called in with rescue boats to rescue all the farmers who were perched on top of the huts." At Potong Pasir, a well-established squatter colony of pig farmers, he said "dead pigs were floating down the river, all the way".

Singaporeans are seen here balloting at Commonwealth Drive in 1965 for the chance to own an HDB flat. Before the HDB built high-rise housing blocks, people had to get by in cramped and often unsanitary accommodation.

Tan and his team resolved the crisis by building big canals and extra drains well ahead of any public housing projects. They worked with HDB early on to determine where they should dig canals to drain excess rain effectively. "The minute HDB had formulated their plans, before the bulldozers went in, the main canal had to be ready. And that was the policy that we adopted after we tackled all the older problems. And that policy holds up till today, that we must always be ahead of land development, and not neglect our drainage systems as many developing countries have."

Bus Stops are not Airports

By the late 1970s, the Singapore economy was experiencing galloping growth. But Albert Winsemius, who visited Singapore a few times a year – and read *The Straits Times* every day, even when he was back home in Holland – thought the nation should diversify its selling points further. His vision? Singapore as a tourism hub. "We can have a runway – our airport. We will receive any airplane and see to it that we always keep a runway that we can receive the largest plane which needs the largest runway," he said. "Then we can have a number of first-class hotels, from elaborate to simple, but every one a quality hotel."

With all that, he added, large planes from global cities such as New York would stop over in Singapore. "People will be tired. We'll put them to bed, tuck them into an air-conditioned room. They can drink from the tap. They can eat whatever they want... on their second day in Singapore, they will spend a considerable amount of money, so we'll see to it that in the neighbourhood of the hotels, there are shopping centres. After a day's shopping, and having spent probably half of their money already, they will go on a smaller plane or bus to KL."

Then, he added, they would return to Singapore within a week and fly home. So tourism became the third pillar of the nation's economy, after manufacturing and financial services.

When you consider how Singaporeans slogged to make their nation viable, it seems only fitting that they should have built the world's best airport. Journalist **Tan Wee Him**, who was an aviation correspondent for *The Straits Times*, recalled how building Changi Airport was a wholly Singaporean endeavour. "The government decided that we would use our own people – our own architects, our own engineers, our own other expertise. That way, the project would be a tremendous learning experience for our people, which would then give them better standing.

> Journalist Tan Wee Him, who was aviation correspondent for *The Straits Times*, recalled how building Changi Airport was a wholly Singaporean endeavour. "The government decided that we would use our own people – our own architects, our own engineers, our own other expertise."

"The people from the Changi Airport Development Division rose to the occasion." They even reclaimed land in record time to build the international airport, which was originally

These passengers are disembarking from Singapore Airlines Flight SQ101, which was the first commercial flight to land at the newly completed Changi Airport at 7.10 am on 1 July 1981. *The Straits Times*' aviation correspondent Tan Wee Him was among them, having sat next to the flight's pilot Capt T.K. Pow in the cockpit.

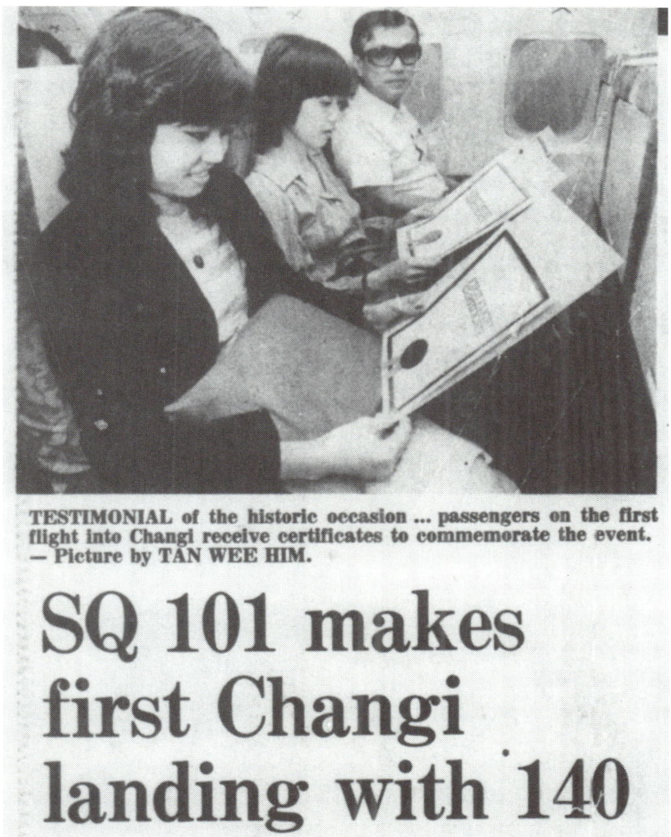

TESTIMONIAL of the historic occasion ... passengers on the first flight into Changi receive certificates to commemorate the event. — Picture by TAN WEE HIM.

SQ 101 makes first Changi landing with 140

Passengers on board Singapore Airlines flight SQ101 from Kuala Lumpur to Singapore on 1 July 1981. The Boeing 727 is the first plane to land at Changi Airport. (*The Straits Times*, 2 July 1981, p. 8)

planned as an expansion of the existing airport at Paya Lebar. But after Prime Minister Lee Kuan Yew visited Boston-Logan international airport on America's east coast, he asked that the site be changed to coastal Changi instead.

Initially, some Singaporeans scoffed at the all-Singaporean effort, saying that local engineers were known for building bus stops and not much else. But the team in charge of creating Changi Airport went around the world, learning the best practices for baggage handling, apron servicing, tarmac layout and so on. "So," said Tan, "when Changi opened, it was one of the most modern airports because we had learnt from the mistakes of others and improved on these."

Incidentally, civil servant turned Haj pilgrimage officer **Haji Mohamed Sidek Bin Siraj** said that Changi got its name from the Javanese phrase "chang-changi", which means to tighten or to tie up.

Tan the journalist could never forget the first plane that landed at Changi, at 7.10 am on 1 July 1981. That was because he was right beside the pilot of that Boeing 727, on Singapore Airlines flight SQ101, which had flown into Singapore from Kuala Lumpur. Tan recalled that Captain T.K. Pow, the pilot, "allowed me to sit next to him in the cockpit when the plane landed for the first time at Changi".

The official opening of Changi Airport on 29 December 1981 was just as unforgettable for Tan – it coincided with the start of his honeymoon. He covered the momentous milestone, officiated by cabinet minister Howe Yoon Chong, and then, as Tan put it, "flew off for my honeymoon from Changi, on the day the airport first opened".

A brand new airport alone in a city would not arrest anyone's attention if the city itself was shabby. When Changi Airport was being built in the mid-1970s till early 1980s, downtown Singapore was decidedly stinky from hawkers and other street vendors dumping their waste indiscriminately into drains. **Lee Ek Tieng**, who was then Permanent Secretary at the Ministry of Environment, recalled.

This is the iconic air control tower of Changi Airport in May 1980. The three-storey bowl-like structure was built on the ground, then pulled upwards painstakingly with four jacks and eight cables at the rate of 6 metres a day.

This man is gazing at the Singapore River in 1983, six years after founding Prime Minister Lee Kuan Yew instructed that it be cleaned up by 1987. The civil servants in charge of doing so achieved that in good time, as shown by the clear waters in this photograph.

When he opened Upper Peirce Reservoir on 27 February 1977, Prime Minister Lee Kuan Yew had actually challenged Lee and his team to clean up Singapore River and its tributaries within 10 years. If they succeeded in doing so, Prime Minister Lee said he would give each of them a gold coin. "It came like a bolt from the blue," said Lee the civil servant.

Tan Gee Paw, then head of the Drainage Department, was tasked to write a Cabinet paper on what and who were polluting the rivers, and how best to tackle such pollution. It cost more than $100 million over 10 years to achieve that. The solutions were sound in theory, but a headache to carry out. "For example," Lee the civil servant pointed out, "you can't just go around collecting the waste hawkers discharged because they washed everything, which went down the drain." City streets stank to high heaven because street hawkers were "slaughtering chickens, even snakes and other wild animals – you name it, they did it – and blood, feathers, everything went down the drain, notwithstanding garbage removal." All the detritus wound up in Rochor Canal and made it a cesspit. The only way to keep the rivers clean was to move hawkers into newly built food centres and embark on an islandwide sewer-building drive.

Lee and his team banished bumboats from the rivers. The filthy boatyards along the Kallang River relocated to Pasir Panjang, and cleared the streets of hawkers and other peddlers. They also got contractors to dredge the bed of the Singapore River by one metre, haul drift mud and debris up and then coat the riverbed with sand, which filtered its currents further. "To our surprise, within a week, the smell disappeared," Lee said.

The clean-up of Singapore's rivers was completed in just under 10 years. Lee and his team received national awards from Prime Minister Lee for their efforts.

Just as essential, if still not widely known, were their efforts to secure Singapore's water supply. Tan, who later became Chairman of the Public Utilities Board (PUB), had drawn up the nation's water master plan in 1972. That plan, he said, was not reviewed till 29 years later. "Up till 2001, the idea of self-sufficiency in water was very remote," he noted. Tan, however, had long been convinced that recycling wastewater was the best way to insure Singapore against future water crises. So he led his PUB colleagues to build a pilot wastewater recycling plant at Bedok.

In 2002, Tan visited the plant to inspect the recycled water, which was stored in a deep well, awaiting its discharge into the sea. "I looked at the water and was completely amazed. It was crystal clear, clearer than the water at the bottom of a swimming pool – and you know how you can see the dirt at the bottom of a pool." The wastewater had been filtered via reverse osmosis, which removed all dissolved substances to produce, as he put it, "water that was better than PUB water, which was well within World Health Organisation drinking limits". "That day," he added, "I realised that we had in our hands a possible solution to the water challenge that we will have to face soon." In 2014, Tan told this author in a separate interview that when he briefed former Prime Minister Lee Kuan Yew on NEWater, as the crystal-clear liquid came to be called, the latter "smiled from ear to ear".

The Highest Praise

While top-class infrastructure was crucial to realising Albert Winsemius' vision of Singapore as a tourism hotspot, the nation also needed icons to capture tourists' imagination. Changi Airport's air control tower became synonymous with Singapore; so too the Merlion, the leonine sea creature thought up in the 1960s by Briton Alec Fraser-Brunner, the curator of the now-defunct Van Kleef Aquarium. The Merlion has since been such a hit with tourists that in December 2017, local news site Mothership.sg reported the existence of three Merlion replicas in the northern Japanese port city of Hakodate. In mid-June 2016, current Prime Minister Lee Hsien Loong spotted another Merlion replica outside a kimono shop in Karuizawa City in eastern Japan. That speaks volumes for the Merlion's popularity.

More recently, the Singapore skyline has been transformed by a succession of stupendous buildings, beginning with the spiky-roofed arts centre Esplanade – Theatres On the Bay, known fondly as The Durian; the integrated resort Marina Bay Sands, designed by Israeli architect Moshe Safdie; and the nation's biggest public park, Gardens by the Bay, whose clamshell-shaped glass domes won the World Building of the Year Award at the World Architecture Festival in 2012.

Singapore's much-loved national icon to date, arguably, is not a building, but furry orang utan Ah Meng. **Bernard Ming-Deh Harrison**, the longtime Executive Director of the

Bernard Harrison, the longtime Executive Director of the Singapore Zoo, was pivotal in drawing hordes of visitors to the zoo with an open-air concept and enabling people to mingle with some of the zoo's most popular attractions, including elephants and orang utans.

Singapore Zoo, recalled that the zoo took in 20 baby orang utans a year from the 1970s, when the government cracked down on those who imported exotic animals illegally. "Singapore was then an entrepot port," he said, "and a lot of traffic came through. We used to have a lot of endangered species here." Foodie **Vincent Gabriel** recalled how at the time, Terengganu Street would be peppered with shops selling live animals such as monster lizards, turtles and rabbits. He revealed: "There was even a rumour that if you wanted to be intelligent, you could buy the brains of a chimpanzee and get it cooked for you."

Harrison said that, at first, the zoo had not set out to have an animal that was iconic of Singapore. It had a gentle elephant, Anusha, which obligingly posed for photographs with visitors. But when he and his team got to thinking about a mascot proper, they were adamant that it should be an Asian species. "We are an Asian zoo," he said, "so there's no point going out with a jaguar as a mascot. Could it be a snake? Well, yes, but snakes don't have the same warmth and appeal as a furry mammal." So he settled on an orang utan – but it was not Ah Meng. "It was a better-looking and more pleasant" ape named Suzie. Sadly, Suzie died of toxaemia during her pregnancy in 1974.

That was how Ah Meng got her job. "Ah Meng was kind of sour-faced," said Harrison. "But she was well-groomed and didn't slouch, which was good for photography." He thought Ah Meng's smile "a bit plastic", but the ape soon drew legions of fans, including King of Pop Michael Jackson, actresses Elizabeth Taylor and Isabella Rossellini, tennis champion Bjorn

Delighted visitors to the Singapore Zoo are seen here getting to know Ah Meng, the zoo's lovable mascot in its hugely popular "Breakfast with An Orang Utan" programme in the 1980s.

Borg and singers John Denver and Donny and Marie Osmond. Ah Meng posed with visitors over a bowl of fruit in the popular programme "Breakfast with an Orang Utan". Hollywood starlet Bo Derek in particular – who was a major sex symbol of the 1980s – was a huge fan. Harrison recalled: "She used to fly to Singapore, jump into a cab and head straight to the zoo to visit Ah Meng – and then fly off. And irritatingly enough, I used to find out that she had visited only after she had left."

Over the years, Harrison took to having Ah Meng in tow whenever he gave school talks. That was how Ah Meng became a household name. "Ah Meng and the term orang utan became as synonymous as Bic and ballpen," he said. "She was quite a character." The ape touched so many hearts that when she died on 8 February 2008, he said at least 1,000 people turned up at the zoo to mourn her. "She touched a generation," he mused. "People between 10 and 15 years younger than me would come up to me and say, 'I remember you used to come to my school with Ah Meng and oh, my gosh, that was amazing'."

The last word on the nation's formative years, during which it chalked up wonder after wonder, should perhaps go to Singapore's first Chief Minister **David Saul Marshall**. Marshall, a formidable defence lawyer who later became Singapore's ambassador to France, criticised the governing People's Action Party (PAP) for the breakneck pace at which Singaporeans were usually expected to perform. Yet, all told, as he later admitted: "I also recognise that, frankly, I don't think I could have been equal to the ramifications of governing the country.

"Watching now from the outside, the activities of the PAP, all in all, it deserves the highest praise - with no background, no real aid from outside to guide their infant steps, to have achieved so much stability, international respect and economic growth."

CHAPTER NINE

WOMEN

I am Woman, Hear Me Roar

If you had 39 gold medals to your name by the age of 19, you might think your future very bright indeed. **Patricia Chan Li-Yin**, who brought such honour to newly independent Singapore between 1965 and 1973, had every reason to expect such a future. After all, she was Singapore swimming's Golden Girl, nigh unbeatable in the pool at regional meets since she was 11 years old.

But Chan was a woman who grew up in an age when her father and his peers – men and women – did not see why women should be ambitious. In 2015, Chan recalled: "There was a part of my father's generation that looked at a woman as being good enough if she could be a schoolteacher… and go and get married.

Singapore's Golden Girl Patricia Chan Li-Yin (second from right) is seen here with her disciplinarian father, Dr Chan Ah Kow, her supportive mother and her three brothers, who were also formidable swimmers.

"So I was holding the national flag in one hand and was the beacon of hope in a new country – and then there were a lot of these comments, such as 'Oh, that's good enough.' It was very confusing as a young teen to look in the mirror and know what you had achieved, and then to be told that I was just going to be... Miss Average, that it didn't matter because I was just a girl."

For much of the 20th century in Singapore, society frowned upon girls who aspired to careers – as well as women who actually held down nine-to-five jobs. Journalist **Khoo Teng Soon** said that, in general, parents and husbands disapproved of their daughters and wives having careers because they would rather they focus on bringing up children and managing the household. Khoo, who grew up under the roof of his tycoon grandfather Chew Boon Lay, said: "Quite a few of my cousins went out to work. At first, of course, there was disappointment in the family especially when my grandmother was still alive; she was rather old-fashioned about it.

"But again, it depended on whose family these cousins belonged to. My No. 1 uncle's daughters married well and the idea was that they should look after their in-laws. It was the system in those days." Some of his other female cousins, he added, married into humbler families, and so they eventually went out to work.

Paternalistic thinking extended to denying many girls an education; after all, they reasoned, what use was education to girls whose fate was to marry, have children and keep house? As Chan realised, even the brightest and most educated women of her time were relegated to careers as teachers.

Gangster-turned-pastor **Neivelle Tan** recalled that Eurasian women and other women who were educated were the earliest to go out and work, usually as schoolteachers. According to Tan, who grew up in the 1930s, "at that time, society looked down on working mothers. Only the Eurasian and other educated wives would work. Our Peranakan tradition is that the mother would always be at home to look after the children, to cook and wait for the husband to come back – and pamper him." Teacher **Mrs Goh Heng Chong née Teo Moh Tet** recalled that Eurasians tended to teach needlework, singing and the scriptures.

Their Dream Job was to Scrub Floors

Then again, even when the destitution of World War II forced society to rethink seriously its opposition to women in the workforce, there were hardly any job opportunities for women, educated or otherwise.

Hedwig Elizabeth Aroozoo Anuar, who graduated from the University of Malaya with a rare First Class Honours in English Literature, had to be content with a $850-a-month job in Kuala Lumpur before Deputy Prime Minister Goh Keng Swee asked her to head the National Library in early 1960. Anuar, who was married and had a son by then, recalled Goh writing to her to ask if she might be interested in a job with Singapore's National Library. That was because the expatriates there were returning home, following the new Malayanisation

Pioneering Singaporean civil servant Hedwig Anuar was known for speaking truth to power, and for speaking up about the unenviable lot of women in Singapore. She is seen here in 2004, having helmed the National Library from 1965 till 1988 as its director.

policy to replace them with locals. "After all," Anuar recalled Goh pointing out, "what was the point of self-government if you go and have a British expatriate for the job?" She had known Goh from her college days.

Anuar, at least, had prospects. Sociologist **Ann Elizabeth Wee née Wilcox** learnt just how grim circumstances were for women in Singapore with no education or relevant job skills. That was after then Minister for Labour and Law Kenneth Byrne invited Wee to chair a committee of the Council of Social Services in 1960. Wee's task was to review the Women and Girls' Protection Ordinance, which the colonial government introduced in 1896. The ordinance followed the establishment in 1888 of the Poh Leung Kuk (or "office to protect virtue") by Singapore's First Protector of Chinese, William Pickering – after whom Upper Pickering Street is named. The Poh Leung Kuk started out as a single room in Lock Hospital, near Kampong Java, and took in young prostitutes, ill-treated girls and the destitute. Under the watchful eye of the Poh Leung Kuk Committee comprising leaders of Singapore's Chinese community, these girls were taught discipline and trained for decent, if menial, jobs.

Wee, an Englishwoman who married a Singaporean lawyer, sieved through piles of government records on social life in Singapore. She also interviewed many locals who were down on their luck. She found that uneducated housewives endured the worst lot of all. Many among them were single mothers, after having divorced or, more usually, after having lost their husbands in World War II or to tuberculosis, which was endemic in Singapore for two-thirds of the 20th century.

Wee said there were few, if any, jobs to be had "beyond washing clothes for others". "There was virtually no factory work. Rubber-packing was mostly monopolised by the *samsui* (female immigrants from Samsui village in Guangdong, China, who worked as construction workers in Singapore) and other single women from China... apart from that, there were only the soft drink factories Framroz and Fraser & Neave. At Henderson estate, there were some glass factories which absorbed local labour." These women would have to wait till the late 1960s before the government, through the Economic Development Board, pulled in enough foreign investors to set up factories here.

Before the blossoming of Singapore's manufacturing industry, the most viable work by far for impecunious, uneducated women was what others called the oldest profession in the world. "If they worked as prostitutes," said Wee, "they could give their children education and I remember one of them was paying for music lessons."

Wee added: "Their dream job was to be a hospital servant, what we called the hospital *ayahs* (attendants). I think that gives you some idea of how little scope there was for women."

They coveted the scrubbing of floors and "doing other dirty work" in hospitals because, she pointed out, it was a government job which meant regular hours and relative job stability. "I always remember that as such a contrast with what became available for women later on."

In fact, she added, the plight of poor women who had to turn to prostitution was her "outstanding memory" of the research she did for the committee she chaired from 1960.

Around that time, winds of change were coming for the lot of women, also through Byrne the minister. In 1961, he tabled the Women's Charter Bill in Parliament. The charter was meant to give wives certain rights against their husbands if their marriages soured, and also sought to address the gaps in the Women and Girls' Protection Ordinance.

Wee recalled the lead-up to the bill's introduction thus: "The People's Action Party's Chinese-educated Women's Wing was active then… against yellow culture or all unclean matters, mainly polygamy and prostitution. The Women's Charter was the response to this."

Mrs Ann Wee is the doyenne of social work in Singapore. An Englishwoman married to a Singaporean lawyer, she was often invited by the government to lead many social service initiatives, including being an advisor to the Juvenile Court in 2007.

She added: "The people who were agitating the most politically for the Women's Charter at that stage, for monogamous marriage, were the Chinese-educated women and schoolteachers, factory workers and even high school girls."

Among other things, Wee recalled, the Women's Charter enabled action to be taken against prostitutes who were aged 21 years or younger, compared with the age limit of 18 years under the Women and Girls' Protection Ordinance.

Seow Peck Leng, who was a member of the Select Committee working on the Women's Charter before it went before Parliament, revealed that when the committee asked Singapore's women to comment on the draft bill, only two women obliged. They were Mrs George Lee and Shirin Fozdar. Both advocated monogamy, and that the Charter should provide for polygamous men to be jailed.

Fozdar, incidentally, founded the Singapore Council for Women in 1952 – with Mrs George Lee its president at one time – and was an indefatigable champion of women's rights after World War II. She was commended by Minister for Culture S. Rajaratnam for her efforts to better the lot of Singaporean women. Fozdar died in 1996, aged 86.

Seow, who was the only female opposition member in Singapore's Legislative Assembly from 1959 till 1963, lamented: "But because of a lack of support from the then government,

Mrs Seow Peck Leng, seen here to the left of Singapore's First Lady Noor Aishah Md Salim (centre, dressed in a *baju kurong*), on a visit to Kampong Amber in 1962. Mrs Seow was a tireless advocate of women's rights for much of her life, and was the first Singaporean woman parliamentarian as well as president of the Persekutuan Wanita Singapura or Singapore Women's Federation.

Mrs Shirin Fozdar was the Secretary-General of the Singapore Council of Women between 1952 and 1961. Strongly believing that women are equal to men, she had begun the fight for the emancipation of women in India when she was just a teenager.

and a lack of support from other women, they failed to be of much use.

"I think the women didn't support them because they felt that it was a personal affair. But if you don't support, polygamy could happen to you... Everybody was thinking of herself." She noted that this was the prevailing sentiment, even though the membership of the Council of Women comprised mostly female factory workers.

That was perhaps somewhat harsh. After all, as Seow herself recalled, a female doctor remonstrated against the charter criminalising polygamy. "The doctor said that for uneducated housewives, if their husbands were put in jail, who was going to look after the household? But I think if she made that remark today, she would be booed."

Seow knew the lot of women in Singapore only too well. A champion of women's causes, in 1954, she set up the Siglap Girls' Club. The club, which taught underprivileged girls life skills, was a throwback to Pickering's Poh Leung Kuk in the 1880s. Then in 1957, Seow founded the Singapore Women's Association and was its president till 1991.

Despite what Seow called the "lackadaisical" attitude of women in Singapore towards punishing polygamous non-Muslim husbands, the charter did eventually outlaw polygamy.

Besides the successful endeavour to make only monogamous marriages legal in Singapore, Seow said a young man protested the draft charter as being too myopic. She recalled: "I very distinctly remember a Chinese-educated chap in his early 20s say, 'Why are we talking about women, women, women? What about old people? You are talking about husband and wife relations. What about parents and children?'"

In response, Byrne the minister replied that the care of the elderly was the responsibility of the state. Nevertheless, Seow thought that the young man had "foresight to say that young people should be made to look after their old people if justice is to done in this country". On 23 May 1994, law don and then Nominated Member of Parliament (NMP) Walter Woon tabled the Maintenance of Parents Bill, triggering heated debates within and outside Parliament as to whether it was necessary for the

"The doctor said that for uneducated housewives, if their husbands were put in jail, who was going to look after the household? I think if she made that remark today, she would be booed."

Women coming out in full force to vote in the 1959 Legislative Assembly general election. This was the first time ever that women were allowed to vote in Singapore. The People's Action Party was the only party to campaign openly on the "one man one wife" slogan.

law to intrude into family affairs to that extent. More than a year later, on 2 November 1995, Parliament passed the bill.

Eventually, the Women's Charter became law later in 1961 and legalised only monogamous marriages by non-Muslim Singaporeans. It was, by the reckoning of Singapore's feminists, a great leap forward for gender parity in the nation.

Seow recalled: "Yes, even at the time, it was the talk of all countries. Every country that I went for conferences, they asked about the Women's Charter." One of the charter's most impactful provisions, she added, was the personal protection order, which a wife could take out against her abusive spouse for her safety. "That was a great step," she said. "Before the charter, the police would say to such wives, 'That's a family matter. We have nothing to do with it'."

Since 2011, noted **Ellen Lee Geck Hoon**, a lawyer and former Member of Parliament, there has been a flurry of amendments to the Women's Charter. The notable changes have been the boosting of the court's powers to ensure that a spouse pays maintenance money while also making counselling and dispute resolution processes more effective. As a backhanded compliment to how far women have come in Singapore, husbands can now claim maintenance from their wives. Lee, added that one issue still being hotly debated among lawmakers is whether or not to criminalise marital rape. As it is, she pointed out, the Penal Code was amended in 2009 to broaden the range of sexual crimes, showing that society abhors violence against women.

But life is a series of a few steps forward – and a few steps back. At the time of writing in 2018, there was a spike in domestic abuse cases in Singapore, serious enough for public buses to carry anti-domestic abuse messages and a hotline for victims to call.

Of Spitfires, Tigresses and Panty Raids

Most women in the 20th century did not speak their mind publicly like lawyer **Phyllis Tan Poh Lian**. Tan, who made history as the first woman president of the Law Society of Singapore, was branded a "spitfire" and a "tigress" by her male peers. She said: "In my day, lawyer R.L. Eber called me Spitfire, you know, one of those aeroplanes in those days.

"And Howard Cashin called me tigress. He was very English and very superior – and here was this punk of a girl just passed out from university asking him for papers. He told me: 'If you have to bang down the phone, say goodbye before you bang the phone down.' So I banged the phone down on him without saying goodbye. From then on, I was the tigress."

She also had the fine instinct of that predator. Referring to the case of Sunny Ang, who was arrested for the murder of his 22-year-old girlfriend Jenny Cheok, a barmaid, after she disappeared on their diving trip, Tan recalled: "Sunny Ang wanted me to probate the will of his girlfriend. And I had looked at the will and felt very uneasy. Women go by intuition. I didn't feel good so I didn't want to do it. I told him I would be going away for a while.

"Then he started talking. He was a charmer and he was trying to boast, 'If you can't find the body, you cannot convict.' He must have looked up the law. He was very intelligent. And then while he was talking, I remember saying, 'And maybe you did it, huh?' It just came out. He just said, 'No, if you can't find the body, you cannot convict'." Ang, a former Singapore Grand Prix driver who went bankrupt before meeting Cheok, stood to gain a total of $400,000 from Cheok's death. Also fishy was the fact that Cheok, a single mother of two, had willed her entire estate to Ang's mother.

While Cheok's body was never found, in May 1965, a jury unanimously found Ang guilty of murdering her, and he was hanged on 6 February 1967.

Predators like Ang have been around since the dawn of time. The reader may, however, be surprised to learn that in the 1950s, panty raids, a mild form of sexual harassment, were sanctioned once a year among residents of Raffles College, the men-only university hostel of then University of Malaya in Singapore. **Carmee Lim**, a former principal of Raffles Girls' School and former resident of the women-only Eusoff College, recalled how she and her girlfriends lived in fear of such raids, during which male hostelites would set off firecrackers in the corridors of their hostel, pull underwear off the girls' washing line and fly the lingerie

Male and female undergraduates are seen here at a lecture in Raffles College in 1948. They lived separately, however, in men and women-only hostels, which led the men to launch "panty raids" on their female counterparts once a year, before final examinations.

high on the flagpole the next day. "It happened once a year," she said, "around the time of our final exams in late January to early February. It was called Cracker War."

She added that, occasionally, her hostel mates caught some among the undie thieves. "They tied one up with rope and put him in our Dining Room," she said. Lim, however, "slept through the whole episode, crackers and all, because I was tired after mugging for exams".

By the 1960s, bolstered by their legal rights under the Women's Charter and an improving economy, more women found work and soon had independent means. In 1964, the Ford car company produced its first advertisement targeted at women in Singapore. Ford's poster depicted a young Asian woman with a chic bob and simple, trendy yellow dress rejoicing at her new acquisition – a Ford Consul Cortina.

But with many men ever on the prowl, working women had to have their wits about them. **Sally Chan née Sally Liew**, who was part of the pioneering counter crew of Malaysia-Singapore Airlines in the 1960s and 1970s, had to fend off many male admirers. "There were occasions when they wanted to have a date with me and all that," she recalled. "I said, 'I have already got my favourite boyfriend; my favourite boyfriend is my husband.' And they would say, 'Oh, okay, okay…' Because if they knew that you are the type that can be taken advantage of, they will not hesitate."

Graduates Should Marry Only Graduates

As employers began requiring university qualifications for better-paying jobs, many women opted for tertiary studies too. The growing number of female graduates from the 1980s presented the government with an unanticipated quandary – the nation relied on its people but many among its female graduates were finding it hard to settle down, as men then were less keen on marrying women with higher qualifications than their own. Those were the findings of Singapore's 1980 population census. As a double whammy, graduate women themselves were either deferring marriage in favour of pursuing careers, or not having children altogether.

So, in his National Day Rally speech in August 1983, then Prime Minister Lee Kuan Yew announced that graduates should marry fellow graduates and, to provide them with opportunities to meet and mingle, the government set up the Social Development Unit in January 1984.

Hedwig Anuar recalled her reaction to the premier's speech: "He shocked us out of our complacency… that there had not been women in Parliament for so long." She and her female friends were "upset" with what the prime minister had said because "how could the government interfere with a thing like this?"

The next year, speaking at a National University of Singapore convocation, Anuar referenced Prime Minister Lee's 1983 speech. Zaibun Siraj took in Anuar's views, and in 1985, she and Anuar co-founded the Association of Women for Research and Action, better known by its acronym AWARE. Anuar retired in 1988, after heading the National Library as its longest-serving director for 23 years, and setting the record as the first woman to helm the institution. In 1969, she was awarded the Public Administration Medal (Gold) and in 1993, named Woman of the Year by *Her World* magazine.

Rocking the Cradle – and the World

Hedwig Anuar perhaps summed up best the relatively speedy emancipation of women in Singapore in 1998: "You young women of today are so fortunate because you have so many choices. In my time, the choices we had were very restricted… we became teachers.

"After my time, a lot of women went into academia… social work was also a new profession like librarianship. And then later we women got into the Civil Service but mostly on the lower rungs, of course."

Many more women have clambered up the career ladder since Anuar's oral history interview in 1998. There are now women cabinet ministers and female permanent secretaries. That is a sea change from the 1960s, when Anuar could count on one hand the number of women who joined the Administrative Service after her. Better yet, she could name all of them: Mabel Puthucheary, economists Lim Leong Bee and Heng Eu Moh, and Lee Seok Tin.

Having secured a foot in the door of the Public Service, these pioneering Singaporean women had to endure occasional chauvinism. Anuar recalled: "P.S. Raman, who was then the Director of Broadcasting, once said, 'Oh, I thought when Hedwig got into the Civil Service, she would change but she's still a woman. She wants to argue about this thing.'"

"He made me think if I had been a man, it wouldn't have been remarked on," she mused. "But because I was a women sticking to my guns, he felt this was a woman's nature." There was, she added, "this feeling that the men were always in charge."

Such jibes stung women especially when most of them used to be paid much less than their male counterparts – just for being women. **Alice Cheang Wye Lan**, the schoolteacher who retired as an inspector of schools, lamented: "We were all inspectors with the same qualifications and the same work but the senior men were Class I and another lady and I were Class II. We were always feeling very bad about this.

"And if you were in Class II, the man would get a $300 allowance, and we would get only $150. And when we retired, we all got pensions – but they all had quite a lot more than we had."

Up till August 1998, Anuar was still saying: "Women are not at the top of the Civil Service very easily... we still have very few women judges and so on. The decision-making is still left largely in the hands of men."

In that light, **Khatijun Nissa Siraj**, who is, incidentally, the mother of the aforementioned Zaibun Siraj, made history when she became the first Muslim woman to work in Singapore's Syariah Court in 1960. She was one among the court's counsellors, and was interviewed by the Public Service Commission before the government appointed her to the court. The Syariah Court adjudicates matters under the Administration of Muslim Law Act (AMLA), which applies to all Muslim Singaporeans.

In the 1960s, the children of Singapore's poor had Khatijun Nissa Siraj to thank for having free, milk to drink regularly in school. Mrs Siraj was also the first woman to work in Singapore's Syariah Court in 1960.

Khatijun did much to persuade her male colleagues to hire more women to counsel troubled married couples because, as she put it to them, "women have got a touch to them; they can understand and reason with the husband and wife."

In fact, spouses intent on divorcing often did not see why they should go to the court at all. That was because, before the AMLA took effect in 1966, they could obtain a divorce easily by just going before a *kadi*, or a religious affairs official.

Khatijun mused: "We had to work hard to convince them to come to court... And

These women were the very first to graduate from the University of Malaya in Singapore in 1950.

then they would wait until both could not take it anymore before coming to us. That was the most difficult part because you cannot mend their ties when they have made up their minds. Then the children were very pitiful."

Ever practical, she also reasoned with her male colleagues in this way: "Islam says the woman cannot ask for a divorce. You must follow whatever your husband says. But if the wife has been beaten up, has no money or food for herself and her children, if you tell her, 'Islam says this and that' do you think she's going to bother? She will tell you, 'Listen, I must save my stomach and my kids' stomachs.'

"So I always tell the Syariah Court president and heads whenever we talk, these are human beings we are dealing with, you must always see things from their point of view. You must always tackle that. It is not about religion; it is about two people fighting."

All working women struggle to juggle career and family but, as Anuar noted, birth control was available worldwide only from the 1960s. Anuar, a single mother of two, marvelled that women today not only have their pick of careers, but also "can decide for themselves whether to marry or not to marry or combine marriage with a career; to have children or not to have children."

"In our time," she pointed out, "there was no birth control. It was not that easy to avoid having a baby if you didn't want to have a baby. You could plan all these things now, make all these choices."

CHAPTER TEN

PERFORMING ARTS
Colour and Light

Many Singaporeans see the arts as a boon to leisure, but also too pricey and hard to grasp. Indeed, Singapore's deeply pragmatic leaders used to consider the arts an indulgence. As its founding Prime Minister Lee Kuan Yew famously told University of Singapore students in 1968: "Poetry is a luxury we cannot afford. What is important for pupils is not literature, but a philosophy of life."

Teacher **Rebecca Chew**, however, showed her students at Naval Base Secondary School how the arts could broaden their horizons and even change their lives for the better.

From 2000 till 2002, Chew was Naval Base's vice-principal and, among other efforts, she mentored at-risk children, that is, those from broken homes or those who had fallen into bad company. She said: "They really needed a structured environment like school to move them through social mobility… to get them out of that cycle and move them into something more stable."

But Chew, whose passion is choral singing, thought they needed something more. "I used the arts to work with the kids," she said. First, she got them to sew a giant quilt for Singapore together. Then, when their art teacher proposed taking them on a trip to Bali, she told that teacher: "Why don't you bring the kids out to Paris?"

"That blew the kids' minds," she recalled. "They never imagined, one, going on an aeroplane and two, going to the Louvre." The Louvre is one of the world's foremost art museums, containing as it does such ancient wonders as the statue of the Venus de Milo. She recalled: "On the day they set off for Paris, their families… cried and came up to me and said, 'I am so thankful that my son can now get on an airplane'." That reminded Chew of families seeing their children off at Paya Lebar Airport in the 1970s, on rare trips abroad. "That wowed the country. That took the imagination."

When the students, some among whom were gangsters, returned from the City of Light, they resolved to make something of themselves by aiming for good jobs, including as port supervisors and aviation technicians. The mentoring, she said, was "very good" for her too, and was "transformative at the heart of it all because it made a difference in the lives of the children and their families". She kept in touch with these students. Speaking in 2014, she said: "Most of them, when they clear their Institute of Technical Education, they would give me a call and say, 'I am now 20-something, finished my army but now I am going to enrol for polytechnic.' It's the best joy when anyone can give you a call like that and say, 'I've earned enough, I can now go to polytechnic'."

Hours Under the Sun

Chew's belief in the transformative power of the arts was realised decades earlier by guitar maestro **Alex Abisheganaden**'s experience with school marching bands. Abisheganaden, known fondly as Singapore's "Father of the Guitar" and whose daughter is chanteuse Jacintha Abisheganaden, recalled how he kept restless youths off the streets. "Today in Singapore, many young boys and girls get jobs in food outlets such as McDonald's and KFC after they finish school. But in the 1960s, getting such jobs was not easy."

At the time, he got the go-ahead from the Ministry of Education (MOE) to form brass bands in schools. "In 1965, the directive from the Cabinet to MOE was to encourage the idea of marching bands." The person in charge of making it happen, he added, was Benjamin Ho, while he was director of school music programmes. Ho and Abisheganaden had their work cut out for them because there were very few school marching bands in Singapore at the time. Anglo-Chinese School had one, so too St Joseph's Institution and St Patrick's School.

So Abisheganaden welcomed everyone to join their school band – never mind whether or not they could read music. "We took in anybody, anyone up to the age of 30. We held classes right up till 10 pm."

Their end in mind? To compete with other schools at the Singapore Youth Festival (SYF) – and to take part in the National Day Parade, which in some years went past Orchard Road. Abisheganaden marvelled: "There would be a Chinese orchestra trying to

This schoolboy was among the 12 primary and secondary school bands taking part in the mass band display at the 1972 Singapore Youth Festival at Jalan Besar Stadium. The yearly festival, aimed at developing students' interest in the arts, kicked off in 1967 and Alex Abisheganaden recalled how these schoolchildren would rehearse for long hours under the hot afternoon sun to make their parents, teachers and friends proud.

"Father of the Guitar" and a leading figure in Singapore's music scene Alex Abisheganaden teaching a young boy how to play the guitar (undated).

play Malay music and Indians would dance to Chinese music. There was this kind of appreciation for inter-racial culture and all the performances were in a big SYF show at the National Stadium, in nightly performances for a week every year."

The Cabinet had likely asked that schools form marching bands for the rigour and focus that these instilled in youths. "You had to practise hours and hours in the sun," said Abisheganaden. "Hours out in the open field, marching up and down, doing all kinds of formations while playing musical pieces. Come National Day, every school had terrific pride in hearing their own school band playing."

Most movingly, he mused: "This school band thing started with teachers who were not really that musically talented, but they captured the vision and the programme really succeeded. Today, it is difficult to think of a school without its own band. I feel this is a wonderful tradition, the pride of the country when you see them on National Day."

Grace and Discipline

Singapore's deeply pragmatic society ranked the arts so low on its list of priorities that many traditional performances were, for many years, in danger of vanishing forever. Choreographer

Som Mohamed Said, who won the Cultural Medallion in 1987, said of her arts-loving Malay-Muslim community: "There are other priorities. Family is one, and there's TV to watch. Then there are the religious classes to attend, then many other things. So many arts forms, including dance, are dying." There were, in fact, so few traditional arts troupes that each did not think of the others as rivals. Besides Sriwana, which was hers, the notable names in classical Malay performances included Perkumpulan Seni and Kemuning.

The lively *ronggeng*, an old Javanese social dance, was popular even among non-Malays in the 20th century, but Malay-Muslims frowned on it because it was a feature of amusement parks. Revellers, who included Alex Abisheganaden, would buy coupons to exchange for turns on the floor with "taxi dancers", as the *ronggeng* women were called. It may have been good, clean fun but to Som, these *perempuan joget* (Malay for "dancing women") were "not a good history in the Malay community, actually".

Som added that it has taken contemporary Malay artists decades to "change the mindset that dance is not just for entertainment" but also a "deepening of grace and discipline" for those who dance.

Singapore's traditional Malay dance doyenne Som Mohd Said, seen here receiving the National Youth Service Award in 1979. The founder of the Sri Warisan dance troupe was awarded the nation's top arts honour, the Cultural Medallion, in 1987 and was inducted into the Singapore Women's Hall of Fame in 2014.

Being an artist, however, is not for the faint-hearted. However talented artists may be, they must wait, often years, before audiences grow to appreciate and support them. Such patience, however, does not pay the bills.

Her hope was that schools would nurture a love of the arts in their students. To that end, she and her fellow artists have been giving lots of talks regularly to students in schools all over Singapore. Som said: "We are trying to educate them to be natural arts lovers, who will automatically in future watch all these art forms. Because, at the moment, it's a sad thing." If nothing else, she added, dance could keep youths from straying into harm's way such as drug-taking. "They simply need a place to exert their energy," she said. "They need to engage their energy in the right direction."

Many who are gifted in the performing arts such as theatre, dance and singing will, of course, be content only when they pursue their calling. Being an artist, however, is not for the faint-hearted. However talented artists may be, they must wait, often years, before audiences grow to appreciate and support them. Such patience, however, does not pay the bills. And so in a market as small as Singapore's, most performing artists have to take on day jobs as teachers, reporters, lawyers, civil servants – or run a business.

Thirunalan Sasitharan was a promising actor when he joined a local newspaper as a journalist. Due to the demands of his work, he had to postpone a rehearsal for a play directed by theatre doyen Kuo Pao Kun. Sasitharan thought it all right to reschedule his rehearsal with Kuo – he would, after all, be missing only a single session.

"When I went in for the next rehearsal, there wasn't a rehearsal," Sasitharan recalled. "Kuo just sat down and spoke to me about what it was to be committed to the work. He said, 'You are now working full-time but that doesn't mean that you play rough and not take rehearsals seriously because you have work. Because this play is also work'." Sasitharan felt "completely terrible" and from then on, did not miss any more sessions with Kuo.

Being with Kuo, a titan of drama in Singapore, was an education in itself. Since Kuo's passing from cancer in 2002, Sasitharan has continued Kuo's legacy through the latter's company, the Theatre Practice and its Practice Performing Arts School. He likened directors to marksmen and had this to say about his mentor: "Pao Kun was a sniper. He wanted to hit the target with every shot. He knew exactly where the target was. Your job as the actor was to get the bullet to the target and he wanted you to do what you needed to do to do that."

"Other directors," he noted, "are machine-gunners, so they will shoot a number of bullets near the target. Some of the bullets would hit it, and some would miss. They would give you some latitude. But with Pao Kun, it always had to be a hit."

Worse yet, Sasitharan said, Kuo would not at any time indicate whether or not the actor had hit the target, as it were. This pushed an actor to breaking point, "until you would know that you had done it".

Guts for Glory

There were, and still are, few homegrown artists who can thrive on the arts alone. Actress **Nora Anny Samosir** said that Lok Meng Chue, a pioneering Singaporean in English-language theatre, was probably the first to quit full-time employment for acting in the 1980s. It took Lok lots of guts to do so then as there were few jobs to be had in a country which went through a huge recession in 1985. Lok got by acting in various productions for TheatreWorks, which was founded in 1985, as well as helping out in its front-of-house needs.

Samosir herself was then dabbling in acting while teaching at Nanyang Junior College. "I was getting flak from my principal about not being focused and all that sort of thing – he was doubting my commitment to the school. So my Head of Department said I should direct a play for the school to give back, share my talent with not just TheatreWorks."

So, in August 1986, she prepared her students to put on the musical *Heartbreak Hotel.* As part of rehearsals, she had them doing acting exercises to loosen up and get into character easier. At first, they protested. "They said, 'Why are we doing these silly exercises, these silly games?'" she recalled. They piped down only after she explained that the best actors did those exercises religiously.

Samosir's desultory students were the norm in the first 30 years of independent Singapore; there was little government support and performing arts were regarded as very

Seasoned actress Nora Anny Samosir (far right) is pensive here in a scene from her 1991 performance in the play *Trojan Women* by TheatreWorks.

Robert Iau Kuo Kwong (centre), with Acting Minister for Culture Ong Teng Cheong and his son Tze Guan, meeting Yoshinao Osawa, the conductor of the Singapore Philharmonic, during the orchestra's concert at the Singapore Conference Hall in 1977.

low on the agenda. Not surprisingly, those gifted in the performing arts were, for many years, denigrated if they followed their hearts. What a world away that was from today; at the time of writing, the arts-focused School of the Arts was celebrating its 10th anniversary. Its founding principal was Rebecca Chew, who had inspired Naval Base's wayward students.

The Singapore Symphony Orchestra (SSO), founded by Deputy Prime Minister Goh Keng Swee in 1977, has global acclaim today, and has performed with such superstars as pianists Lang Lang and Martha Argerich, and violinist Igor Yuzefovich. But few in Singapore today know that there was another symphonic orchestra that preceded it.

In the 1970s, **Robert Iau Kuo Kwong** gathered some leading lights in Singapore's media and legal professions to start a symphony orchestra of amateurs. Iau, himself a musician, knew Yoshinao Osawa, who conducted the Tokyo Chamber Orchestra, one of Japan's top ensembles. With Osawa, he set up the Singapore Philharmonic, or what he called "a scratch orchestra" of 70 amateurs. Among them was violinist Pamela Tan, whose daughter Vanessa-Mae Vanakorn Nicholson also became a violinist and sold several million albums, becoming the wealthiest British entertainer under the age of 30 in 2006.

Iau, who was awarded the Public Service Medal in 1988 for his contributions to the arts in Singapore, recalled that the Singapore Philharmonic was "supported strongly" by the banks and commercial houses in Singapore. This was so even though the Osawa-backed orchestra was a throwback to the Syonan Kokkaido Orchestra, conducted by one Watanabe, during the Japanese Occupation of Singapore. Incidentally, the wartime ensemble had at least one local musician – Abisheganaden's brother Paul, a violinist, who was later very supportive of local composer Zubir Bin Said in Zubir's efforts to shape "Majulah Singapura", the national anthem.

The Singapore Philharmonic held about five concerts yearly and, in a first for Singapore then, would announce upcoming concerts right after they had finished each performance. Iau said: "The Japanese section leaders couldn't speak a word of English and our local chaps couldn't speak a word of Japanese. And yet it was one of the most moving things to see when they got down to working together through a piece of Tchaikovsky, Beethoven or a Mozart sonata. All of a sudden, you realised that language was no barrier, that all communicated in a totally new language, a universal language."

Getting the Show on the Road

Dr Uma Rajan said that the Ministry of Culture, which oversaw the performing arts from the 1960s till the 1980s, relied on radio programmes and road shows to bring arts to the people. The Aneka Ragam Rakyat (Malay for "Varied Rhythms of the People") community concerts were especially popular. Rajan used to sing film songs and perform traditional dances then. Through such road shows, the government tried to bring Singapore's diverse communities closer. Robert Iau, a polymath, was a founding member of the National Theatre Trust when it was set up on 1 April 1982 to replace the Aneka Ragam Rakyat. He said: "Aneka Ragam was an early series of public concerts with multi-racial performances to reinforce Singapore's multi-ethnic culture." In format and spirit, Aneka Ragam mirrored the SYF.

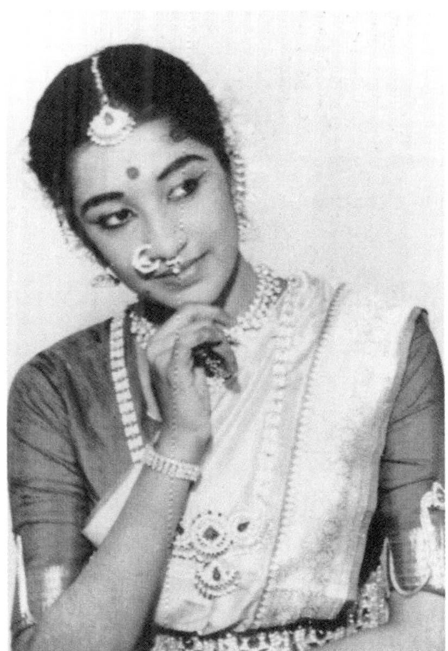

Dr Uma Rajan, a school health doctor, was also an accomplished classical dancer. She advised the National Arts Council for some years and led the first Festival of Asian Performing Arts.

Indeed, Rajan pointed out, the government had "always made a conscious move" towards ensuring that Singapore's different ethnic groups were represented in government-supported arts performances. The People's Association has been a particular champion of this; as recently as 2017, they invited even the tiny Nepalese community in Singapore to take part in the yearly Chingay parade.

Rajan, a medical doctor and retired Indian classical dancer, thought one good way to be authentically Asian was to allow the young to innovate ancient art forms. "I feel innovation keeps the tradition alive. For *bharatanatyam* (a genre of Indian classical dance), you have to allow students to innovate. If we keep the links with our grandparents, the family relationships will not die."

Appealing to as wide an audience as possible also made sound business sense, noted Rajan. Given Singapore's small market for everything in general, she said: "You have to be cross-cultural to reach audiences in the other ethnic groups; to be more visible you need an art form that is appreciated not just by one community, but also by other ethnic groups, that raises your profile further."

When the National Theatre Trust took over the role of Aneka Ragam, Robert Iau changed its programming somewhat, bringing in various performance troupes from mainland China. These included Hainanese, Teochew and Cantonese opera singers. He managed to do so despite the then prevalent political sensitivities about Singapore befriending a communist country. "By the 1980s," he said, "street operas in Singapore had begun disappearing... and the Chinese shows were quite an eye-opener." These foreign acts performed at the open-air National Theatre, which was then the only big arts stage in town. It could seat up to 3,500 people, but had no air-conditioning, which proved most uncomfortable given the sultry Singapore climate.

Iau said Britain's ballet troupe Sadler's Wells, for one, liked the venue. "They were all praises for the dimensions of the stage, which was about 100 feet wide and 70 feet deep. It gave them an enormous amount of room to move around and express themselves vigorously."

Where Have All the Playwrights Gone?

Artists pride themselves on pushing boundaries for fresh insights on humanity. But considering how difficult it was to shape Singapore as a nation, the government had little time for alternative views of how things could be. In the 1980s, playwright and educator **Robert Yeo Cheng Chuan** learnt just how chary the government was about this when, in the 1980s, he tried to stage his play, *One Year Back Home*.

Written in 1977, the play had a character named Fernandez who, he said, "stands up and makes clever speeches and criticises the People's Action Party and, in the end, he's arrested for his so-called Marxist affiliations". The government, through its Public Entertainment Licence Unit (PELU), took one-and-a-half years to approve its performance. PELU itself was born out of a need for the government to rein in mass public assemblies which, in the 1960s, sometimes set off riots.

Pioneering Singaporean playwright Robert Yeo Cheng Chuan is a longtime cultural critic and from 1977 till 1994, he chaired the government's Drama Advisory Committee and Drama Review Committee.

In 1980, *One Year Back Home* was finally staged by the Experimental Theatre Club. That inspired a commentary in the *New Nation* newspaper with the headline "We need more local plays". In it, its writer considered that the play's "success showed there was a market for homegrown drama. Yet there are few local plays and even fewer playwrights." The writer noted further that Yeo "had difficulty" in finding backers for his play. "One was scared. Another disdained local playwrights," went the commentary.

Decades later, with the maturing of Singapore's political landscape, Yeo did see his play performed by at least two other theatre groups, TheatreWorks and Arts and Acts, with funds from, among others, the National University of Singapore Society.

It must be said, however, that Yeo was not rapped for his political views. In fact, from 1977 till 1994, the government had him chair two arts advisory panels, the Drama Advisory Committee and the Drama Review Committee. Yeo, a former Fulbright Scholar and alumnus of the University of Iowa's prestigious international writing programme, said: "In 1974 or 1975, I was writing this cultural column for the *New Nation* called Saturday with Robert Yeo. I suppose the people at the Ministry of Culture might have taken note of that and said, 'This guy is opening his big mouth every three or four months in the *New Nation*. Let's give him something to do and see what he makes of it'." The two committees were disbanded after 1994, but in recognition of his services to English-language theatre in Singapore, Yeo received the Public Service Medal in 1991.

Yet, the gingerly attitude of PELU persisted throughout much of the 1990s. **Dr Robert Liew**, an impresario who did much to bring top Western performance artists to Singapore, recalled how he struggled to organise the inaugural Singapore International Comedy Festival in 1998. "The scripts had to be vetted, which was hard because comedy is meant to be spontaneous and improvised."

One of the most spontaneous and successful plays in Singapore's theatre history, *Emily of Emerald Hill*, won its creator **Stella Kon née Lim Sing Po** the 1983 National Playwriting Competition. Curiously, this heart-wrenching one-woman play about a Peranakan matriarch was first performed in Kuala Lumpur by Malaysian actress Leow Puay Tin in 1984. It was only a year later that Singaporean actress Margaret Chan made the role her own. Emily was so uniquely Singaporean that Britain invited Kon and Chan to stage the play at its Commonwealth Arts Festival as well as the prestigious Edinburgh Fringe Festival in 1986.

Actress Margaret Chan, seen here with President and Mrs Wee Kim Wee and her son Jonathan, was among the very first to bring Stella Kon's *Emily of Emerald Hill* to life. They are seen here at the very first opening night of the play at the Jubilee Theatre in Raffles Hotel.

> One of the most spontaneous and successful plays in Singapore's theatre history, *Emily of Emerald Hill*, won its creator Stella Kon the 1983 National Playwriting Competition.

Kon, a great-granddaughter of Dr Lim Boon Keng, a prominent figure in Singapore society in the early 20th century, remembered how the British received her play: "The Commonwealth Arts Festival was an assemblage of literarily sophisticated people from many cultures who were perfectly adaptable to reading Chinua Achebe and were very open to other cultures... They were perfectly willing to absorb the exotic parts and go to the heart of the story. That was not a problem at all."

In her oral history interview in 2006, Kon let on that she moulded facets of Emily on her own mother, who studied acting at London's vaunted Royal Academy of Dramatic Art (RADA). "My mother acted in a play called *I Remember Mama* when she was at RADA. The play was about a Swedish mama; imagine my dear Chinese mother trying to do a Swedish accent. But now that I come to think of it... that was the prototype of an ethnic character like Emily."

She added: "There was a scene when the Swedish mama told you how to make meatballs, that you must use stock in the meat, 'not vater' as how the Swedish pronounce 'water'.

Those words were the prototype for some of Emily's recipe-giving which was not just about imparting information but a big revelation about the ethnic roots and the meaningfulness of recipes in ethnic identity."

To date, Kon's *Emily* is one of Singapore's best-travelled plays, having been performed in 17 cities in seven countries on four continents, at the rate of 300 shows over 30 years. Among the most consummate actors to tackle the demanding role of tortured Emily Gan was Ivan Heng, founder of groundbreaking theatre company Wild Rice, which established a yearly week-long theatre festival that is a firm favourite on Singapore's arts calendar. Kon's success inspired her younger compatriots to dream just as big; other homegrown playwrights who have since made their mark include Alfian Sa'at, Jean Tay and Geoffrey Tan.

Are You There, Singapore?

Trying to use straitjackets on artists can seem like containing water in a colander. While dramatists in Singapore have painstakingly worked their way around the authorities' restrictions and reservations, they stayed true to what motivated them. At TheatreWorks, this meant working on socio-political issues or, as its managing director **Tay Tong** put it, "what it is about us being here".

TheatreWorks, the nation's first homegrown professional arts company, was co-founded in 1985 by film school graduate Lim Siauw Chong – who was also its first artistic director – journalist Lim Kay Tong and architect Justin Hill. To date, it is Singapore's most widely travelled company, having staged more than 2,500 productions abroad.

In 1988, lawyer Ong Keng Sen, who is Tay's childhood friend, joined the company and is now its artistic director. He explores facets of being human through such thought-provoking productions as *Descendants of the Eunuch Admiral, The Lady of Soul and Her Ultimate 'S' Machine*, and *Six of the Best.*

To TheatreWorks, art, like charity, begins at home. Speaking on the 25th anniversary of his company in 2010, Tay mused: "When we were founded in 1985, there was a dearth of Singapore writing. The company was very interested in locating the Singapore voice, a Singapore identity on stage. Up to that point, a lot of works in drama we saw on stage were adaptations of American, British, Russian or even Japanese and mainland Chinese writings. But none were really about Singapore."

So, he added, one of TheatreWorks' earliest missions was to nurture Singapore playwrights. Between 1987 and 1996, the company devoted much of its time, energy and money in its Writers' Lab, an incubator for budding playwrights, with quarterly readings of plays to build a following for their works.

Local theatregoers were soon appreciating original musicals such as *Army Daze* and *Beauty World*, both dreamt up by playwright Michael Chiang. They found that such local content resonated with them.

By 2009, TheatreWorks was taking Writers' Lab into the wider community, beginning with the Southeast district.

Actor and raconteur Hossan Leong hams it up in a staging of Michael Chiang's musical *Beauty World* for the President's Star Charity show in 1998.

As local and international interest in the stories of Asia grew, TheatreWorks gravitated towards another mission: documentary performance. An example of this was their collaboration with dancer and choreographer Goh Lay Kuan. Goh, the wife of Kuo Pao Kun, who had joined the Australian Ballet Company in Australia, returned to create many iconic dances for Singapore. "She was a major force in dance in Singapore," said Tay.

The play based on her life was titled, simply, *Goh Lay Kuan & Kuo Pao Kun*, and debuted to sold-out houses in April 2010 as a work in progress and, in 2012, was presented as a fully fleshed-out production. Before the telling of Goh and Kuo's lives through a drama, TheatreWorks had done something similar with Cambodian court dancer Em Theay, who suffered under the Pol Pot regime. This production, titled *Beyond the Killing Fields*, has been staged in Berlin, London, Lyon and many other global cities since.

Artists Need to be Loved

The biggest shot in the arm by far for artists in Singapore was when then Minister for Culture Ong Teng Cheong introduced the Cultural Medallion award in 1979. Ong was himself a consummate musician who, as President of Singapore, once conducted the Singapore Symphony Orchestra (SSO) in 1993.

The inaugural medallion recipients were the SSO's founding conductor Choo Hoey, poet Edwin Thumboo, dancer Madhavi Krishnan, musician David Lim Kim San, dramatist Bani Buang and painter Wee Beng Chong.

Their award was really from the people, said **Chia Wai Hon**, who was a Cultural Medallion judge for many years. The selection process was "very democratic", he stressed, because the artists were chosen by Singaporeans in the street. "The public nominates the artists and submits its nominations. Anyone can nominate an artist." After the National Arts Council has vetted the nominations and pared them down to the finalists, Chia and his fellow judges would deliberate on each nominee's merits. "There was a lot of arguing," he recalled with mirth. "There was a lot of work involved." Since 1979, the Cultural Medallion has been conferred on 125 artists.

Robert Iau recalled the Singapore performing arts scene in the 1970s and 1980s as "unstructured" and "a little cluttered" from a distinct separation between the various art forms and genres within each art form. For example, the best-followed Malay performance art then was drama, via the television programme *Sandiwara*, which ran for 20 years. "It was a very powerful thrust in Malay drama," he recalled.

Then, in 1991, there was an even bigger change – in place of the Ministry of Culture, there would now be a National Arts Council (NAC). "It was a clear endorsement from the government to have artists as a major component of Singaporean life," said Uma Rajan.

The government entrusted the formation of the NAC to **Professor Tommy Koh Thong Bee**, a law don and uber-diplomat. In 1971, Koh had written a letter to the *New Nation* newspaper, lamenting the dearth then of ballets, operas and other performing arts shows

Among those at this picnic in Fort Canning Park to usher in the 1999 Singapore Arts Festival are three movers and shakers of the Singapore arts scene, Ambassador-at-Large and National Arts Council (NAC) founding Chairman Professor Tommy Koh (left); then Minister for Information and the Arts George Yeo Yong Boon (to the right of Koh), and architect and then NAC Chairman, Liu Thai Ker (extreme right).

in Singapore. He never let up on his conviction that the nation should, and could, be more culturally vibrant.

By 1988, Singapore had bounced back from a debilitating recession in 1985, and the government even threw everyone a street party. Known as Swing Singapore, it drew half a million revellers on New Year's Eve. It was around that time that Koh saw a need for the NAC, to help a thousand flowers bloom in a country that was then a cultural desert. "I felt Singapore had arrived at the point in its overall development where the bread-and-butter issues had basically been solved. We have a well-educated young generation who are more culture-loving than their predecessors and that the time was very ripe for us to do something."

In setting up the NAC from 1991, Koh said he saw himself as a "bridge between the government and the artistic community". So he made it a point to have dialogues with local artists every month. He also attended art shows and exhibitions every chance he got. "I used to drag my wife to every performance and exhibition until she got angry with me," he recalled. "Because I told her that artists not only need financial support but they also need to be loved. Because they lead… very often a life of sacrifice.

"They needed to be loved and I needed to be there to show them respect and love." He also helped them fund their performances by introducing them to prospective corporate sponsors. Koh's overall vision was "Singapore as being culturally a natural meeting place between the Malay, Chinese, Indian and Western civilisations".

To that end, he launched the Festival of Asian Performing Arts in 1993. It was a hit. "The first year, we sold 60 percent of all tickets, the second year 70 percent and the third year 80 percent," he said. In 1999, to better streamline arts offerings, NAC merged that festival with the Festival of the Arts to form the Singapore Arts Festival (SAF). But Koh was glad to note that SAF's programme directors continued to ensure that at least half of all shows it put up had Asian flavours. As Rajan put it: "The main thing is that the Asian concept should not be lost. We don't want to be another Edinburgh or Adelaide," referring to two renowned global arts festivals.

The SAF had a precursor of the same name in 1977, but the only dramas performed at the earlier festival were in Chinese, not English, said long-time arts administrator **Liew Chin Choy**, a former Vice-President of the Nanyang Academy of Fine Arts.

Rajan pointed out that, slowly but surely, the idea of Singapore as a cultural hub blossomed. "People started to mark the SAF on their calendars. And artists started enquiring about SAF and how they could contribute to it," she noted.

It took some time for Singapore's civil servants to become comfortable working with artists who were, by nature, expressive, often assertive and sometimes downright mercurial. Koh said that, as Chairman of NAC, his biggest challenge, besides fund-raising, was "to break the old mindset of the bureaucrats and to say working with artists calls for a completely different mindset from other areas of the Civil Service, that you cannot manage artists the way you can manage other citizens." He exhorted them to be more open-minded, creative and "not so focused on just rules, rules, rules that you lose sight of what you are trying to do".

Esplanade – Theatres on the Bay under construction in 2000. Some say it resembles a durian, others say it reminds them of a giant microphone. To all, it is Singapore's premier arts centre, which opened with much fanfare on 12 October 2002 and has been a crowd-pleaser ever since.

Artists, he added, used to tell him: "We like you very much but we don't like your staff." Koh urged them to consider the big picture. "Listen," he told the artists, "it's necessary to have a bureaucracy because you need an administration. If the rules are not good, we will fix it. But to argue that we don't need rules is wrong, you know?"

> To work with professionals, you have to connect with them as professionals and to work with artists, you have to respect them as artists.

Koh's unstinting efforts to develop local artists such that they could be on a par with the world's best had the media referring to him as "Renaissance Man" throughout the 1990s.

The strongest indication of recognition for the importance of the arts in Singapore came in 1994, when plans for an arts centre for Singapore were set in motion.

Around that time, Ong Teng Cheong, who was then President of Singapore, visited vaunted auditoriums around the world with **George Yeo Yong Boon**, Minister for Information and the Arts from 1990 till 1999. Yeo recalled: "When we were planning the Esplanade, I went with Ong Teng Cheong on a tour of arts centres around the world. We were looking at halls such as The Barbican in London, in Birmingham, the Paris Opera House and possibly La Scala in Milan. Ong had an eye for buildings, and I learnt from him." In particular, Yeo said, he liked how Ong, an architect, respected greatly the individuality of his fellow architects. At the time, Ong chaired the steering committee to create Esplanade – Theatres on the Bay. But after he became President of Singapore in 1993, Yeo took over the reins, although Ong continued to keep close tabs on the project.

"He left the gory details to me," Yeo said, "but on the big things, he would state his views. And when architects made presentations, many among us on the committee would instinctively want to talk about details but he would just make his points and leave it to the architects to work out the expressions." As Yeo put it, Ong taught him that while those managing a project could state their objectives and air their views to those executing their vision, "in the end, the totality of the work must be organic and emanate from within the architect".

"That impressed me – that to work with professionals, you have to connect with them as professionals and to work with artists, you have to respect them as artists."

To that end, Ong, Yeo and Iau also sought the views of artists from China, India, Indonesia, Japan and Thailand to ensure that the arts centre could accommodate Eastern art forms such as percussion traditions.

Everyone on the project took great pains to make the centre "fit for purpose", Yeo said, and that meant making sure designs were friendly to the disabled and infirm. "We wanted it to be something which would stand out internationally; we knew we had only one shot – you can't rebuild the Esplanade. So the responsibility to get it right was quite heavy."

Iau, who was heavily involved in planning the arts centre, recalled advising the steering committee: "If we're going to do something in Singapore for Singaporeans, attempting to repeat or copy in any way an existing icon would be the worst disservice that we could do for Singaporeans.

"So we had to find our own way and our own concept."

He also suggested that the new arts centre should be easily accessible via the MRT. "At that time," he said, "the MRT was kicking off in a very big way and the arts centre needed to generate traffic because it had to have its own resources."

It helped that the site for the Esplanade sat within Singapore's leafy Civic District, flanked by the Padang, Victoria Concert Hall, what is now the National Gallery Singapore and the belt of national museums.

Making Passion Possible

When the new millennium dawned in 2000, more money rolled in for the arts in Singapore, said Uma Rajan, who used to be part of the NAC. The spike in funds came from greater confidence among the artists themselves as they staged performances that were sometimes on a par with the world's best. That, in turn, enabled the NAC to dream bigger; it began marketing Singapore artists and their works to regional, and then international, markets. A case in point was the Esplanade-initiated Mosaic, a yearly jazz and soul festival that, in time, hosted legends such as Pat Metheny, Youssou N'Dour and the late Shirley Horn.

"The only question I posed to artists was if they made sure that the money that came went towards the artists much more than all the frills," she said. By frills, Rajan meant costly technical set-ups such as sound systems. She stressed: "You have to make sure that the artist got a fair share of the dollars and cents."

Robert Iau said that after more than 30 years of progress, the average Singaporean began warming to the arts because they were "looking for a better quality of life and opportunities for self-expression and the opportunity to leave something behind which may not be related entirely to material things".

The growing awareness of artists in Singapore dovetailed nicely with the momentous opening of the Esplanade on 12 October 2002, to much fanfare and fireworks.

George Yeo mused: "Now, when you go there in the evenings and see how happy people there are, soaking in the ambience and enjoying the sea breeze... this is the work of generations."

To hear Tay Tong of TheatreWorks tell it, the success of homegrown artists is a happy problem. "The quantum of support for the arts has increased. However, costs have also increased and at the same time, there are more players in the scene. So although there's a bigger pie, there are more people fighting for the larger pie. So, percentage-wise, I think that kind of remains the same.

"I also find it not very interesting to talk about a lack of resources," he added. "I think what is more interesting is to talk about how you create from limited resources that you have, and how you create."

Struggling against constraints, he thinks, gives what an artist creates more impact. Artists could, of course, try for corporate sponsors but Tay thought that, too, was constraining. "Corporate sponsorship is from the marketing budget. So if you have a product that suits the marketing campaign, that brings in a certain audience profile, you will get the corporate dollar." The rub, he pointed out, was choosing that route meant having to cajole, perhaps even pander to, potential sponsors.

All told, Tay said Singaporean artists should aim for audiences beyond the nation's shores, lest they risk being "a little myopic" and wind up "limiting" themselves. "You need a passion for the arts... and the feeling that you can make an impact or difference."

CHAPTER ELEVEN

SPORTS
Game, Set and Match

Few fans are as uproarious as soccer supporters. Raucous punters in the stands have been known to hurl whistles, water bottles and whatnots at the pitch whenever a game is not going their team's way.

So it was that an *epok-epok* (Malay for curry puff) went whizzing across Johor's Larkin stadium – just as Singapore's soccer captain **Dollah Kassim** was about to let fly a crucial kick towards goal during a Malaysia Cup match in the 1970s.

Then *thwack*! – but the sound was not of his boot hitting the ball. Dollah recalled: "I was hit by an *epok-epok* in my face when I wanted to take a corner.

"I broke the *epok-epok* in two, bit into one half and threw the rest down… it was so painful."

Imagine how loud the people of Singapore roared when the nation won the Malaysia Cup for the first time as an independent nation in 1977, defeating Penang 3-2.

Yet, being a sportsman to the last, Dollah brushed that off. "I was not angry," he said. "This is part and parcel of the game." The Singapore team lost to Johor that night and, he recalled, "we got scolding from A to Z. We just lived with it."

Dollah was likely sanguine about such dressings-down because he knew that his countrymen backed his squad to the hilt. "What I really treasured," he said of his years in football, "was the atmosphere." He was referring to the legendary Kallang Roar, or the thunderous Singaporean cheers that reverberate throughout sporting arenas whenever Singapore scores against its rivals. "Our Singaporeans, I love them," he added. "The way they shout, support us, so patriotic. That kind of Singapore feeling."

So imagine how loud the people of Singapore roared when the nation won the Malaysia Cup for the first time as an independent nation in 1977, defeating Penang 3-2. He said: "We were so happy we won for them. And they came down to see us, shaking our hands non-stop. Everybody wanted to be a part of us, that's what made me so happy."

His then fiancé (now wife) who lived in Toa Payoh before they wed, told him that her "whole HDB block was shouting with joy" when it had been "so quiet" earlier that night. "The whole of Singapore was behind us," he recalled. "It was really a good sign."

Singapore's national team vying for the 1990 Malaysia Cup in this match against Perlis, which triggered the first Kallang Wave from Singapore fans. Such good cheer was a far cry from the 1970s, when Singapore's then captain Dollah Kassim was hit in the face by a curry puff hurled by an onlooker just as he was about to take a corner kick.

The win bode well indeed for the then 12-year-old nation of many races who were, for the most part, getting on well as they built their future.

But, as you read of artists in the preceding chapter, those who pursued sports as a calling in Singapore were frowned upon for many years. The ever-pragmatic founding Prime Minister Lee Kuan Yew, whose views held much sway, strongly dissuaded Singaporeans from pursuing a career in athletics.

With little encouragement from the government at first, the development of sports in Singapore limped on from the 1960s till the early 1990s, without much direction and purpose. As Prime Minister Lee famously said when he opened the original National Stadium at Kallang in 1973, Singaporeans should "not waste time going especially out of our way to produce gold medallists, whether for (the) Olympic Games, Asian or Southeast Asian Peninsular (SEAP) Games".

To the credit of Singapore's sports community, the athletes continued giving their all whenever they represented the nation at home and abroad. At the 1993 Southeast Asian (SEA) Games in Singapore, for example, swimmer Joscelin Yeo alone contributed nine of the nation's 50 gold medals. In fact, Singapore clinched its best SEA Games medal haul ever – 164 in total – at that meet. According to retired army colonel **Kwan Yue Yeong**, this accomplishment led the government to have a change of heart towards sports.

Kwan, a former Executive Director of the Singapore Sports Council (known as Sport Singapore since 2014), said that "the government had plans to develop and promote sports

The Singapore sports scene has become more vibrant in recent years. Today, the world's largest sports dome, which cost a cool $1.6 billion, encompasses the new National Stadium at the Singapore Sports Hub in Kallang.

in Singapore especially after the success of the 1993 SEA Games". Founding premier Lee, in fact, personally drove Singapore's bid to host the inaugural Youth Olympic Games in 2010. With Singapore a thriving global city by then, Lee saw that such a prestigious event could do much to bolster the nation's reputation internationally – which, as it turned out, it did.

The Singapore sports scene has become more vibrant in recent years. Today, the world's largest sports dome, which cost a cool $1.6 billion, encompasses the new National Stadium at the Singapore Sports Hub in Kallang. Singaporean billionaire Peter Lim owns stakes in Spanish football club Valencia FC and English football club Salford City. Global household names such as Cristiano Ronaldo, Lionel Messi and David Beckham have conducted football clinics for Singaporeans. And, of course, at the Summer Olympic Games in 2016, swimmer Joseph Schooling won Singapore's first Olympic gold in the men's 100m butterfly, beating his American idol, Michael Phelps.

A Nightmare on the Psyche

Singapore had won the Malaysia Cup once before its 1977 triumph – when the tournament was still known as the Malaya Cup – on 1 August 1965, eight days before Independence. Strikers Quah Kim Swee, part of the famous Quah family of footballers, and Majid Ariff thrashed traditional champions Selangor 3-1. It was the sweetest birthday present for a newborn nation that would later produce Fandi Ahmad, the first Singaporean to play for a European football club and who, consequently, became Singapore's first millionaire sportsperson.

It helped that Dollah Kassim and his mates were coached by the shrewd game technician Choo Seng Quee, known fondly as Uncle Choo. "He read our opponents well," Dollah said. "He made us learn their weaknesses. There are not many coaches who can do that. I am glad he was around when I was playing."

That was so even though Choo could be an exacting taskmaster – and somewhat of an eccentric to boot. He had a long list of "No's" before any match: no cold or fizzy drinks. No haircuts. And, most of all, no disturbing him before kick-off.

Tough love was the lot of many among Singapore's champion swimmers too. They included the nation's Golden Girl **Patricia Chan Li-Yin**, whose coach was her formidable father, Dr Chan Ah Kow. She recalled: "He would peg a mark for you to beat and you went for it. And you would do whatever was necessary to beat that mark because you have become aware, as a young person, that you are only as good as your last performance." It was, she said, "a nightmare on the psyche when you wanted to sit down and just relax; that becomes very difficult."

Singapore's former national football team captain Dollah Kassim (right) warming up with Quah Kim Lye (left). Quah is one of the four famous Quah brothers, who include Quah "Mercurial Speed Demon" Kim Song.

Singapore's Golden Girl Patricia Chan Li-Yin (left) and sprinter C. Kunalan (right) were two among Singapore's brightest sports stars in the 1960s and 1970s. Here they are at the Istana in 1970, with their trophies for being Singapore's Sportswoman and Sportsman of 1969.

Woe betide if she slackened off in the pool. Dr Chan, who in his younger days had been a hurdler known as "The Fiery Flying Hams" for his bulging thighs, would, she recalled, "yank me physically out of the pool, slap me until I would fall back into the water. And then you get going." But, she stressed, "he wouldn't do that to another child". Dr Chan lived till the ripe age of 84, having coached his daughter to 39 gold medals at the SEAP Games between 1965 and 1973.

Chan's successors – Junie Sng Poh Leng and Joscelin Yeo among them – had no less stick from their coach, former national water polo player **Kee Soon Bee**.

Oon Jin Teik, former Chief Executive of the Singapore Sports Hub and Chief Executive of the Singapore Sports Council from 2004 till 2010, recalled training under the late Kee: "I don't remember him missing a single training session. He always had four things with him – sunglasses, a stopwatch, a loudhailer and a stick about eight feet long." Oon said Kee used the stick to prod his trainees' limbs to correct their swimming technique, but they came to see it as a "cane", a reminder of how strict a disciplinarian he was. He was also a stickler for "clocking mileage", making them swim more laps than what other coaches demanded.

Oon recalled that every session at Toa Payoh Swimming Complex began at 5.30 am. One had to wonder what residents near the pool made of Kee, shouting instructions through his loudhailer at that unholy hour. It did not help that Oon was clad in polyester swimming trunks – sewn by his mother. "If I say it was curtain-like material, I am not exaggerating," he averred.

The no-nonsense national swimming coach Kee Soon Bee (seated, third from left in a suit) is seen here with Singapore's water polo team which represented Singapore in the 1956 Olympic Games in Australia.

Oon Jin Teik, former Chief Executive of the Singapore Sports Hub and former Chief Executive of the Singapore Sports Council, was a national swimmer in his salad days. He recalled his mother sewing swimming trunks for him out of "curtain-like material".

He said Kee would frequently select two or three promising swimmers to stay over at his home on weekends. "His wife would cook," Oon recalled. "And he would literally brainwash us with a very positive view of the critical success of being an elite swimmer."

In his interview with the Oral History Centre in March 1998, Kee gave insights about his "brainwashing": "I would lecture my trainees in this way: there is a lion that sees a zebra from afar. He starts going for it at 60 miles an hour. But he loses his energy and the zebra escapes. And the lion now has its tail between its legs. Then a wild dog chases and chases and chases the zebra until the zebra collapses. So the wild dog ends up eating the zebra."

Kee mused: "Junie Sng said, 'I want to be the wild dog.' So that's why she went for distance swimming. She was a very intelligent girl." At 11, Sng first represented Singapore at the 8th SEAP Games in 1975 – and clinched a gold medal in the 800m freestyle. "She frightened everybody," Kee recalled. Sng went on to wow Singaporeans anew, bagging two gold medals and one silver, at the 1978 Asian Games. He added: "No one had ever achieved two golds and one silver against Japan and China."

However stentorian Kee was, he actually cared more about his trainees' overall well-being than their sporting prowess. He said: "Any coach in any sport should not tell a fellow what to do. All the time, (the swimmer you are training) memorises all the strokes, thinking and rehearsing in his mind… and you are going to teach him a new learning situation? Absurd!"

Junie Sng's (centre) swimming coach Kee Soon Bee said she "frightened everybody" with her sheer prowess and laser-focused determination, which led to her bagging two golds and one silver medal at the 1979 Asian Games. No Southeast Asian had achieved that before her. She capped her career with a total of 38 gold medals from the Southeast Asian Games.

He stressed: "If you change the system, you have lost the race." So he likened coaches who told their trainees what to do to "backseat drivers" whose "Hey, don't go there!" admonitions would "cause accidents".

In that 1998 interview, Kee also asserted: "Don't try to share your knowledge... like 'you must follow this, you must do that'... you are not the swimmer."

With the benefit of Kee's deep understanding of what made them want to swim their best, it was small wonder that Sng and Yeo triumphed beyond Singapore's wildest dreams. In all this, you might be surprised to learn that Kee made it a point not to accompany his charges to major sporting events. The reason, he said, was this: "I have confidence in my swimmers... Most of them don't like their own parents to follow them. Once they are alone, they feel free to do things. That's good."

Down but not Out

Former professional boxer **Lim Kee Chan** would agree. As a boy, Lim was skinny and "sickly looking" and was picked on by others larger than him. So he learnt boxing at the Katong Boy's Club because "I never liked bullies". He took a "hell of a beating" whenever he fought back.

His eldest brother, a medical student, baulked when Lim decided to leave school for good after 10 years of education. "He asked me if I could continue two more years of studies, learn a little bit of medicine and what-have-you because he was going to start his own practice, so he wanted me to help him." Lim said no. "In the end," he recalled, "like my father, he ended up having to accept it because I made a name for myself. And they were quite happy."

Lim started out as a boxer with a day job as an audit clerk at the now-defunct firm of Turquand, Youngs & Co., thanks to his eldest brother's recommendation. But Lim soon resigned when he realised that "for half an hour's appearance in the ring, I get $300 whereas I have to work three months to get the same amount of money".

Lim was a professional boxer for a total of five years, during which time he was invited to fight in places such as Manila, as well as against the world's fourth best fighter, Belgium's Pierre Cossemyns. Of the latter, he recalled: "None of the papers gave me a chance to last six rounds. Some said I would not last three rounds. But I lasted 10 rounds. And I had a swollen eye and a cut lip. I was badly beaten. But I lasted 10 rounds." The following day, his company doctor, who was himself a former boxer, looked at Lim's face and put him on three days' medical leave. "And when I went back to give it to my boss," Lim recalled, "he said, 'No, you can't take three days' MC'."

You might put down such an apparent lack of sympathy for a sportsman's plight to work-related issues or a boss's disdain for his subordinate. But how would you explain the lack of support from your own sporting fraternity? Bodybuilder and weightlifter **Harold De Castro**, who was Mr Singapore 1948, was floored by how lukewarm his fellow weightlifters' reception was to Tan Howe Liang winning Singapore's first Olympic medal at the 1960 Olympics in Rome.

Bodybuilder and weightlifter Harold De Castro, who was Mr Singapore 1948, was floored by how lukewarm his fellow weightlifters' reception was to Tan Howe Liang winning Singapore's first Olympic medal at the 1960 Olympics in Rome.

De Castro said they tended to make only "surface" remarks and did not like to speak about what they felt about anyone or anything. "When somebody wins a silver medal, we don't go around and pat him on the back and say, 'Hey, you did a good job!' We don't. So what? You got a silver medal, that's all."

De Castro trained with Tan for international meets and later had to forgo competing in his favourite lightweight category so that Tan could try his luck in it. To De Castro, their ostensibly physical exertions were all about mind, not body, control. De Castro said: "Weightlifting is more of the mind; in other words, you keep reminding yourself how good you must be and what you should lift... like hypnotising yourself."

And that, he added, was exactly how Tan achieved his Olympian feat. He lifted 155 kg, setting an Olympic record in the clean and jerk lightweight division. "Tan is what we call a crazy guy... he will just hypnotise himself and he will just go there and lift... he does not know how many pounds he is lifting... he is crazy, because he has no barrier, no limits. That's the reason why he can improve."

Champion weightlifter Tan Howe Liang (left) chats with Singapore's Yang di-Pertuan Negara Yusof Ishak at a tea party which Mr Yusof held in his honour at the Istana. This was after Tan had won Singapore's first Olympic Games medal with a silver at the 1960 Olympic Games in Rome.

Tan had no barrier or limits, but he certainly had a heart. **Goh Teck Phuan**, who was Singapore's chef de mission to the 1970 Commonwealth Games in Edinburgh, Scotland, remembers just how big a heart Tan had. Swimmer Junie Sng has an elder sister, Elaine, who was swimming for Singapore at the games. Junie, who was then six years old, was with their mother to cheer Elaine on.

Goh recalled Junie's mother telling him: "I want Junie to see a big game and I want her to swim in the pool." So Goh arranged everything and made sure that Junie got to swim in an Olympic-sized pool at the games. Goh added: "We encouraged her because her sister was representing Singapore."

But while Junie and her mother had found accommodation near the games village, having enough food to last them for their trip was a concern. Goh recalled: "For them to get food outside would be so difficult. You'd have to go so far to buy the food."

Enter Tan Howe Liang and his fellow weightlifters. They, along with all the other competitors, had their meals within the games village. So after breakfast every day, Tan and his teammates would, Goh recalled, "da bao" (Mandarin for "take away") lots of milk, bread, butter and other foods, storing these in Goh's room for Junie and Mrs Sng. Goh said: "They told the Games organisers, 'We weightlifters have got to eat more. We want to bring back to the room.' So that is how Junie and her mother were fed during the whole period. Credit goes to Tan Howe Liang and all the weightlifters."

And to think that Tan himself often had to scrape by to keep his Olympic dreams going, scrimping all he could to buy the attire and gear he needed to train and compete.

No Shoes, Free Vitamins and Donated Eggs

The lot of a Singaporean national athlete was, for many years, as humble as could be. Champion sprinter and long-time athletics coach **Canagasabai Kunalan**, better known as **C. Kunalan** or Mr K, recalled how he and his fellow athletes relied on "free vitamin samples" and "donated eggs" from well-wishers to energise themselves just before a race. He was fortunate that his wife, whom he married in 1966, would brew Chinese herbal tonics for him, fortified with fish, chicken and sometimes mutton, to boost his stamina. He stressed that financial and medical support for athletes, including from the government, "has improved as the years have gone by" but it has still "by and large been a huge sacrifice for Singapore's athletes to train for their nation's glory".

A case in point: Umaglia Kancanangai Shyam Dhuleep, better known as U.K. Shyam who, on 27 August 2001, broke Kunalan's 33-year-old national record of 10.38 seconds in the 100m sprint. Kunalan mused: "It was despite the SAAA (Singapore Amateur Athletics Association). He did not get the right kind of support from it but he was so determined to break the national record. There were days when he would sit in my office and talk to me about how he was going to break it."

Kunalan said he was convinced Shyam would do so; for one thing, he noted from the registration book at the gym where Shyam trained that the latter was almost always the last person to sign out every night.

Sprinter C. Kunalan, who held the 100m national record for 33 years, is seen here training in the 1970s. Over three decades, he clinched five gold medals at the Asian Games and 15 at the Southeast Asian Games.

In this photo-finish from the 100m sprint at the 1966 Southeast Asian Games in Bangkok, Singapore's C. Kunalan lost the gold medal to his friend, Mani Jegathesan of Malaysia, by 0.01 seconds.

The game-changer for Shyam's bid to break Kunalan's national record, however, was champion swimmer Ang Peng Siong, who won the World's Fastest Swimmer award at the 1982 United States Swimming Championships. Kunalan said: "The main person who really helped him [Shyam] to break the record was Ang Peng Siong because Peng Siong took him under his wing and said, 'Okay, let me sponsor you'. Gave him a job as a gym instructor and then gave him time to train and I think that really helped."

"Ang Peng Siong," he added, "was a buffer against all the negatives."

How did Kunalan himself fend off all the negatives to set that 33-year-old national record at the 1966 Asian Games? The wiry, soft-spoken gentleman, whose daughter Mona Kunalan later followed in his footsteps, had his family's full support – and, as he says, was "always serious" about training such that "if the coach asked me to do something 10 times, I would do it 12 times".

That approach, as it turned out, took him to the finals of the 1966 Games. He confessed: "I was very nervous. Then I was leading in the finals, up to 99 m and I threw up my hands and then my friend from Malaysia, Mani Jegathesan, he stuck his neck out so beautifully – and won by an Adam's apple."

Swimmer Ang Peng Siong, who is among Singapore's most admired and respected sportsmen, clocked the world's fastest time in the men's 50m freestyle event at the 1982 United States Swimming Championships in Indianapolis.

It had been a photo finish and, as the duo flopped onto the track after the race, for a good half an hour, they didn't know who had won. Kunalan recalled: "I remember Jega telling me that he had made so many sacrifices because he was a medical student and so he had trained for the Games while doing his medical studies.

Sprinter Glory Barnabas steeled herself after a personal tragedy to run for the nation at the 1975 Southeast Asian Games in Bangkok. Here she is in 1962, training in a Swift T-shirt at the Farrer Park Stadium.

"And then they announced the results." Jegathesan, dubbed The Flying Doctor for his speed, was declared the winner. "And I didn't feel sad or anything," Kunalan averred. "I felt okay... because everybody was appreciative and sympathetic at the same time. They said, 'Wow, you were so close.'"

"That," he added, "was my most satisfying run. Would have been better if it had been gold. But I don't think it was any less significant at that time for me, a *kampung* boy.

"My wife also did not feel bad because we had not expected such a result. It was the Asian Games... previously. I was fourth in the Southeast Asian Peninsular Games. And suddenly, in the Asian Games, a silver medal."

Kunalan and, later, Shyam were just two among countless Singaporean sportsmen who gave their all, no matter how trying their personal circumstances.

Sprinter **Glory Barnabas** knew that only too well. Barnabas, who grew up without running water in Lorong Low Koon in Hougang and whose first love was netball, was all set to race at the 1975 SEA Games in Bangkok when she received the worst news. She recalled: "One of my younger brothers met with a car accident and, at that time, I was actually running at the SEA Games. The guy in charge of the Singapore soccer team, Mr Ganesan, told my coach the news and that's how I knew about it.

"I rushed home for the funeral then after that, everybody said: 'Please go and run. We're sure it would have been your late brother's wish.' So I went back." She ran only the relay events, though, as she decided to pull out of all the individual races.

An athlete's commitment often knows no bounds. Long-distance runner **P. Chinakaruppan Suppiah**, better known as **P.C. Suppiah** or **P.C. Sam**, ran the 5,000m and 10,000m barefoot in his early days because he simply could not afford shoes. He suffered

National hurdler Ahmad Osman Merican receiving his gold medal for the 110m hurdles at the 3rd Southeast Asian Peninsular (SEAP) Games in Kuala Lumpur in 1965. His time of 14.5 seconds was a national record that lasted 43 years. Osman used to joke that leaping over neighbour's fences as a boy helped him be a champion. His disciplined living and having a good coach also garnered him a gold medal at the 1966 Asian Games.

blisters aplenty, but at the 1972 Munich Olympics, he powered through to become the first Singaporean to finish the 10,000m under 32 minutes, clocking 31 minutes and 59.2 seconds. It would be 41 years before Soh Rui Yong broke that record.

Most Singaporean athletes took such personal struggles in their stride. Among them was champion hurdler **Ahmad Osman Merican**, who said he actually enjoyed the lean living. Ahmad, a rookie cop who brought the highest honours to the nation in the 110m hurdles, said: "I liked the clean life of athletes. They had a routine timetable. After training, we might go for a drink… and then as we were very tired, we would go home and sleep. No alcohol. No cigarettes. It was a very healthy concept. I like that kind of feeling."

In the early years after Independence, many athletes such as Ahmad, were so skint that they could not afford coaches. Ahmad recalled praying silently that the distinguished athletics coach Tan Eng Yoon would train him.

Ahmad, who as a boy used to leap over fences after stealing his neighbour's tapioca, recalled: "I was dying for a coach… because I couldn't see whether my technique was correct or not... You need someone to watch if you are spending too much time in the air or not putting your whole leg through." Happily, Tan took him on and worked him such that Ahmad hurtled to gold medals at the 1965 and 1967 SEAP Games – and, best of all, a gold medal at the 1966 Asian Games.

A Shoo-in for the Shuttle King

The first sport in which Singapore stamped itself on global consciousness was not athletics, boxing, swimming or football. It was badminton that got the rest of the world sitting up and taking notice of the tiny island that could. And the shuttlers that took Singapore to the great high – the All-England championships – were Wong Peng Soon and **Ong Poh Lim**.

Between the two, Wong was more often on the winner's podium. The world knew him as "The Great Wong" as he was the first Asian to win the coveted All-England title in 1950. By then, he had an unbroken string of national badminton victories under his belt. Ong, who was Wong's big rival on court and firm friend off it, was the only person who managed to break Wong's winning streak at home in 1954.

Wong and Ong bonded, perhaps, over the fact that they each had famous granduncles. Wong's paternal granduncle, Wong Ah Fook, was a good friend of Sultan Abu Bakar of Johor and built the Istana Besar for the royal. You might recognise the granduncle's name as a major road in downtown Johor Bahru is named after him.

Ong's paternal granduncle, Singapore-born Ong Tiang Swee, was once the Chinese *kapitan* of Sarawak, that is, the leader of the Malaysian state's Chinese community. Ong said of his granduncle: "I was a small fly. But he invited me to see him before he died. I was then a world champion… he told me, 'I want you to sign (your) autograph (for me)'."

Ong was, in many ways, Wong's successor. Wong had been Singapore's top shuttler from the late 1930s till the 1950s. Besides the All-England – which he won in 1950, 1951, 1952 and 1955 – he also won the Danish Open, the Indian Open and the Philippines Open, just to name a few. This was in an age when most people outside Asia could not point to where Singapore was on a map.

Wong Peng Soon had been Singapore's top shuttler from the late 1930s till the 1950s. Besides the All-England – which he also won in 1950, 1951, 1952 and 1955 – he also won the Danish Open, the Indian Open and the Philippines Open, just to name a few. This was in an age when most people outside Asia could not point to where Singapore was on a map.

He also led the then Malayan team to prestigious Thomas Cup triumphs in 1949, 1952 and 1955. He was the team's captain in 1955 – and retired from competitive badminton on a high that same year. He was only 33 years old.

Wong moved on to coach budding badminton talents at the Singapore Youth Sports Club and, later, Singapore's national teams to various meets. Although he had retired, the world did not forget him. He was awarded the highest accolades in his field almost every decade after hanging up his racket.

Upon retirement in 1955, Wong was awarded Britain's Member of the Order of the British Empire (MBE) for services to sport. In 1962, he was the first and still only sportsperson

Fleet-footed shuttler Wong Peng Soon stamped Singapore's global dominance of badminton with his string of All-England and Thomas Cup wins. He is seen here with the Thomas Cup in 1949, won by a Malayan team he had led.

to be conferred the Sijil Kemuliaan (Certificate of Honour) by the Singapore government.

Then in 1985, the Singapore Sports Council gave him its Distinguished Service Award, also for services to sport. The following year, he was inducted into the Singapore Sports Museum's Hall of Fame. A decade later, in May 1999, he was inducted posthumously into the International Badminton Federation's Hall of Fame.

Ong said Wong's death from pneumonia on 22 May 1996 was long and slow. That was because Wong had suffered a stroke in 1981, which left him partially paralysed thereafter. Ong, whose entire immediate family died of strokes, recalled: "My good friend Wong Peng Soon also got a stroke… At that time, he was 63 years old. There was an 18-year-old girl, who was a world champion from Denmark, who came to Kuala Lumpur and wanted to play Wong Peng Soon."

Ong added that $50,000 was up for grabs if Wong agreed to spar with the girl in 1981 Whoever lost the match would still get $25,000. "The person who arranged the match was also a badminton player, Abdullah Perus, a good friend of Dr Mahathir Mohamad." Ong mused, "The girl said something like, 'What? This old man (Wong) is nothing'."

But, Ong added, the upstart did not know that Wong was still fighting fit then. Wong had about three months to train for the showdown with her. Ong recalled: "So Peng Soon asked his wife to give him the same treatment as she had when he was younger. Every morning, he took three half-boiled eggs with fresh milk. At noon, he had bacon and at night he had beef, chicken and all that."

The champ likely pushed himself too hard. After one-and-a-half months of training, Wong suffered a stroke at 3 am. "It was a very big stroke," says Ong. "He nearly died… From that day on, until he died, he dragged on."

And while Singapore may be tiny alongside the other nations of the world, sometimes the smaller one is, the better one stands out. Singapore's former chef de mission Goh Teck Phuan knew this. He was at the 1970 Commonwealth Games in Edinburgh, but did not march with the Singapore contingent at the opening ceremony. He was, instead, in the Royal Box with Britain's Queen Elizabeth II and Singapore's then Minister for Social Affairs Othman Wok. Goh recalled: "When Singapore marched in, the crowd was screaming, 'Bugis Street! Bugis Street! Bugis Street!' because a lot of sailors from HMS *Terror* were there. The Queen turned around and asked what were they shouting? What was it all about?

"Othman Wok merely said, 'It's a famous street in Singapore'."

A TIMELINE OF THE ORAL HISTORY CENTRE

Year	Milestone
1978	• Deputy Prime Minister and Minister for Defence Dr Goh Keng Swee initiates a nationwide oral history programme, with George E. Bogaars, Permanent Secretary in the Ministry of Finance, as chair of the Oral History Advisory Committee.
1979	• David Lance, Keeper of the Department of Sound Records at the Imperial War Museum, London, is asked to advise on the setting up of the Oral History Unit. • The Oral History Unit (OHU) sets up office in Grange Road with a team of five officers. The Unit comes under the care of the National Archives and Records Centre (NARC), the predecessor of the National Archives of Singapore. Lily Tan, Director of the NARC, is concurrently appointed Director of the OHU.
1980	• OHU undertakes two oral history projects: "Pioneers of Singapore" and "Political Developments in Singapore, 1945–1965". • A Documentation Unit is created in December to ensure the systematic cataloguing and archiving of all oral history interviews.
1981	• OHU embarks on its third and fourth oral history projects, "The Japanese Occupation" and "Special Project". The latter aimed to collect interviews on aspects of Singapore's social and cultural history. • OHU merges with the NARC to form the Archives and Oral History Department (AOHD).
1983	• AOHD moves from 15 Grange Road to the Old Hill Street Police Station at 140 Hill Street. • The oral history project "Communities of Singapore" is launched.
1984	• Minister for Foreign Affairs and Culture S. Dhanabalan officially opens AOHD's new premises at Hill Street on 25 May. • AOHD publishes *Pioneers of Singapore: A Catalogue of Oral History Interviews*, the Documentation Unit's first attempt at publishing a retrieval aid for a completed oral history project.
1985	• AOHD organises "Japanese Occupation: Singapore 1942–1945", the first-ever exhibition on Singapore's Occupation years. • AOHD is split into two entities: the National Archives, headed by Lily Tan, and the Oral History Department (OHD) led by Kwa Chong Guan.

Year	Milestone
1986	• OHD launches an oral history project on "Vanishing Trades".
1988	• OHD publishes the first edition of *The Oral History Manual*, which provides a guide to oral history methodology. • OHD compiles interview extracts for a 13-part radio series, "People and Places", which was broadcast over Singapore Broadcasting Corporation's Radio 5.
1989	• OHD participates in the ASEAN Committee on Culture and Information project to collect nursery rhymes from around the region.
1992	• OHD hosts the ASEAN Oral History Colloquium. • OHD participates in Heritage Day, in collaboration with the National Museum and the National Library, to commemorate the 50th anniversary of the fall of Singapore to the Japanese.
1993	• OHD and the National Archives merge to form the National Archives of Singapore (NAS) on 1 August, under the National Heritage Board. • OHD is renamed Oral History Centre (OHC).
1997	• OHC begins digitising its analogue collection.
1998	• NAS moves from Hill Street to the former Anglo-Chinese Primary School at 1 Canning Rise. • Oral history metadata is made available online to facilitate research.
1999	• A Chinese book, 雪泥鸿爪 (*Imprints in Time*), is published to commemorate OHC's 20th anniversary.
2001	• OHC separates from NAS and becomes part of the Heritage Services Division under the National Heritage Board. • Pitt Kuan Wah is appointed Director of NAS.
2003	• The National Heritage Board's Heritage Services Division is dissolved and OHC comes under the charge of NAS again.
2004	• OHC collaborates with Mediacorp to produce a radio programme titled "Reflections".
2006	• The book, *Reflections and Interpretations*, is published to commemorate OHC's 25th anniversary.

Year	Milestone
2007	• The book, *Memories and Reflections: The Singapore Experience*, is published, a substantial update to the 1988 *Oral History Manual*. • Oral history transcripts are made available online.
2011	• Eric Tan is appointed Director of NAS.
2012	• NAS becomes an institution under the National Library Board.
2013	• Eric Chin is appointed Director of NAS. • Full oral history recordings are made available for online streaming.
2014	• NAS' online oral history portal is revamped with enhanced search options such as voice-to-text technology and time-stamping features.
2015	• NAS launches the Citizen Archivist Project, an online crowdsourcing initiative inviting the public to help transcribe archival records, including oral history interviews.
2017	• Minister for Communications and Information Dr Yaacob Ibrahim announces the Community Oral History Committees initiative to engage and encourage the Chinese, Malay, Indian and Eurasian communities in Singapore to collect oral histories from their respective communities. • Wendy Ang is appointed Director of NAS.
2018	• Senior Oral History Specialist Mark Wong is elected Vice-President of the International Oral History Association. • OHC begins offering a course in oral history at the Civil Service College.
2019	• The book, *The Sound of Memories: Recordings from the Oral History Centre, Singapore*, is published to commemorate the NAS' 50th anniversary (2018) and the OHC's 40th anniversary (2019).

LIST OF INTERVIEWEES

1. **Alex Abisheganaden (Accession no.: 001461)** is a musician and educator. Although known as Singapore's "Father of the Guitar", he played many other musical instruments too. In 2007, he was awarded the nation's highest arts honour, the Cultural Medallion. Singaporean jazz singer Jacintha Abisheganaden is his daughter.

2. **Abu Bakar Bin Haji Abdul Halim (Accession no.: 000625)** was a supervisor at Radin Mas Religious School in Mt Faber Road. He was later Chairman of the school's administration committee from 1979 till 1984.

3. **Ahmad Osman Merican**, also known as **Osman Merican (Accession no.: 002672)** was a national hurdler in the 1960s, setting the national record of 14.5 seconds in the 110m hurdles in 1965. The Inspector of Police was appointed Acting Assistant Superintendent of Police in August 1980.

4. **Christabelle Alvis (Accession no.: 002828)** was educated in Myanmar and India. She taught at Naval Base Secondary School throughout her entire teaching career, from 1958 till 1986.

5. **Alwee Alkaff (Accession no.: 000124)** was a real estate agent and valuer, and the scion of one of Singapore's pioneering Arab families. At one time, he was honorary secretary of the Singapore Malay Chamber of Commerce and Industry.

6. **Mangalesvary Ambiavagar (Accession no.: 001981)** was an educator who taught at Raffles Girls' School in the late 1950s. She later rose in her career to become a principal.

7. **Ang Chit Poh (Accession no.: 004159)** was a bus driver who witnessed how the private bus business was affected during the Severe Acute Respiratory Syndrome (SARS) crisis from March till July 2003. Born into a family of 12 children, his father ran a provision shop and also drove a pirate taxi.

8. **Hedwig Elizabeth Aroozoo Anuar (Accession no.: 002036)** is the daughter of Percival Aroozoo, the first local principal of Gan Eng Seng School from 1938 till 1955. She is the first local to head the National Library and was its Director from 1965 till her retirement in 1988.

9. **Haji Aziz Bin Rahim Khan Surattee (Accession no.: 000284)** was an old boy of St Joseph's Institution, and later an assistant mechanic at Nissan Motors during the Japanese Occupation. Post-World War II, he was an attendant at Tan Tock Seng Hospital.

10. **Guy Joseph Janvier Barbe**, also known as **Brother Vincent (Accession no.: 000468)** was born in Canada. An alumnus of King's College London, the Catholic priest was a prisoner-of-war who taught interned boys in Changi Prison during the Japanese Occupation. Post-war, he founded the reformative institution called Boys' Town.

11. **Glory Barnabas (Accession no.: 002712)** was a national sprinter who competed for Singapore well into her 70s. A physical education teacher, she was 71 when she won Team Singapore the gold and silver medals for the high jump and long jump events, respectively, at the 2013 International Gold Masters in Japan.

12. **Rupchand Bhojwani (Accession no.: 000452)** was born in Sindh, India. The managing director of J B Rupa & Company, he was President of the Sindhi Merchants' Association in the 1980s.

13. **Marie Ethel Bong (Accession no.: 001390)** was the elder sister of Hedwig Elizabeth Aroozoo Anuar. During the Japanese Occupation, she bought and sold pianos to help her family get by. She was Principal of Katong Convent from 1971 to 1985.

14. **Sheila Bruhn-Allan (Accession no.: 002740)** gave one of the most chilling accounts of Japanese brutality during World War II. Interned at Sime Road Camp during the Japanese Occupation, she later became a paediatric nurse. She also wrote a memoir of the war titled *Diary of a Girl in Changi* (1994).

15. **Harold De Castro (Accession no.: 002968)** was a bodybuilder who won the Mr Singapore title in 1948. He trained with weightlifter Tan Howe Liang, who was Singapore's first Olympic Games medallist in 1960.

16. **Shuki Ram Chandra née Davies (Accession no.: 002039)** was an old girl of St Hilda's School. She started out as a junior club secretary at the Young Women's Christian Association and later worked as a clerk in the government treasury and later, in the Public Works Department.

17. **Chan Kai Yau (Accession no.: 001707)** was born in Hong Kong. A mathematician by training, he was Singapore's Director of Education from 1975 till 1982. He was later Executive Director of the Singapore Chinese Chamber of Commerce and Industry from 1985 till 1987.

18. **Chan Kwee Sung (Accession no.: 000962)** was a tutor and a prolific writer of bygone days in Singapore. He had a column in *The Straits Times* titled "Long Life" from 1998 till 2002. His memoir, *One More Story to Tell*, was published in 2005.

19. **Patricia Chan Li-Yin (Accession no.: 002629)** gave newly-independent Singapore much hope as its "Golden Girl" of swimming. She won a total of 39 gold medals at regional swimming meets between 1965 and 1973, beginning her breathtaking haul at the tender age of 11.

20. **Sally Chan née Sally Liew (Accession no.: 002353)** was among the pioneering batch of ground hostesses of Malayan Airways in 1958. She was later a public relations manager with Malaysia-Singapore Airlines and then Singapore Airlines.

21. **Alice Cheang Wye Lan,** also known as **Mrs Hwang Chung Yun (Accession no.: 000237)** was born in Guangdong, China. Her family moved to Singapore, where she attended Raffles Girls' School from 1919 until 1922. She was Principal of Balestier Girls' School from 1949 until 1955, and then an Inspector of Schools from 1956 till 1960.
22. **Lucy Chen née Lim Seok Hui (Accession no.: 003130)** was a granddaughter of tycoon Lim Nee Soon, after whom the residential town of Nee Soon, now Yishun, was named. She was a teacher before becoming a bookkeeper at the Southeast Asia Film Company.
23. **Cheong Quee Wah (Accession no.: 001611)** enjoyed a distinguished career in public service. He was Permanent Secretary at the Ministry of Home Affairs when Hotel New World collapsed in March 1986, and helped direct the search-and-rescue operations.
24. **Dr Andrew Chew Guan Khuan (Accession no.: 001620)** was a medical doctor in government service who went on to distinguish himself in public service. He was Head of Civil Service from 1984 till 1994 and then Chairman of Public Service Commission from 1998 till 2008.
25. **Rebecca Chew (Accession no.: 003856)** is a choral expert and an educator with a distinguished career, which includes being the first Principal of Singapore's groundbreaking School of the Arts from 2009 till 2012.
26. **Chia Cheong Fook (Accession no.: 003028)** narrowly escaped being executed by Imperial Japanese Army (IJA) soldiers during the Sook Ching killings. He later distinguished himself in public service, including being the Permanent Secretary of the Ministry of Foreign Affairs from 1975 till 1987.
27. **Felix Chia (Accession no.: 001553)** wrote many books on Peranakan culture. He survived the Sook Ching and went on to work as a food distribution clerk for the Imperial Japanese Army during the Japanese Occupation.
28. **Chia Wai Hon (Accession no.: 001886)** has been an artist, an arts educator and an arts critic. He headed the Art Education Department at the Institute of Education from 1980 till 1987. He was a member of the National Arts Council's Arts Resource Panel and a judge for the Cultural Medallion.
29. **Jap Chong Chow Pin (Accession no.: 003192)** co-founded The Quests in 1961. The Quests became Singapore's most successful band of the 1960s and Chong was its rhythmic guitarist till 1971.
30. **(Lieutenant-General) (Retired) Winston Choo Wee Leong (Accession no.: 002343)** served as Chief of Defence Force in the Singapore Armed Forces from 1974 till 1992. After his retirement from the armed forces, he continued to serve Singapore as a diplomat.

31. **Elizabeth Choy née Yong Su Moi (Accession no.: 002827)** was a war heroine. In 1943, during the Japanese Occupation, she and her husband Choy Khun Heng were detained by the Imperial Japanese Army for anti-Japanese activities. She was released only after being tortured for 193 days by the Kempeitai (Japanese military police). Britain awarded her the Order of the British Empire in 1950, and she was later an educator and councillor in Singapore.

32. **Chua Eng Cheow (Accession no.: 000722)** was a master potter from Fengxi Village in Chao An County, China, which is known for its fine porcelain. He learnt how to make coarser ceramics only after he emigrated to Singapore in 1930. He went on to become a master in firing ceramic wares in dragon kilns.

33. **Frederick Arthur Chua (Accession no.: 001465)** read law at Cambridge University and was among Singapore's pioneering local-born legal officers. He was elevated to the Bench and was a judge of the Supreme Court from 1957 till 1992.

34. **Jennie Chua (Accession no.: E000658)** was synonymous with the fabled Raffles Hotel after she made history by becoming its first Singaporean and its first female General Manager in the 1990s. Born into a family of 12 children, she started out as a typist but rose through the ranks to become the first woman to chair the Singapore International Chamber of Commerce in 2009.

35. **Chua Jim Neo (Accession no.: E000059; not publicly accessible as yet)** was the mother of Singapore's founding Prime Minister Lee Kuan Yew. Married at 15, she had three other sons and a daughter. She was among the most renowned cooks of her time. In 1974, she published the definitive *Mrs Lee's Cookbook*. She died at age 73 in 1980.

36. **Vernon Christopher Cornelius (Accession no.: 001711)** became lead singer of the Singapore band, The Quests, in 1966. Known as the Cliff Richard of Singapore, he was for a time a disc jockey for Rediffusion.

37. **Joseph Anthony Desker (Accession no.: 001433)** survived the malaria-infested settlement of Bahau in Negeri Sembilan during the Japanese Occupation. He went on to become a senior civil servant in the Ministry of Finance, and later the Ministry of Foreign Affairs in the 1960s and 1970s.

38. **Dollah Kassim (Abdullah Bin Kassim; Accession no.: 002793)** was one of Singapore's most gifted footballers of the 1970s. Dubbed the "Gelek King" (*gelek* in Malay means "sashaying") for his extraordinary ability to dribble deftly past opponents, he was a top goal-scorer who helped Singapore clinch the Malaysia Cup in 1977.

39. **Ee Boon Lee (Accession no.: 003045)** was among *The Straits Times*' star reporters from 1956 till 1963. He then carved out a career at Radio Television Singapura between 1963 and 1981 as a News Editor, and from 1981 till 2000 as an Editor.

40. **Rita Fernando (Accession no.: 002044)** grew up in a village in Siglap. An alumna of St Anthony's Convent, she became a teacher.
41. **Fong Chiok Kai (Accession no.: 000185)** was a long-time grassroots leader and a keen observer of Singapore Chinese culture. He became Chairman of the Kreta Ayer Community Centre Administrative Committee in 1982.
42. **Merrilyn Fong Wai Lye (Accession no.: 003590)** is proud that her father Peter Fong was a fighter pilot in World War II's Flying Tiger squadron, defending mainland China against its Japanese invaders. She was a producer-presenter at Mediacorp from 1993 till 1996, before becoming a freelance writer.
43. **Vincent Gabriel (Accession no.: 002909)** was a gourmand who faithfully tracked developments in Singapore's food scene, particularly its hawker culture. He was a teacher at St Patrick's School from 1960 till 1971. After 1989, he became a consultant in the local food industry.
44. **Goh Heng Chong née Teo Moh Tet (Accession no.: 001392)** was born into a wealthy family. An alumna of the Methodist Girls' School, she was a teacher from 1940 till her retirement in 1964.
45. **Alfred Goh Kok Kee (Accession no.: 003208)** was the aide-de-camp (ADC) to Singapore's fourth President, Wee Kim Wee, as well as his successor, Ong Teng Cheong. At 1.82 metres, he was told that his height was a big reason why both presidents chose him as their ADC. He joined the Singapore Armed Forces as a regular in 1986 and by 1990, was working in the Office of the President.
46. **Goh Lay Kuan (Accession no.: 002410)** is a dance pioneer and the widow of Kuo Pao Kun, the doyen of Singapore theatre. She and Kuo founded The Theatre Practice in 1965. She was awarded the Cultural Medallion in 1995.
47. **Goh Teck Phuan (Accession no.: 002128)** was Singapore's chef de mission to the 1970 Commonwealth Games in Edinburgh. He was also a respected athlete, coach, mentor and all-around champion of sports. The Akira Swift Goh Teck Phuan Memorial Age Group Cross Country Championships is named after him.
48. **Goh Yong Hong (Accession no.: 002241)** was Singapore's Commissioner of Police from 1979 till 1992. A lawyer by training, he introduced, among other things, neighbourhood police posts.
49. **Nirmala Gopiendran (Accession no.: 003814)** was a social worker who contributed much to the plight of those being cared for by the Singapore Association for Retarded Children.

50. **Dhanalakshmi Govindasamy (Accession no.: 000140)** is the daughter of the great Singaporean philanthropist P. Govindasamy Pillai (1887–1980). A man of austere tastes, her father co-founded the Singapore Indian Chamber of Commerce in 1937 and the Ramakrishna Mission. Pillai was also the main benefactor of the Sri Srinivasa Perumal Temple in Serangoon Road.

51. **Bernard Ming-Deh Harrison (Accession no.: 003217)** was the Executive Director of the Singapore Zoo from 1981 till 2002, and the Chief Executive of Wildlife Reserves Singapore from 2000 till 2002. He introduced exciting concepts such as the open-air Night Safari and the hugely popular "Breakfast with an Orangutan" programme.

52. **Mary Hee Sook Yin (Accession no.: 002206)** was a midwife from 1961 till 1999 and remembered the massive floods in Singapore of the 1960s and 1970s.

53. **Heng Chiang Ki (Accession no.: 000152)** was a canteen boy and then cashier for a food supplier to the Imperial Japanese Navy during the Japanese Occupation.

54. **Amanda Heng Liang Ngim (Accession no.: 002891)** is among Singapore's most well-known women artists. A former tax officer, she is a performance and installation artist, and co-founded The Artists Village in 1987.

55. **Captain Ho Weng Toh (Accession no.: 002364)** was, like Merrilyn Fong Wai Lye's father, a bomber pilot in the American-trained Flying Tigers 1st Bomber Squadron, defending China against the Japanese in World War II. In 1950, he joined Malayan Airways as a pilot and was later a training captain for Singapore Airlines.

56. **How Mun Heng (Accession no.: 002320)** is a historian by training. He was, among other things, a Deputy Director in the Prime Minister's Office from 1984 till 1985 and the Director (Administration) in the Ministry of Community Development from 1985 till 1998.

57. **Bryant Hwang Tchuan Thau (Accession no.: 003164)** was among the relatively few Singaporeans who went to boarding school in Britain. He then trained as a stockbroker there, before returning to Singapore to work as a stock market dealer for much of his life.

58. **Robert Iau Kuo Kwong (Accession no.: 002275)** was a polymath with a varied career. He helped shape the National Service programme as the Director of Manpower in the Ministry of Defence from 1967 till 1971. A talented musician, he was also Chairman of the Singapore Arts Centre (which was renamed Esplanade – Theatres on the Bay) from 1994 till 1998.

59. **Ismail Bin Zain (Accession no.: 000601)** was an old boy of Raffles Institution. During the Japanese Occupation, he worked as a clerk at the Central Police Station.

60. **Joshua Benjamin Jeyaretnam**, better known as **J.B. Jeyaretnam (Accession no.: 002932)**, was for many years a leader of Singapore's opposition. A former district judge and Registrar of the Supreme Court, he won the Anson by-election in 1981.

61. **Rajabali Jumabhoy (Accession no.: 000074)** was born in India, but made his fortune in Singapore. The chairman of Jumabhoy & Sons Ltd, he was also a founding member of the Singapore Indian Chamber of Commerce. From 1955 till 1959, he was a Legislative Assemblyman.

62. **Kannusamy s/o Pakirisamy (Accession no.: 000081)** lived most of his life in or around Serangoon Road. He was born in 1914, early enough to remember the cowherds and goatherds of yore. He made a living as a tutor.

63. **Kee Soon Bee (Accession no.: 001808)** was an Inspector of Police who distinguished himself as a national water polo and swimming coach. Among his most accomplished charges was Junie Sng, Singapore's Golden Girl in the pool who won 38 gold medals at various regional meets. He was also a founder of the People's Association Youth Swimming Club.

64. **Khatijun Nissa Siraj (Accession no.: 001663)** was the first woman to work in Singapore's Syariah Court and the Registry of Muslim Marriages from 1960 till 1970. Her daughter, Zaibun Siraj, has continued her mother's good work as a strong advocate of women's rights in Singapore.

65. **Khoo Teng Soon (Accession no.: 000475)** was the grandson of Chew Boon Lay, a great philanthropist after whom Boon Lay housing estate is named. Khoo rose from being a clerk at Cold Storage supermarket to Chief Sub-Editor, Managing Editor and then Group Editor at *The Straits Times* between 1949 and 1979.

66. **Cedric Buher Kleinman (Accession no.: 002943)** served as one of the pioneering officers in the Singapore Armed Forces. He was the platoon commander of A Company of the 2nd Singapore Infantry Regiment and at one time chaired its Advisory Board for Deferments and Exemptions. He was later Head Instructor at the Singapore Armed Forces Training Institute.

67. **James Koh Cher Siang (Accession no.: 002847)** had a schoolmate whose home was razed in the Bukit Ho Swee Fire of 25 May 1961. Koh was Permanent Secretary in the Ministry of Education from 1994 till 1997, and later became Chairman of the Housing & Development Board in 2007.

68. **Dr Koh Eng Kheng (Accession no.: 002000)** was among Singapore's most beloved family physicians. He opened Chung Khiaw Clinic in 1957 and was still seeing patients a few months before his death in July 2006. In 1972, he was appointed President of the Singapore Medical Association and was later President of the College of General Practitioners Singapore.

69. **Professor Tommy Koh Thong Bee (Accession no.: 002021)** is a hugely respected international lawyer, law professor and diplomat. He is Ambassador-at-Large at the Ministry of Foreign Affairs, having served Singapore with distinction as its Permanent Representative to the United Nations. He is also Special Adviser to Singapore's Institute of Policy Studies and Chairman of the National Heritage Board.

70. **Stella Kon née Lim Sing Po (Accession no.: 002996)** is a pioneering Singaporean playwright whose work, *Emily of Emerald Hill*, has been performed globally. Her paternal great-grandfather is Lim Boon Keng, while her maternal great-great-grandfather is Tan Tock Seng, after whom the hospital is named. Kon won the prestigious SEA Write Award in 2008.

71. **Canagasabai Kunalan**, better known as **C. Kunalan (Accession no.: 002572)** is among Singapore's most admired and revered national sprinters. In 1966, he clinched a silver medal for the 100m sprint in the Asian Games, losing the gold to his friend Mani Jegathesan of Malaysia by just 0.01 seconds. His 100m national record of 10.38 seconds at the 1968 Olympic Games in Mexico City was broken only after 33 years, by U.K. Shyam in 2001.

72. **Captain Chitharanjan Kuttan (Accession no.: 002697)** was the Comptroller of the Port of Singapore Authority from 1971 till 1974 and its Deputy Port Master from 1974 till 1992.

73. **Colonel (Retired) Kwan Yue Yeong (Accession no.: 003101)** did much to shape sports as a viable career, one that brought great glory to the nation, after he was seconded from the Ministry of Defence to the Singapore Sports Council. He was for many years the council's Executive Director.

74. **Dr Lau Wai Har (Accession no.: 001501)** was the Director of the Institute of Education from 1976 till 1979. She did much to help Chinese-educated teachers master English so they could use English as their medium of instruction competently after a change in the nation's education policy.

75. **Lee Ek Tieng (Accession no.: 002832)** was among the 12 civil servants involved in the clean-up of the Singapore River. A former Head of Civil Service, he has also been Group Managing Director of the Government of Singapore Investment Corporation (GIC).

76. **Ellen Lee Geck Hoon (Accession no.: 004115)** is a Consultant with law firm Belinda Ang Tang & Partners, and President of the Singapore Table Tennis Association. She was a Member of Parliament for Sembawang Group Representation Constituency from 2006 till 2015.

77. **Samuel Lee Jian Wei (Accession no.: 003409)** is Asia's first test-tube baby, born on 19 May 1983 to a security supervisor and a secretary. He was named Samuel by Professor S.S. Ratnam, the surgeon who carried out in-vitro fertilisation to aid his conception.

78. **Lee Khoon Choy (Accession no.: 000022)** was a journalist who later entered politics. He was a Parliamentary Secretary in the Ministry of Culture in the late 1960s before being appointed Singapore's envoy to Egypt and Indonesia. He was also ambassador to Japan and South Korea in the mid- to late 1980s.

79. **Lee Liang Hye (Accession no.: 000651)** was an old boy of Raffles Institution. He later joined the Administrative Service and, among other postings, worked at the Statistics Department from 1951 till 1958.

80. **Lee See Sin (Accession no.: 003736)** painted huge cinema posters which could be several storeys high and so he often had to climb up very tall scaffolding. He was also a well-trained artist who mentored budding painters in the community.

81. **Professor Lee Seng Teik (Accession no.: 002632)** was among Singapore's pioneering plastic surgeons. He was Senior Registrar at the Department of Plastic and Reconstructive Surgery at the Singapore General Hospital in 1975. He was one of the doctors who treated victims of the *Spyros* oil tanker explosion in October 1978.

82. **Raymond Leong Kum Hon (Accession no.: 003192)** grew up in Tiong Bahru with Jap Chong Chow Pin, his fellow bandmate from the band The Quests, which they co-founded in 1961, naming it after an abbreviated form of the name of their alma mater Queenstown Secondary Technical School.

83. **Liak Teng Lit (Accession no.: 003867)** is the former Chief Executive of Toa Payoh Hospital, Changi General Hospital, Alexandra Hospital and Khoo Teck Puat Hospital. Under his watch, Alexandra Hospital had the fewest patients suffering from Severe Acute Respiratory Syndrome (SARS) when the epidemic hit Singapore in 2003.

84. **Carmee Lim (Accession no.: 002590)** studied and lived in her first school, Yang Zheng Primary. She went into teaching and, by 1984, was an Inspector of Schools. She distinguished herself as the Principal of Raffles Girls' School from 1989 till 1999, having taught there from 1969 till 1977.

85. **Lim Kee Chan (Accession no.: 002068)** gave up his studies to pursue his passion – professional boxing – and competed in quite a few regional meets against world-famous boxers. He later switched to journalism, becoming the chief sports writer of *The Straits Times* in the 1960s.

86. **Lim Siam Kim (Accession no.: 002587)** was Director of Operations at the Ministry of Home Affairs when Hotel New World collapsed in March 1986. He was later Chief Executive of the National Heritage Board, among other posts he held during his illustrious career.

87. **Loo Yew Kim (Accession no.: 003501)** grew up in the grounds of Kwong Wai Shiu Hospital, where her foster parents were cleaners. Upon leaving school, she became a patient care assistant – a post we would now refer to as a nurse – at the hospital.

88. **Haji Maarof Salleh (Accession no.: 002818)** is an educator who has been a Senior Fellow at the Institute of Southeast Asian Studies. He is Past President of the Muslim Religious Council of Singapore (MUIS).

89. **Ian MacLeod (Accession no.: 002914)** was born in Singapore on 23 January 1922 and lived here till 1929. His father fought, and survived World War II, but his mother succumbed in a prisoner-of-war camp in Singapore. He is the author of the book, *The Day That Singapore Fell 70 Years Ago*.

90. **David Saul Marshall (Accession no.: 000156)** was Singapore's first Chief Minister from 1955 till 1956. He founded the Workers' Party in 1957, and was later its chairman. After a stint as a Member of Parliament for Anson in the early 1960s, he became Singapore's ambassador to France, Portugal, Spain and Switzerland from 1978 till 1993.

91. **Keki Medora (Accession Number: 000295)** was born in Mumbai, India, where she lived with 22 other family members under one roof. She later worked as a social worker in Singapore, raising funds for various causes. She was also a former President of the Leprosy Association.

92. **Haji Mohamed Sidek Bin Siraj (Accession no.: 001255)** was a clerk in the Colonial Secretary's office before the Japanese Occupation. From 1955 till 1970, he was an executive officer in the Social Affairs Department of the Ministry of Home Affairs.

93. **Rudy William Mosbergen (Accession no.: 002983)** was, among other postings, the Principal of Raffles Junior College from 1982 till 1987. He was later the Deputy Director of Curriculum Development at the Institute of Education.

94. **Dr Edmund Hugh Monteiro (Accession no.: 001956)** treated many among Singapore's first HIV/AIDS sufferers. He is former Director of the Centre for Communicable Diseases. He got his smarts, wisdom and compassion from his father, the trailblazing doctor Ernest Steven Monteiro.

95. **Professor Ernest Steven Monteiro (Accession no.: 000488)**, the father of Dr Edmund Hugh Monteiro, was the first Asian to hold the Chair of Clinical Medicine at the University of Malaya, and later Dean of the Faculty of Medicine at the same university. He succeeded in cultivating an anti-polio serum in goats and, through his concerted anti-polio campaign, was able to rid Singapore of poliomyelitis within 20 years. He was later a diplomat to the United States and Brazil.

96. **Jeremy Ian Monteiro (Accession no.: 003016)** is Singapore's foremost jazz musician. He led his first band while he was still in his teens, and has jammed with many among the world's giants in jazz. He was awarded the Cultural Medallion in 2002.

97. **Haji Muhammad Ariff Bin Ahmad (Accession no.: 000798)** was the man whom Zubir Said, composer of Singapore's national anthem, consulted for the lyrics to the anthem. Haji Muhammad Ariff was a respected authority on Malay language, customs and culture, and was also once the honorary secretary of the Malay Education Council.

98. **Mun Chor Seng (Accession no.: 002582)** was a cameraman with the Singapore Broadcasting Corporation from 1970 till 2000. On 29 January 1983, he was about to attend a colleague's wedding when he was recalled to work – to film the risky efforts to rescue passengers trapped mid-air on the Sentosa cableway.

99. **Nadesan Ganesan (Accession no.: 003279)** was a lawyer and former Chairman of the Football Association of Singapore. He survived the Japanese Occupation, and vowed never to touch tapioca or sweet potato again.

100. **S.R. Nathan or Sellapan Ramanathan (Accession no.: 004030)** was the sixth President of Singapore from 1999 till 2011 – making him Singapore's longest-serving president to date. A pioneer of medical social work in Singapore, he started out as a Seaman's Welfare Officer in 1956, rising to become Director of Intelligence in the Security and Intelligence Department of the Ministry of Defence. From 1979 till 1982, he was the first Permanent Secretary of the Ministry of Foreign Affairs, High Commissioner to Malaysia, ambassador to the United States and then President of Singapore.

101. **Ng Kah Ting (Accession no.: 000139)** was the Member of Parliament for Punggol from 1963 till 1991. He was also Advisor to the Punggol Citizens' Consultative Committee.

102. **Dr Ngiam Tong Tau (Accession no.: 003117)** was a veterinarian who helmed the Primary Production Department in the 1980s, the Agri-Food and Veterinary Agency thereafter, and then became Executive Vice-President at United Engineers Limited.

103. **Dr Farleigh Arthur Charles Oehlers (Accession no.: 000421)** was the 12th of 12 children in a distinguished Singaporean family. Among his brothers was Sir George Oehlers, Singapore's first Speaker of Parliament. Dr Oehlers was a Singapore-trained dentist.

104. **Ong Poh Lim (Accession no.: 001932)** was among Singapore's most successful shuttlers and a great friend of his main rival, Wong Peng Soon. He and Wong represented Malaya and won the Thomas Cup in 1949, 1952 and 1955.

105. **Oon Jin Teik (Accession no.: 003592)** is a former national swimmer who trained under Kee Soon Bee, competing at the 1984 Olympic Games in Los Angeles. He was the Chief Executive of Sport Singapore (formerly Singapore Sports Council) from 2004 till 2010, and Chief Executive of the Singapore Sports Hub from 2017 until 2019.

106. **Othman Wok (Accession no.: 000133)** was a descendant of Singapore's first settlers, the Orang Laut. He was a journalist with *Utusan Melayu*, before becoming Singapore's Minister for Social Affairs and then a diplomat.

107. **Charles George Peall (Accession no.: 002496)** joined the British Army in 1940 and was a motor engineer there. He and his fellow soldiers set sail for the Far East and landed in Singapore on Christmas Day 1941. When the Japanese invaded, he was taken prisoner and sent by train to Thailand, where he survived its barely habitable prison camps.

108. **Noel Arthur Pereira (Accession no.: 000423)** was an engineer who, as a child, grew up on Pulau Bukom and had to take the ferry to school on mainland Singapore daily. During the Japanese Occupation, he had to run engines with palm oil as petrol was scarce.

109. **Saravana Perumal (Accession no.: 000335)** was born in Sri Lanka. He emigrated to Singapore and was a male nurse at public hospitals here between 1947 and 1980. In 1980, he worked as a nurse at the remand prison in Jalan Penjuru.

110. **Vilasini Perumbulavil (Accession no.: 002437)** is an alumna of Raffles Girls' School and the University of Malaya in Singapore. From 1976 till 1983, she was Head of the Central Library at the National Library and then Head of the Asian Collection at its Children's Library from 1984 till 1991.

111. **Dr Uma Rajan (Accession no.: 002567)** was among the few women graduates of the University of Malaya's medical school. She was with the School Health Service from 1972 till 1999. Trained in classical Indian dance, she was an advisor to the National Arts Council for some years.

112. **Professor S.S. Ratnam,** also known as **Shanmugaratnam s/o Sittampalam (Accession no.: 001936)** was a pioneering gynaecologist in Singapore, who introduced in-vitro fertilisation here. He trained in medicine at the University of Malaya in Singapore between 1953 and 1958, and later headed the University Unit of what is now KK Women's and Children's Hospital. On 19 May 1983, he delivered Asia's first test-tube baby, whom he named Samuel.

113. **Nora Anny Samosir (Accession no.: 001811)** is a seasoned stage actress and educator. An alumna of Canada's York University and Britain's The Central School of Speech and Drama, she taught at Nanyang Junior College and, most recently, the National University of Singapore.

114. **Jessie Sarkies (Accession no.: 003479)** was the grand-niece of Armenian brothers Martin, Tigran, Aviet and Arshak Sarkies. Tigran and Aviet founded the Raffles Hotel in 1887. She was a home-based food caterer.

115. **Thirunalan Sasitharan (Accession no.: 003466)** is a theatre educator. He is co-founder and director of the Intercultural Theatre Institute, formerly known as the Theatre Training and Research Project. He worked closely with Singapore's theatre doyen Kuo Pao Kun for many years, until the latter's death in 2002.

116. **Kasinather Saunthararajah,** better known as **K.S. Rajah (Accession no.: 002088)**, trained in Singapore as a teacher but later switched to law, graduating in 1963 from the law faculty of the University of Malaya in Singapore. He headed the civil and criminal divisions of the Attorney-General's Chambers in the 1970s and was a Judicial Commissioner of the Supreme Court of Singapore from 15 May 1991 till 2 March 1995.

117. **Seow Peck Leng née Chua Seng Kim (Accession no.: 000721)** was a politician and advocate of women's rights. In 1954, she founded the Siglap Girls' Club for underprivileged girls, which became the Singapore Women's Association. She helmed it till 1991. In 1959, she became the first female opposition parliamentarian.

118. **Professor Kanagaratnam Shanmugaratnam (Accession no.: 001562)** was a pathologist who came to be known as Singapore's "Father of Pathology". He established Singapore's Cancer Registry in 1967 to track the nation's cancer trends. His son Tharman was formerly Deputy Prime Minister in Singapore, and currently Senior Minister.

119. **Professor Thomas Henry Silcock (Accession no.: 000180)** was the first Professor of Economics and Head of the Economics Department at Raffles College. He survived internment during the Japanese Occupation.

120. **Sin Leong (Accession no.: 003146)** is among Singapore's Four Heavenly Kings of Chinese cuisine, the others being Hooi Kok Wai and the late Tham Yew Kai and Lau Yeok Pui. They are the creators of *yusheng* (raw fish salad). Sin owns Red Star Restaurant in Chin Swee Road with Hooi.

121. **Soh Guan Bee (Accession no.: 000310)** was a fitter who worked in Japanese organisations during World War II. He was occasionally also a professional gambler.

122. **Soh Siew Cheong (Accession no.: 003274)** grew up in Chinatown in the days when gangsterism was rife. He trained as an engineer and was among the pioneering batch of local civil servants in Singapore.

123. **Som Mohamed Said (Accession no.: 001812)** is the doyenne of Malay classical dance in Singapore. The founder of much-awarded performance troupe Sri Warisan, she was conferred the Cultural Medallion in 1987.

124. **Subramaniam s/o Munian (Accession no.: 003036)** had a simple carefree childhood but in his 20s, had the onerous responsibility of proofreading all the documents in Tamil relating to Singapore's independence from Malaysia on 9 August 1965.

125. **Sukarti Binte Asmoin (Accession no.: 002576)** is an *ustazah* (female religious teacher) and is a council member of the Singapore Islamic Scholars and Religious Teachers Association (PERGAS).

126. **Sumitera Mohd Letak (Accession no.: 001915)** started out as a midwife, travelling to and from mainland Singapore to the outlying islands to care for women there. She later took up nursing and continued to help mothers in need, winning volunteerism awards along the way.

127. **P. Chinakaruppan Suppiah (Accession no.: 002662)**, also known as **P.C. Suppiah** or **P.C. Sam** was the first Singaporean to compete in the 10,000m event at the 1972 Munich Olympic Games. He sometimes ran his races barefoot as he could not afford sports equipment. He also won gold medals at the Southeast Asian (SEA) Games.

128. **Tan Sri Syed Esa Almenoar (Accession no.: 000013)** was a lawyer with his own practice, and also a former Secretary-General of the Singapore United Malay National Organisation (SUMNO). He contested, but did not win, the ward of Changi in the 1963 General Election. He was among those who tried to defuse the race riots of 1964.

129. **Tan Gee Paw (Accession no.: 003170)** was the architect of Singapore's Water Master Plan in 1972, and helped clean up the Singapore River between 1977 and 1987. He was also among the brains behind NEWater. He was Chairman of Singapore's water agency, PUB, from 2001 till 2017.

130. **Tan Guan Chuan (Accession no.: 000414)** volunteered in the Air Raid Precautions (ARP) corp before the onset of World War II. During the Japanese Occupation, he worked in the Office of the Custodian of Enemy Property, which seized assets of those opposed to the Imperial Japanese Army.

131. **Neivelle Tan (Accession no.: 001600)** is a nephew of Tan Cheng Lock, who fought for Malaya's independence from the British. At 14, he joined a gang and by the age of 17, was found culpable in a gangland murder but was spared the gallows because he was younger than 18 years. In prison, he became a Christian and founded the Church of God (Evangelical). He is now a pastor.

132. **Tan Peng Ann (Accession no.: 002659)** started out as a secondary school teacher but found his calling with the Singapore Armed Forces from the 1960s. He retired from the army and became a principal training consultant.

133. **Professor Tan Ser Kiat (Accession no.: 003084)** was the Group Chief Executive of SingHealth from its inception in 2000 till 2012. An Emeritus Consultant in the Department of Orthopaedic Surgery at the Singapore General Hospital, he is also President of the Singapore Medical Council. He has been a member of the Public Service Commission since 2013.

134. **Tan Siew Mong (Accession no.: 003326)** is a practitioner of traditional Chinese medicine who saw first-hand how Singaporeans were gripped by fear during SARS. He is Chairman of the Public Free Clinic Society.

135. **Richard Tan Swee Guan (Accession no.: 003859)** is a pioneer of Singapore's dance scene. He was active in the Singapore Armed Forces' Music and Dance Company for many years, and continues to choreograph performances put up by Singapore's Peranakan community.

136. **Tan Wee Him (Accession no.: 003058)** joined *The Straits Times* on 1 May 1970 as a photographer. He rose through the ranks to become the newspaper's aviation correspondent and was in the cockpit of the first flight – SQ101 – when it touched down at the newly-completed Changi Airport on 1 July 1981.

137. **Dr Tay Chong Hai (Accession no.: 002537)** is the first Southeast Asian to have had a disease named after him – Tay's Syndrome. In the late 1990s, he discovered another disease, eosinophilic arthritis. With his wife, Dr Caroline Gaw, they first alerted Singaporeans to the existence of Hand, Foot and Mouth Disease.

138. **Tay Tong (Accession no.: 003458)** was the managing director of pioneering Singapore drama company TheatreWorks for 30 years. He left it in April 2018 and is now a cultural advisor, including helping freelance artists through the National Resource Centre for Arts Freelancers.

139. **Tee Tua Ba (Accession no.: 002323)** is a law graduate who became a hero of the 1974 *Laju* ferry hijacking. He was Commissioner of Police from 1992 till 1997. He is now Chairman of the Singapore Red Cross Society.

140. **Teh Lee Thong (Accession no.: 001302)** came from a family who had been breeding chickens for eggs since the 1930s. In the 1960s, he enlarged his family business by investing in automated hatchery equipment to boost its yield significantly.

141. **Gnanasundram Thevathasan (Accession no.: 000345)** was born in what is now Sri Lanka. After marrying and moving to Singapore, she taught children living in slums and educated their mothers on birth control methods. For her efforts, she was later made a Justice of Peace.

142. **Dr Victor Mathuraretnam Samuel Thevathasan, also known as Dr Victor Madura Ratnam Thevathasan (Accession no.: 002171)** was among the last batch of students to graduate with a Licentiate in Medicine and Surgery from Raffles College in 1949. An old boy of Anglo-Chinese School and an alumnus of University College London, he was a Senior Health Officer in the government's Public Health Division from 1962 till 1973.

143. **John Ting Kang Chung (Accession no.: 002927)** is an architect and was President of the Singapore Institute of Architects from 2002 till 2004.

144. **Dr Charles Toh Chai Soon (Accession no.: 002159)** is a leading cardiologist who is still in private practice. He became an Associate Professor of Medicine in 1970. He is a member of the Public Service Commission.

145. **Toh Lim Mok (Accession no.: 002969)** was in his teens when he founded a private ambulance service for the poor in Singapore. He has been Chairman of Fengshan Citizens' Consultative Committee and was once Chairman of the Kampong Glam Community Centre Management Committee.

146. **Toh Mah Keong (Accession no.: 000001)** was one of the very first persons to be interviewed by the Oral History Unit (now Oral History Centre) on 27 December 1979. He was a businessman who was partly educated in Singapore.

147. **Dr Tow Siang Hwa (Accession no.: 001920)** was among Singapore's pioneering gynaecologists. As Head of what is now KK Women's and Children's Hospital from 1960, he secured accreditation for it from the prestigious Royal College of Obstetrics and Gynaecology in Britain. He later went into private practice and set up The Tow Yung Clinic. He was also a church pastor. He died at age 93 in 2019.

148. **Abdul Kader Tyebally (Accession no.: 000161)** is the scion of the Bombay Trading Company, founded by his father Fidahusein. Tyebally was born in India, but studied at Raffles Institution in Singapore. He helmed many other companies during his lifetime.

149. **Richard @ Ricky Uy (Accession no.: 002324)** was born in Shanghai and graduated with a degree in Theology, but went into the Asian film business. He was an Assistant Producer for global film giant Shaw Brothers and remained in the movie and entertainment industry for close to half a century.

150. **Wang Cheow Ah (Accession no.: 001259)** was born in 1927. He attended Sing Hua and Yock Eng schools and later became a pastry chef and partner of the fabled Nam Fong Biscuit Shop here.

151. **Ann Elizabeth Wee née Wilcox (Accession no.: 001623)** is the doyenne of social work in Singapore. An Englishwoman married to a Singaporean lawyer, she joined the Department of Social Studies at the then University of Malaya (now National University of Singapore) in 1957 and was Head of the Department of Social Work from 1968 till 1986. In 2017, she released her memoir titled *A Tiger Remembers: The Way We Were in Singapore*.

152. **Peter Wee Ban Kheng (Accession no.: 002100)** was President of The Peranakan Association Singapore General Committee from 2010 till his death in 2018. His name was synonymous with his business, Katong Antique House.

153. **Eugene Wijeysingha (Accession no.: 001595)** began his career as a teacher at Raffles Institution (RI) in 1959. Among his students was Singapore's future second Prime Minister Goh Chok Tong. He was later Principal of Temasek Junior College from 1980 till 1985 and then Principal of RI from 1986 till 1994, when he retired.

154. **Dr Albert Winsemius (Accession no.: 000246)** was the highly respected Dutch development economist who helped shape Singapore's economic development strategy between 1961 and 1984. He died in 1996.

155. **Yau Chung Chii (Accession no.: 000427)** was steeped in Chinese kitchen wisdom. She was by turns a salesclerk at Daimaru departmental store, a telephonist and a typist.

156. **Robert Yeo Cheng Chuan (Accession no.: 002578)** is a poet, playwright, novelist, essayist and cultural critic who had a newspaper column in the 1970s. He was for many years a lecturer at the Institute of Education, becoming an Associate Professor of English Literature. He was Chairman of the Drama Review Committee of the Ministry of Culture and then Ministry of Community Development from 1977 till 1991. He has also taught creative writing at Singapore Management University.

157. **George Yeo Yong-Boon (Accession no.: E000003)** helmed the Foreign Affairs, Trade and Industry, Health and Information and the Arts ministries between 1990 and 2011. Prior to politics, he was a Brigadier-General in the Republic of Singapore Air Force. He has also been Chairman of Kerry Logistics Network, and Chairman of Nalanda University.

158. **Dr Yong Nen Khiong (Accession no.: 003548)** was among the Chinese residents of Singapore who settled in the Japanese wartime settlement of Endau in Johor in the mid-1940s. He later became a heart surgeon.

159. **Yoong Siew Wah (Accession no.: 002603)** was Director of the Internal Security Department from 1971 till 1974, after stints as Director of the Corrupt Practices Investigation Bureau and the Singapore Special Branch. He had joined the Singapore Police Force in 1950.

160. **Zamroude Za'aba (Accession no.: 000241)** was a part-time announcer and newsreader with Radio Malaya in 1941, before the onset of the Japanese Occupation. She then worked as a clerk at the Japanese Police Training School in Thomson Road.

IMAGE CREDITS

All images in this book are from the National Archives of Singapore except the following:

Page 11:	Sharon Siddique
Page 19 (top):	Robert Tan
Page 23:	The Straits Times © Singapore Press Holdings Limited. Reprinted with permission
Page 25:	Urban Archiver
Page 30:	Raffles Hotel Singapore
Page 37:	Carmee Lim
Page 39 (bottom):	Raffles Institution
Page 45:	Reproduced from *Katong Convent Secondary School Official Opening Celebration, 30 July, '88*
Page 46 (top):	National Library Board
Page 50:	PUB, Singapore's National Water Agency
Page 56:	Wikimedia Commons
Page 61:	Vernon Cornelius (photo by Peter Robinsons Studio)
Page 62:	Jeremy Monteiro and Singapore Jazz Association (photo by Norhendra Ruslan)
Page 65:	Ronni Pinsler
Page 70:	State Library of Victoria (Argus Newspaper Collection of Photographs, H99.200/652a)
Page 71:	Australian War Memorial (011529/10)
Page 74: (bottom)	Nederlands Instituut voor Oorlogsdocumentatie (Beeldbank WO2 – Image Bank WW2 – NIOD)
Page 81:	Wikimedia Commons
Page 83:	The Straits Times © Singapore Press Holdings Limited. Reprinted with permission
Page 84:	Australian War Memorial (045424)
Page 89:	Ho Weng Toh
Page 92 (top):	National Archives and Records Administration
Page 92 (bottom):	State Library of Victoria (Argus Newspaper Collection of Photographs, H98.103/4171)

Page 94:	State Library Victoria (Argus Newspaper Collection of Photographs, H98.101/177)
Page 97:	Singapore Tourism Board
Page 99:	ISEAS-Yusof Ishak Institute
Page 102 (top):	ISEAS-Yusof Ishak Institute
Page 108:	National Library Board
Page 109:	The Straits Times © Singapore Press Holdings Limited. Reprinted with permission
Page 116:	Singapore Memory Project
Page 131 (top and bottom):	The Straits Times © Singapore Press Holdings Limited. Reprinted with permission
Page 133:	The Straits Times © Singapore Press Holdings Limited. Reprinted with permission
Page 134:	The Straits Times © Singapore Press Holdings Limited. Reprinted with permission
Page 144:	The Straits Times © Singapore Press Holdings Limited. Reprinted with permission
Page 145 (right):	Dr Edmund Hugh Monteiro
Page 149:	Reproduced from *Living the Singapore Story: Celebrating our 50 Years 1995–2015*
Page 152:	Public Service Commission
Page 167 (top):	Singapore Airlines Limited
Page 168:	Civil Aviation Authority of Singapore
Page 169:	Kouo Shang Wei Collection, National Library Board
Page 171:	Bernard Harrison
Page 172:	Registered Tourist Guides Association of Singapore
Page 174:	The Straits Times © Singapore Press Holdings Limited. Reprinted with permission
Page 176:	National Library Board
Page 179:	Reproduced from *Shirin Fozdar: Asia's Foremost Feminist*
Page 184:	Khatijun Nissa Siraj
Page 188:	National Arts Council (Retrieved from PictureSG)
Page 189:	Som Mohamed Said
Page 191:	TheatreWorks (Singapore) Ltd

Page 192:	Ong Teng Cheong
Page 193 (left and right):	Dr Uma Rajan
Page 195:	Wesley Loh
Page 201:	Xypex Chemical Corporation
Page 207 (top and bottom):	The Straits Times © Singapore Press Holdings Limited. Reprinted with permission
Page 210:	Sport Singapore
Page 213 (left):	Sport Singapore
Page 213 (right):	C. Kunalan
Page 214:	Singapore National Olympic Council
Page 215:	Glory Barnabas
Page 216:	Ahmad Osman Merican
Page 218:	Sport Singapore